# LAST VOYAGES
*Cavendish, Hudson, Ralegh*

THE ORIGINAL NARRATIVES

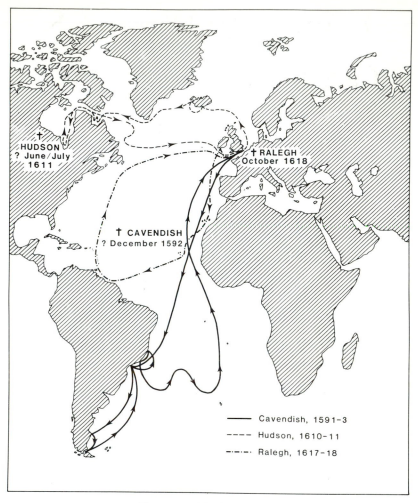

† HUDSON
? June/July
1611

† RALEGH
October 1618

† CAVENDISH
? December 1592

——— Cavendish, 1591-3
- - - Hudson, 1610-11
-·-·- Ralegh, 1617-18

The routes of the three voyages

# LAST VOYAGES

## *Cavendish, Hudson, Ralegh*

### THE ORIGINAL NARRATIVES

INTRODUCED AND
EDITED BY
PHILIP EDWARDS

CLARENDON PRESS · OXFORD
1988

Oxford University Press, Walton Street, Oxford OX2 6DP
Oxford New York Toronto
Delhi Bombay Calcutta Madras Karachi
Petaling Jaya Singapore Hong Kong Tokyo
Nairobi Dar es Salaam Cape Town
Melbourne Auckland
and associated companies in
Berlin Ibadan

Oxford is a trade mark of Oxford University Press

Published in the United States
by Oxford University Press (USA)

© Philip Edwards 1988

British Library Cataloguing in Publication Data
Last voyages: Cavendish, Hudson, Ralegh.
1. Voyages by sailing ships, 1591–1618.
Biographies. Collections
I. Edwards, Philip, 1923–
910.4'5
ISBN 0–19–812894–0

Library of Congress Cataloging in Publication Data
Last voyages—Cavendish, Hudson, Ralegh: the original narratives/
introduced and edited by Philip Edwards.
p. cm. Bibliography: p. Includes index.
1. English prose literature—Early modern, 1500–1700. 2. English prose literature—Early
modern, 1500–1700—History and criticism. 3. Voyages and travels. 4. America—Discovery and
exploration—English. 5. Cavendish, Thomas, 1560–1592. 6. Hudson, Henry, d. 1611.
7. Raleigh, Walter, Sir, 1552?–1618. I. Edwards, Philip.
910.4'09'032—dc19 PR1295.L37 1988 88–4244
ISBN 0–19–812894–0

Set by Wyvern Typesetting Ltd.

Printed in Great Britain
at the University Printing House, Oxford
by David Stanford
Printer to the University

The stars be hid that led me to this pain

SIR THOMAS WYATT,
'My galley charged with forgetfulness'

# *Preface*

OF the many debts I have incurred in preparing this book, the greatest is to my colleague David Quinn, for the help and encouragement he has given me and for allowing me to make free use of his edition of Cavendish's narrative of his last voyage. (My thanks go as well to the publishers of that edition, the University of Chicago Press.) I am also deeply grateful to the owner of the manuscript of the narrative, Paul Mellon, for giving me permission to base my text on the manuscript and for his kindness in bringing the volume personally from the United States to London for me to consult.

Among those who have helped me over stiles of various kinds I should like especially to thank Elizabeth Danbury, Nick Davis, John Fisher, John Gledson, Maria Guterres, Agnes Latham, Paul Laxton, Sandra Mather, Malcolm Lewis, Pauline Round, Richard Ruggles, Germaine Warkentin, and Margaret Wilkes. My wife Sheila and my daughter Kate both gave generous assistance in checking my texts.

A modernizing editor is a servant of two masters, Fidelity and Clarity, and he will never rid himself of compromise and consistency in trying to accommodate the two. Apart from the usual difficulties faced when giving a modern-spelling version of sixteenth- and seventeenth-century writings (e.g. travel/travail; see p. 109), I have had special problems with the names of people and places, which appear in bewildering variety, particularly surnames (e.g. Chidley/Chudleigh, Thornhurst/Thornix, Woodhouse/Wydowse, Faner/Funer/Fanner/Farmer). I have tended to standardize the names of people to avoid confusion; original forms are normally given in the Notes. But I have given latitude to the individual spellings of place-names, especially the many versions of Rio de Janeiro and the Orinoco.

References to books and articles in the introductions and the commentary are normally by means of the surname of the author, date of publication when necessary, and page numbers. The full titles of these works are listed in the References section at the end of the book, on pp. 253–7.

All dates are given in the 'Old Style', as used in England at the time of these voyages, except that the year is given as from 1 January, not 25 March. Thus I have headed Ralegh's letter to Winwood (p. 217) '21

March 1618', whereas his own dating, at the end of the letter, is '21th of March, 1617'.

The narratives which form the main substance of the book have been given marginal line-numbers, in tens, on each page. Cross-references in the introductions and the explanatory notes give page number followed by line number—thus 'p. 123/12' refers to line 12 of page 123.

This line-numbering facilitates reference from the text-notes (at the foot of the page) which record all important variants in the texts of the narratives. The sources of these variants are given in abbreviated or conventional form; fuller information is given in the introductions. When only one manuscript is in question, 'MS' is used. Where there is more than one, the collection is named for each (e.g. Sloane, Harley, PRO). For printed editions, either the editor's name is given (e.g. Purchas, Schomburgk, Cayley) or the date of the edition (e.g. 1650, 1829). I use the form '1650+' to indicate the edition of 1650 and subsequent editions.

In the explanatory notes which are also to be found at the foot of the page I have done my best to provide the information necessary for the fuller understanding of the narratives. Readers who have an advanced knowledge of the ships of this period must try to forgive the mistakes I have no doubt made in explaining seafaring terms, though some of the more recondite ones defeated the highest authorities.

P.E.

*Oxton, Birkenhead*
*1987*

# Contents

# List of Maps and Figures

# GENERAL INTRODUCTION

THE narratives of Elizabethan and Jacobean voyages (sedulously collected by Hakluyt and Purchas) have always been, in a rather vague way, part of 'English literature', but when after the Second World War the British Empire broke up and the New Criticism came to dominate literary study, these writings almost completely disappeared from sight. On the one hand they had lost their appeal as stirring accounts of the empire-builders, and on the other they lacked every necessary constituent of the well-wrought literary artefact. But in recent years the changed climate of critical approach has led to a welcome increase of interest in the literature of discovery, colonization, and travel,[1] and it seems opportune to conduct this experiment in a post-imperial presentation of sixteenth- and seventeenth-century voyages. The direction I am taking is different from that of a number of recent studies, which set out to establish patterns of colonial discourse and are as attentive to fictions such as *The Tempest* or *Robinson Crusoe* as to the records of the historical voyages. I want to concentrate on the voyage narratives and let them speak for themselves with a minimum of interference from me. I shall argue in this introduction what I hope my book as a whole will demonstrate, that these narratives, written by the voyagers themselves, are a special kind of writing with distinctive values of its own.

I have fashioned a triptych out of three well-known voyages, the final voyages of Thomas Cavendish (1591–3), Henry Hudson (1610–11), and Sir Walter Ralegh (1617–18). Each of these men was obsessed by a dream of personal honour and wealth achieved in a triumphant national enterprise. Each failed disastrously, bringing himself and many of those whom he had involved in his venture to the extreme edge of suffering and eventual death. The story of these voyages is presented by means of the narratives of those who were involved. I have provided an explanatory framework for them, but my introductions and notes have the function of display-cases and nothing more. The narratives are

---

[1] Some examples relevant to the voyaging period covered in this book are Greenblatt 1985 and chs. 4 and 5 of Greenblatt 1980; Hulme; Marienstras, ch. 7, 'Elizabethan Travel Literature and Shakespeare's *The Tempest*'; and many of the articles in Hunter and Rawson.

given in modern spelling, but they have all been newly edited from the original manuscripts or printings.

Cavendish's dream was to reach the Far East a second time and, besides becoming the first man to sail round the world twice, to exploit the contacts he had made on his first voyage and so establish for England a trading empire with the fabulous East. But his ships never got through the Magellan Straits, and he died (probably by his own hand) on his way back to England. The presentation of this voyage is as in Browning's *The Ring and the Book*, except that the narratives are genuine. The voyage is seen through the eyes of five separate participants and one contemporary commentator. I begin with Cavendish's own paranoid self-justification, written at sea just before he died. This hectoring recital is challenged by the reductive account of one of his victims, Anthony Knivet, from the early part of his story of his long years as a captive of the Portuguese after being put ashore by Cavendish to die. A more conscious challenge to Cavendish is John Jane's history of the voyage, which he wrote to defend his captain, John Davis, whom Cavendish accused of wilfully ruining the expedition. Davis also speaks in his own defence. The writer Thomas Lodge was one of the gentlemen volunteers on board the Galleon Leicester, 'at sea with Mr Candish, whose memory if I repent not, I lament not', and I include a few passages by him related to the voyage. I also reprint Purchas's fizzy introduction to the original (censored) printing of Cavendish's narrative.

Hudson inherited from Martin Frobisher and John Davis the mission to search out a sea-passage to China by a northern route, north-east or north-west, which would immeasurably increase the accessibility of Eastern wealth to English trade. His three attempts, in 1607, 1608, and 1609, to find a north-eastern passage and then a North American route had failed, and the voyage of 1610 was to explore the possibility of a north-western passage via the 'furious overfall' that John Davis had reported at the entrance of what is now Hudson Strait. Winter overtook his ship in Hudson Bay, and in the Spring his men mutinied and set him and a few others adrift in the shallop, never to be heard of again. This voyage is the only one of the three in which the voice of the leader does not dominate. Apart from a few uncommunicative pages from Hudson's log and a few pages about trouble on board 'found in the desk of Thomas Wydowse, student in the mathematics', the voyage is seen only through the refracting lens of Abacuck Pricket's narrative, which he carefully fashioned to absolve himself from any charge of complicity in organizing the mutiny.

Sir Walter Ralegh had gone to Guiana hoping to find gold and to establish an English presence there when he was in the shadow of Queen Elizabeth's disfavour in 1595. His second expedition was undertaken to free himself from the far worse burden of King James's disfavour, manifesting itself in his long imprisonment in the Tower under a suspended sentence of death for alleged treason. He accepted the impossible task of finding and bringing back Guiana gold without upsetting Spain. He found no gold, he upset Spain, his son was killed, and on his return he was executed on the fifteen-year-old charge of treason (which involved conspiracy with Spain!).

For the first two voyages I give all the contemporary accounts. But for Ralegh's voyage there is an overwhelming mass of contemporary comment, and to make a selection from the arguing voices would inevitably have imposed a personal view on events. I have therefore concentrated on Ralegh's writings alone. I give his journal, which has not been reprinted for many years, his 'Apology', and the letters to Winwood, his wife, Carew, and King James.

Although this book corrects and amplifies the historical record at quite a number of points, it is not offered as a contribution to the history of the voyages. Its purpose is to call attention to the writings which these voyages produced or provoked, and to ask what claims this participant literature has on us, a literature that in its language and structure is usually much inferior to the better works of fiction of the period. To balance the word 'fiction' I am using the word 'report' for writings about actual events in which the authors participated; it is less clumsy and misleading than such phrases as 'the literature of fact' or 'documentary literature'.

Voyage narratives (which are only one small area of report) have their own characteristic features, which may seem to create a special problem. There is hardly a narrower or more distorted and less shareable manner of life than that of a sixteenth-century long voyage—except perhaps life in prison. Here in the first place is an entirely male society. Not only are women wholly absent from these narratives, but sexual matters are never even mentioned. There are a few obscure hints of homosexual affections. The silence does not seem to be entirely a matter of reticence—or of censorship by Hakluyt and Purchas. Ralegh's orders to his fleet included dire warnings against molesting 'any woman, be she Christian or heathen, upon pain of death', but the constant discomfort of life aboard ship, shortage of food and water, the fight for survival aboard in the face of disease and ashore in the face of the enemy, seem to have obliterated or at least relegated sexual problems. The Renaissance voyage of discovery was of course commonly imaged as a male sexual exploration. The ship ploughed the sea so that its men might penetrate virgin land.

> And now a wind as forward as their spirits
> Sets their glad feet on smooth Guiana's breast.

So wrote Chapman in his 'Carmen epicum' (Hakluyt, x. 447). The image was so common that Donne could wittily invert it to refer to his personal sexual conquest: 'O my America! my new-found-land' (Elegy xix). So perhaps sexual energy was further diminished by being subsumed within the enterprise itself.

Next, the social structure on board these ships was of a strange composition. In the Cavendish and Ralegh voyages the seamen, from the master downwards, were probably outnumbered by the landsmen: gentlemen and hangers-on of indeterminate social class who had come along to do the fighting and the plundering. The interests and wishes of these two groups might be very far apart. The landsmen were bonded by feudal ties of loyalty and (often) kinship to the leader they had enlisted under—usually the captain of their ship, who might be more a military man than an expert seaman. Indecision and faction were fatally built into a sea-going society which more than most others depends for its continuance on co-operation.

The second voyage is an exception because there was a single ship, because Hudson was a seaman first and last, and because there were very few landsmen aboard and no soldiers. But all three leaders shared a privileged position of absolute authority for which, in communities of that size, there is scarcely a parallel in ordinary civilian life then or now. The authority of all three leaders was openly and seriously challenged, as will be seen, and to a greater or lesser extent each had to temporize and yield in the face of mutinous opposition. But the despotic power granted to the leader of these expeditions had at all times a profound effect on the thoughts, emotions, and conduct of the 'general' and his temporary subjects, and it gives a special tincture to all the writings gathered here. The force of the law which guarded that power can be seen in the slow, myopic movement of the enquiry by the High Court of Admiralty into the Hudson mutiny.

The remoteness of these voyages from our own lives is, however, most obvious in the adversities encountered. These are stories of men under continuous stress from perils little known to us, ranging from scurvy and other consequences of an insufficient, monotonous, and ill-balanced diet, to violent encounters with completely unknown peoples, and manœuvring cumbersome sailing ships through thick ice or the sandbanks of tropical rivers.

It is probably the very unusualness of the conditions and the adventures that made voyage literature so popular over the centuries. Stay-at-home readers wanted to know what the world was like, and enjoyed living vicariously with those who had freed themselves from monotony and security and hazarded themselves in the severities of wind and weather in unknown seas and on strange shores among ferocious or gentle savages. The reverend Samuel Purchas, in his Preface to the narratives of Cavendish and Knivet (p. 54), blandly suggested to the reader that God had delivered Knivet from his adversities 'that thou out of his manifold pains mayst gather this posy of pleasures, and learn to be thankful for thy native sweets at home, even *delights in the multitude of peace*'.

So the argument that these voyages are too outlandish and unfamiliar can be met by the argument that it is precisely their unfamiliarity that is so fascinating. But this in itself is not their justification. At this point Shakespeare can help. He made the fascination of Othello's tale of 'most disastrous chances / Of moving accidents by flood and field' the trigger of his great tragedy.

> This to hear
> Would Desdemona seriously incline.
>
> She gave me for my pains a world of sighs;
> She swore, in faith, 'twas strange, 'twas passing strange.
>
> She loved me for the dangers I had passed,
> And I loved her that she did pity them.
> This only is the witchcraft I have used.

The attraction Othello's tales had for Desdemona was neither what Iago thought it was ('bragging and telling her fantastical lies') nor the complacent 'posy of pleasures' described by Purchas. She recognized in the exotic a quality of difference, and was awed by it. Her marriage was an attempt to reconcile difference and normality, to transform normality by domesticating difference. That it was a disastrous failure indicates what a terrible risk she ran, but does not invalidate her idea. Her recognition of human life as somehow growing larger and more intense in the wild scenes Othello spoke of and yet not becoming separated from civil existence but being able to return to it with the power to irradiate it—this recognition seems to me to be the justification of these voyage narratives and their foreignness. It is certainly the recognition that Coleridge made when he turned his reading of voyage narratives into 'The Ancient Mariner', in which the poet brings home the new knowledge which his seafarer brought home.

The bizarre adventures of these ill-equipped ships were strange beyond strangeness to those who were in them, even the experienced seamen. John Jane's appalled account of the return of the remnant of the *Desire's* company, 'lost wanderers upon the sea' (pp. 119–20), is a very good example of the sense of being wrested out of the known conditions of life. The subtleties and complexities in the chemistry of personal relationships became simplified in these conditions. Hunger, fear, jealousy, greed, pain, frustration, hatred dominate. Watching these voyagers move out of the shelter of society, their expectations in a constant state of defeat, their elementary needs and emotions magnified, we are tempted to think of them as characters in a vast stage tragedy. And indeed the careers of these three leaders constantly call to mind what was going on in the tragic theatre of those times. 'True it is, that as many things succeed against reason and our best endeavours, so it is most commonly true that men are the cause of their own misery, as I was of mine.' So wrote Ralegh, sombrely trying to work out a theory of failure on his way back to his execution (p. 229). Many years earlier he had pictured himself in his misfortune as being like one who

> Alone, forsaken, friendless on the shore,
> With many wounds, with death's cold pangs embraced,
> Writes in the dust, as one that could no more—
> Whom love, and time, and fortune, had defaced.
>
> ('Ocean to Cynthia', 89–92)

These metaphors become a reality in the voyage narratives. Determination and obstinacy drove Cavendish, Hudson, and Ralegh after a vision of riches and glory through a landscape of cold and heat, storm and calm, aggression and violence, sickness, suffering, and death, which seems a literalization of tragic myth. It *is* life, though it is life distorted and in upheaval. For all their peculiarity and unfamiliarity, these narratives present a living theatre of misfortune which is in the end no more exotic or remote from us than are the vicissitudes of the stage tragedies which distort and exaggerate in order to illuminate and clarify our dilemmas.

Their masculinity, however, is a continuing limitation. It is a temptation to say that if there is an absence of women there is also an absence of men in these narratives—an absence of gender; so that these stories are outside rather than without sex. But that argument leads to the suggestion that male experience is the paradigm of all human experi- ence. These are stories of what men do. They emphatically present male activity (and they don't do it much credit). Their translation into general human experience must begin from this one-sidedness.

Another way in which the restricted conditions of these voyages can be seen as embryonic metaphors is that they are journeys, and inevitably take on the potency of the journey as an image of life. That potency has been shown in countless writings, from the Anglo-Saxon poems, *The Wanderer* and *The Seafarer*, to Conrad's *Typhoon* and beyond, which frame the passing of time as a confident setting out, an encounter with the adversity of the elements, and a chastened arrival in harbour. It has also been shown in a recognition of the symbolic power of single incidents, as when Cowper, towards the end of his life, went back to an incident he had first read years before in the narrative of Anson's voyage, and in 'The Castaway' made his tremendous identification with the sailor lost overboard:

> We perish'd, each alone;
> But I beneath a rougher sea;
> And whelm'd in deeper gulphs than he.

Our narratives make little conscious use of the metaphoric power of a voyage. But that power is always latent, giving an extra suggestiveness to the confidence of the departure, the bewilderment and disarray of misadventure, and the exhausted return.

If, seen from afar, there are strong resemblances between each of these three voyages and the patterns we are familiar with in Elizabethan and Jacobean tragedy, or the great sea-fictions of Conrad and Melville, there is not the faintest resemblance in the quality of the writing. There are by any standards of judgement some very moving passages in the narratives which follow; but by and large, even with as fine a poet as Ralegh among the authors, the writing is awkward, laboured, and thin, stumbling along with inadequate vocabulary and tangled syntax. That is because the authors of the narratives are participants in the events; they are the characters in the story, not the authors of the story. Their writings are an extension or a continuation of their participation, as (for the most part) they reshape events in the effort to assert themselves, defend themselves, justify themselves. There is a difference between

writing for your life and writing for a living. This distinction is
fundamental. Given the plots, Marlowe, Shakespeare, Jonson, Webster
would have transformed the linguistic energy of the stories. But these
writings are not literary productions; they are the voices of the characters in the drama, offering their own commentary on the action, writing
their own dialogue. The hero composes his own dying speech, literally
(both Cavendish and Ralegh). The result is certainly histrionic, but
frankly it is not of the same order as the dying speeches to be heard in the
real theatre. You might wish to make a distinction here between Knivet,
Jane, and Pricket, who were acting out parts devised for them by the
leaders, and Cavendish, Hudson, and Ralegh, whose imaginations set
these voyages afoot. But they are all in the same boat. Perhaps the
leaders started out as Author; but they were demoted to Character, and
became bewildered participants in someone else's script.

It is worth noting how much the act of writing was considered to be an
indispensable part of making voyages. Hudson insisted on bringing with
him Henry Greene, who ironically (according to Pricket) became the
instigator of the mutiny. 'This man our master would have to sea with
him because he could write well' (p. 153/2). John Jane was the nephew
of John Davis's chief financial backer and travelled with him regularly as
that backer's representative; but his role changed to that of Davis's loyal
historian, his press and publicity officer, as it were. Ralegh's journal
started out as a matter-of-fact log, but soon expanded into the preliminary material for the eventual 'official narrative' that Ralegh must have
had in mind. It is obvious that the backers of Hudson's unsuccessful
voyage had a close interest in the shape the written record of the voyage
took (pp. 129–30). And Hakluyt was always waiting to encourage the
production of writings which, suitably edited and placed, would become
part of the record that argued England's imperial future. For the
Elizabethan voyager, writing was participation, as necessary to the
eventual outcome of the voyage as hauling on ropes or joining a
shore-party.

> A thing inseparate
> Divides more wider than the sky and earth

It is difficult, perhaps impossible, to make a clear distinction between
writings in which people describe events they participated in, or report,
and imaginative writings, or fiction. There is no record of events that
does not stray into fiction, and no fiction that is wholly divorced from the

writer's personal experiences. Every life story weaves together fact and fancy, intentionally or unintentionally, and the combinations are infinite. The dividing line between history and myth gets harder to discern. Narrative is defined as interpretation, imposing meaning even as it tries to record.[2] A writer organizing facts falls into the same patterns of discourse as a writer organizing the world by means of fiction. The gods in charge of writing demand obeisance; both observation and make-believe culminate in narratives with a strong family likeness.[3]

It is an understandable temptation to stress that which writings of all kinds have in common, and that which separates them all from the world of actuality which most of them claim to describe or refer to. But, while recognizing the extreme difficulty of penetrating the disguises of language and the infidelity of the human mind, we should at all costs avoid manœuvring ourselves into a corner and declaring that after all we live in a world of words and there is no difference in the end between writings about things that have happened and writings about things that have not happened. In *Tropics of Discourse* (1978), Hayden White said in one of the essays, 'I wish to grant at the outset that *historical events* differ from *fictional events* in the ways it has been conventional to characterize their difference since Aristotle' (p. 121). He writes as though the difference were of academic interest. 'It does not matter whether the world is conceived to be real or only imagined; the manner of making sense of it is the same' (p. 98).

To refuse or make light of an ultimate distinction between historical writing, however fictional, and fictional writing, however historical, seems to me to risk confusing the categories on whose distinction human relationships depend. To have outgrown what we believed when we were children, that telling the truth was one thing and telling stories another, is an emancipation that has its perils. As readers and critics we ought to be cautious about joining the world of politicians, in which the record of real happenings, being of infinite malleability, declines into unimportance. Historical truth may be unknowable, but there is such a thing as falsehood.

The great privilege of fiction is its freedom to reassemble the world of happenings without being charged with falsehood. It has no obligation to follow the linear course of events and experiences; it remains tenacious to its own idea. It is true to experience, but it blends and fuses

---

[2] A classic statement of this position is Frank Kermode's study of biblical narrative, *The Genesis of Secrecy*.

[3] For recent writings on this subject, see Martin, pp. 222–3 and 237–8.

the experiences it is true to. Conrad wrote in the Author's Note to *Typhoon and Other Stories* (1919), 'None of them are stories of experience in the absolute sense of the word. Experience in them is but the canvas of the attempted picture.' And concerning another sea-story, *Redburn* (1849), Melville, more picturesquely, wrote that 'divine imaginings, like gods, come down to the groves of our Thessalies, and there in the embrace of wild dryad reminiscences, beget the beings that astonish the world' (Gilman, p. 175). In her attempt to re-create in words the very quality of experience itself, Virginia Woolf transferred her family holidays in Cornwall to the Scottish settings of *To the Lighthouse*.

'Now for the poet, he nothing affirms, and therefore never lieth.' Sir Philip Sidney was here reframing a traditional idea; it sounds like a joke but it is an idea of fundamental importance. The truth of imaginative literature lies somewhere other than in its adherence to recorded fact, and its allegiance elsewhere frees it from any charge of falsifying the record, or lying. You can accuse D. H. Lawrence of bad faith towards Jessie Chambers but you cannot accuse him of lying about Miriam Leivers in *Sons and Lovers*; everything he says about her is of equal truth. You can accuse Wordsworth of greed in appropriating to himself the experiences he relates in 'Daffodils' or 'The Solitary Reaper', but you cannot accuse him of being a liar. His use of the first person is an essential stratagem in communicating his ideas.

The definition of report is that it is a form of literature which cannot be granted the freedom permitted to 'the poet' and which can legitimately incur the charge of lying or falsification. Given the sturdy presence of writing and the paucity of otherwise-recorded facts to challenge its assertions, this definition may not seem to have much practical value in sorting out literature into its two kinds, but at least it proposes a criterion by means of which separateness can be recognized. Participation in actual events is where we start. From that point on, whether the contract between writer and reader is of allegiance to the course of history or allegiance to the general truths of fiction is often a matter of personal judgement and *ad hoc* decision. The need for fiction to seem true has led many writers to claim truth. Defoe went to great trouble to make his fictional voyages (like *A New Voyage Round the World* and *Robinson Crusoe*) as dull and episodic as he could in order to gain credence. In the Preface to *Typee*, Melville spoke of his 'anxious desire to speak the unvarnished truth', although in that book, as in all his 'autobiographical' work, reminiscence is liberally interspersed with invented material. Neither Defoe nor Melville can be brought to court for lying—except for their claim to be telling the truth.

The writers in this book were (obviously) not great literary artists using every resource of their talents to create a sense of the actual. They were wrestling with the actual, trying to avoid being smothered by it, using the whole of their limited resources to tame it and reduce it to order. Even on the many occasions when we have no means of verifying what they say, it is legitimate to wonder if they are lying. The invitation to the reader is different from the invitation in fiction; we are not invited to share the illusion of lived life; we are invited to detect or infer the throb and pulse of lived life lurking below the evasions and inadequacies of the assertions in the narratives.

Fiction moves towards self-sufficiency, self-definition; towards the autonomy of the worlds it creates (as the Dublin of 16 June 1904 is moved towards the autonomy of *Ulysses*). Report always remains incomplete, part of something else; it is always in relationship with a series of actual happenings which can never be fully or truly known; it depends for its meaning on this relationship. Even historical fiction does not have this dependence. Shakespeare's *Richard III* has interesting links with what happened in England towards the end of the fifteenth century, but its meaning does not depend on those links. Sometimes fiction imitates the dependence of report. With an enigmatic work like *Hamlet* one is continuously pushing out from the text to 'happenings' outside the text in order to explain the text: whether Gertrude slept with Claudius before her husband's death, whether she knew her husband was murdered. This is to relate visible fictions to invisible fictions, and, while it adds to verisimilitude, the quality of the relationship is quite different from that between writing and event in reports.

The exact distance of each of our narratives from the events they purport to describe can never be known because the events can never be known, but something of the quality of the bias in each will soon be apparent to the reader. Cavendish is determined to lay all the blame on John Davis, Pricket is determined to lay all the blame on the dead Henry Greene, Ralegh is determined to lay all the blame on the dead Lawrence Keymis. Here there is obvious and conscious shaping of the evidence and the record. Cavendish's is the most carefully designed and plotted of all the narratives, foreseeing its end in its beginning. Knivet's is the least plotted (although only a small part of his very long narrative is printed here); it is basically a list of episodes, and even in the full version it has no ending, but breaks off. Pricket's narrative is notable for one

mature and uncharacteristic literary device; he postpones the entry of
his villain, Henry Greene, until he has reached the wintering of the
Discovery in James Bay, and then with a sophisticated flashback relates
the way he boarded at Harwich and explains what kind of a man he was.
It is possible in all the main narratives to detect the suppression or
omission of information, and these occasions are pointed out in the
notes.

Apart from these matters of design, interpretation, and presentation
in narratives which as often as not were as keen to make out a case as to
give a faithful record of events, there are imponderable forces pushing
these accounts away from 'what actually happened'. Knivet's literary act
of recall seems to me to be the most honest attempt of all of them to be
faithful to the past. But as he sat down in London after the long years of
his captivity in Brazil to give Hakluyt the narrative he had no doubt
pressed him for, the quite unconscious sifting and rearrangement that
time, memory, and language must have imposed are incalculable.[4]

There are in all the narratives which follow some passages which
render human experiences in so vivid and vital a way that it does not
matter at all whether we are reading report or fiction. They stand in their
own right, whether they are true or untrue, as usable images of life. But
most of the time, as I have suggested, we are absorbed in relating what is
said to a hypothesis of 'what actually happened'. The power comes from
the tension between what is said and the imagined facts. It is perhaps a
coincidence that there is a darkness at the centre of each of my three
voyages. It is now quite impossible to discover or reconstruct the
happenings at the critical moment at which things went wrong finally
and irretrievably. For the Cavendish voyage it is the separation of the
ships on coming out of the Magellan Straits. For the Hudson voyage it is
the development of the conspiracy against Hudson on the night of 21/22
June 1611. For the Ralegh voyage it is the failure to reach the gold-mine
after the capture of San Thomé.

The particularly intense darkness at these critical moments is only an
intensification of the darkness which exists all the time. The power of
these narratives lies in a tension, yet one of the two elements in the
tension is hidden from us. Rightly enough, you want to know if these
witnesses are telling the truth, but you are aware from the beginning that
the truth can never be told. To read these texts in a constant state of
distrustful extrapolation from what they say to what we think was really

[4]  See P. Edwards, p. 297.

happening is not a matter of trying to catch the writer out. It is a matter of trying to find the writer's human position in the drama which he has not authored. Writers of realist fiction learned of the great value, for verisimilitude, of the 'unreliable narrator' and the indeterminate event. These voyage narratives give you the real thing, with narrators who lived through and influenced the events they inadequately describe, events which really happened, although just how they happened we shall never know.

It is worth reflecting on what we might mean by this mist-hidden crag of 'what actually happened'. Here is the first stanza of Wallace Stevens's 'Metaphors of a Magnifico':

> Twenty men crossing a bridge,
> Into a village,
> Are twenty men crossing twenty bridges,
> Into twenty villages,
> Or one man
> Crossing a single bridge into a village.

A wholly objective view of one of these voyages, disregarding all the prejudices and partial perceptions of those who were involved. Spaniards and English, the leaders and the led, the healthy and the sick, the seamen and the soldiers, would be a very curious affair. Even if we could attain the unattainable knowledge to provide this view, once we have emptied out all the subjective perceptions we should be left with nothing but a barren, aseptic, diagrammatic record of the strength of the winds, the course and distance sailed, the numbers slain, and so on. In *The View from Nowhere* (1986), Thomas Nagel argues that a view of reality must incorporate the subjective views of that reality. 'The subjectivity of consciousness is an irreducible feature of reality' (p. 7). Twenty men crossing a bridge are twenty men crossing twenty bridges, or one man crossing a single bridge. If we are to have a total view of 'what actually happened' on these voyages we should need to include the subjective and partial experience of everyone who was involved. We should need to include the quantifiably objective facts—the actual strength of the winds, the courses and distances sailed, the secret orders given, the number of shots fired—but also the fullness of every incident as it appeared to Cavendish, to Jane, to Davis, to Knivet, to Lodge, and to everyone else. This is the 'intersubjectivity' of which Nagel talks: 'There is a close connection between objectivity and intersubjectivity' (p. 63). But of course there is no 'being of total imaginative flexibility'

who could ever 'project himself directly into every possible point of view'
(p. 17). And if there were, there would be no way of conveying this
infinitely multiplied honeycomb of subjective experience to mortal
understandings.

Given the fatuity of imagining that we can ever be more than a step
along the road towards gaining a total view of 'what actually happened',
we are in a better position to see the three points of our triangle: the
narrator, the event, and the reader. These voyages did happen, outside
the narratives that mediate them to us. But (practically) nothing exists
except as it is perceived, and nearly four hundred years afterwards
nothing is perceived except as it is communicated. The communications
are flawed renderings of the perceptions—flawed by defect of language
and failure of memory and self-protective falsehood—but even in their
prejudiced imperfections they are as vitally a part of the drama of the *real*
voyage as were the individual perceptions from which they grew. As
readers we are in no god-like position to judge where exactly these
writers falter in their faithfulness towards what they did and what they
saw. These texts incorporate us as secret sharers on the voyages. We are
(we flatter ourselves) more enlightened, more compassionate than our
shipmates. Although for a great deal of the time we are shut up below
decks in ignorance, and know less (much less) than each narrator knew
at the time, we also, moving Ariel-like from one text to another, know
much more than any single narrator. Our final knowledge, however
reliable and extensive its sources, remains not only vicarious but
personal, partial, and subjective. Our measurement of the distance of
each narrative from the actual happenings is a comparison of one partial
glimpse of the truth with another.

Each of the narratives that follow is, for all its literary and historical
inadequacy, a living constituent part of a complex and intense series of
happenings and, for all its prejudice and self-interest, a contribution to
an understanding of those happenings. These writings have considerable importance as testimonies to and commemorations of events that
actually happened. Of course they are unreliable. They do not, will not,
cannot describe the events themselves as they really were. We position
ourselves as readers between the texts and the unknowable events,
balancing the one against the other, assessing the credibility of Knivet or
Pricket or Ralegh on whatever evidence we have, but knowing that we
remain partial and unreliable interpreters ourselves.

The texts which follow have their importance in a relationship with
real events, and can only be understood in that relationship. To that

extent they are qualitatively different from fictional writings, whose relationship to real people and real events is immaterial. It does not matter much, as regards the quality of our texts, whether the real events they relate to were of great or trivial historical significance. In point of fact, those events were a small but not negligible part of the shaping of the world in which we now live, a visible speck in our *damnosa hereditas*, and for that reason as well as others have a special claim on our attention.

In my book *Threshold of a Nation* (1979), I made a study of the relationship between the nationalism of an expanding England in the Elizabethan–Jacobean period and the drama of that time. In this book, presenting actual documents of the early, unsystematic gropings which were rapidly leading to the formation of the British Empire, I am less concerned to make out a case or offer judgements. Quite clearly these three unsuccessful ventures could not be put forward as instances of heroism, courage, daring, and far-sighted political vision. But equally they are not put forward in order to denounce the European scramble for land and booty of which they form part. It is impossible to read the annals of European expansion into the Americas, Africa, and the Pacific, with the exploitation, enslavement, displacement, or extinction of the inhabitants, without revulsion and indignation. But it is late in the day to be a knight in shining armour protesting against these evils. There were precious few when it really mattered. We have inherited the mess, and we may as well cut out recrimination and devote our energy to the problems before us, bequeathed to us by the centuries of European expansion.

It so happens that there is little of the arrogance, intolerance, cruelty, and hypocrisy we associate with colonialism in the narratives that follow. For Cavendish and Ralegh the antagonists were their competitors the Spaniards rather than the indigenous peoples. And Hudson was looking only for a sea-route to the East, not for conquest. Ralegh was of course an ardent, dedicated, life-long imperialist; saluted by his successors in spite of his failures in Virginia and Guiana.[5] But his complacent belief that the native chiefs of Guiana had freely surrendered their land to Queen Elizabeth (see pp. 182, 246/7) is almost a whiff of comedy in the prolonged tragedy of the expropriation of the Americas.

All three men were fully aware of where they stood in the history of their country and where they wished to stand in that history. But they

[5] Quinn 1947.

were also victims of history; their dreams of personal and national triumph were not self-generated. They were inevitably creatures of the movements they helped to create. This is partly why the incompetence and misfortune which marred the end of their lives have tragic over-tones; they are by no means accountable for all the things that happened to them. I do not regard the three protagonists in this book as very admirable or even very agreeable people. There are great differences among them. It is hard to find any enthusiasm at all for the personality of Cavendish, whereas Ralegh was a remarkable and very gifted person in spite of all his failings (which I have not tried to disguise), and he had to endure intolerable malice and injustice. Hudson is the unobtrusive one of the three, strangely so; perhaps more of an enigma than the others because of this quietness about him.

But moral judgements on the three leaders are not the most important judgements to make on the material before us. In this respect at least the leaders are like tragic heroes. Our calculation of responsibility for the disastrous outcome of tragedies, while it continually triggers our moral approval and disapproval, tends to move forward to fundamental questions about the guidance of human affairs which are not to be answered in terms of the merits of individuals or judgement on their conduct. Defects of personality and errors of judgement abound in the voyages, as they do in the tragedies; they give the course of disaster its special direction, but not its inner energy. Kyd, Marlowe, and Shakespeare went to great lengths in their plays to suggest the mysterious power of unidentifiable forces to which all human will and striving were subject. The authors of the voyage narratives, by contrast, offer us a simple understanding of transcendental control. 'But God would not suffer me to die so happy a man,' wrote Cavendish (p. 77/21). 'When I saw all these men dead I praised God that had rid them out of their miserable estate,' wrote Knivet (p. 93/31). 'Now in this extremity it pleased God to give us sight of land,' wrote Pricket (p. 170/23). As I have said, these authors are not the Author. They write as characters in the drama, like the pious Albany in *King Lear*. What Shakespeare might have made of Ralegh's last voyage if he had lived to hear of it and had wished to make a fictional tragedy of it is worth pondering. In the real-life tragedy, the Author remains as invisible and as inscrutable as Shakespeare would no doubt have made the ultimate direction of affairs in his stage play.

Cavendish's desire for glory, Ralegh's desire to regain freedom and power, the desire of the gentlemen who enlisted with them for adventure and riches, the desire of the mariners for a livelihood, were all given their shape within the controlling climate of competitive nationalism. In the writings which have collected about these desires it is not really possible to take a view of the whole cloth of early imperialism, though it envelops them. Their value is different; they magnify the close weave.

I

*The Last Voyage of*
*Thomas Cavendish*
*1591–1593*

FIG. 1. Thomas Cavendish. Engraving by Crispin van de Passe from *Effigies Regum ac Principum* (Cologne, 1598). The legend 'Extremos pudeat rediisse' is from Virgil, *Aeneid*, v.196 ('It would be shameful to return last of all'); possibly the allusion is to Cavendish's refusal to return with dishonour. (Reproduced by permission of the National Maritime Museum, Greenwich)

# INTRODUCTION

## 1. *Cavendish and his Voyages*

WHEN Thomas Cavendish, 28 years of age, arrived back in Plymouth in 1588 as the third man to have sailed round the world, the Armada had just been defeated; and the great success of his voyage, a deep inroad into the Spanish monopoly of the Pacific, was welcomed as a further contribution to England's triumph over Spain. Cavendish's proud letter to Lord Hunsdon on the accomplishment of his mission, reporting how by navigating, burning, spoiling, capturing, and exploring he had opened up to England the riches of the East, I have placed as a prologue to the events of three years later (p. 50). From Plymouth, Cavendish took his ship, the Desire, round to the Thames to sail past the Queen at Greenwich. Even the heavy rain could not obliterate the splendid ostentation of the occasion. The sails of the ship were of blue damask, said a Spanish report, the standard of blue silk and cloth of gold. 'It was as if Cleopatra had been resuscitated.' Cavendish dined the Queen on board; the cabin was hung with cloth of gold and silver. Ballads were published, and rumour inflated the value of the booty to colossal figures (*CSP Spanish*, iv. 487–8, 491, 493).

Cavendish's attempt to repeat and outdo the triumph of 1586–8 is the subject of the first part of this book.

Thomas Cavendish—more properly Candish or Caundish (he usually signed himself 'Caundyssh')—was born in 1560, an heir to large estates in Suffolk. He spent some time at Cambridge without taking a degree and then, like his younger sister Anne, who became maid-in-waiting to the Queen, was attached to the Court. His election to Parliament in 1584 for Shaftesbury in Dorset and in 1586 for Wilton clearly marks a relationship with the great Earl of Pembroke's circle (Quinn 1975, p. 8). In 1585 Cavendish's maritime adventures began in connection with Ralegh's first expedition to Virginia. He fitted out his own bark, the Elizabeth (50 tons), and sailed as captain in her. His position in the expedition was as high marshal under the commander Sir Richard Grenville, responsible for law and discipline (Quinn 1955, p. 158). According to Ralph Lane, the leader of the settlement on Roanoke Island, Cavendish did not get on with Grenville (ibid. 210). It seems he preferred to rule rather than to serve. He was not one of the settlers himself but did not return in Grenville's company; the Elizabeth (it seems) came back separately (Quinn 1975, p. 8).

Almost at once Cavendish, 'thus fleshed and somewhat hardened unto the sea' (Hakluyt 1589, p. 809), began to prepare for his world-voyage. On 21 July 1586, some six years after Drake's circumnavigation in the Golden Hind, a fleet of three ships sailed from Plymouth: the Desire, a new ship of 120 tons, the Content (60 tons), and the Hugh Gallant (40 tons). The vivid account of the voyage which Hakluyt printed in 1600, replacing the briefer and starker narrative by 'N.H.' given in the 1589 collection, was by Francis Pretty of Ely, one of the gentlemen soldiers. It is as well to remember that England was at war with Spain, and that Cavendish's expedition (however much a private initiative) was part of the struggle for possession of the Far East. For the story is of a party of sea-borne marauders, plundering and burning and looting as they made their way down the west coast of Africa, the east coast of South America, through the Magellan Straits, and north up the west coast of the American continent as far as California. Cavendish could be ruthless in using thumbscrews and half-hanging to make his victims talk, but he was also courageous in heading his own raiding parties. There were full-scale military engagements with Spanish forces as well as the more frequent raids upon settlements. ('We burned the church and brought the bells away,' says Pretty once.) The English force had its losses as well as its triumphs. One of the striking features of Pretty's account, worth remembering when reading of the manifest under-provisioning of the later voyage and the consequent privation of the ships' companies, is the endless availability of water, meat, and grain ashore, and shipping afloat, for those hardy enough to seize them.

The great triumph of the voyage was the capture of the Santa Ana off the Californian coast. She was the richly laden Manila galleon heading for Acapulco; she surrendered only after a long and arduous fight. Cavendish took what he could in gold, pearl, silk, etc., but was unable, as his letter indicates, either to man the captured ship or accommodate all her cargo. The crew and passengers of the galleon were humanely treated and set on shore and the ship was burned.

In the long voyage across the Pacific Cavendish was reduced to the one ship, the Desire. The Hugh Gallant had been abandoned as a liability, and the Content was lost without trace after leaving the American coast. Cavendish reached the Philippines and explored southward through the Moluccas to Java. Then it was westward to the

Cape of Good Hope and north for St Helena and home. The East Indian part of the voyage was much more peaceful than the American part. Cavendish entertained Javanese potentates and disaffected Portuguese expatriates with banquets and music aboard the Desire. (The same musicians had trumpeted his men to the final successful onslaught on the Santa Ana.)

The circumnavigation occupied just over two years. Three years later Cavendish had equipped another fleet to repeat the voyage, to capitalize on the knowledge gained and the contacts made. He had bought two large ships, the Roebuck and the Galleon Dudley, and sent them out on privateering expeditions in 1589 and 1590. He then replaced the Dudley with the Galleon Leicester (which had been Edward Fenton's ship in his unsuccessful voyage to Brazil in 1582–3), refitted the Desire, and acquired the Black Pinnace—famous as the ship that had brought Sir Philip Sidney's body back to England from the Netherlands in 1587. He then got the interest of the widely experienced navigator John Davis, who agreed to sail with him and bring the Dainty, which he co-owned with Adrian Gilbert, on the understanding that he would part company off California to explore for a western end to the northern passage whose eastern entrance had eluded him on three separate voyages.

So, as John Jane tells us in his first paragraph (p. 98), on 26 August 1591, 'three tall ships and two barks' sailed from Plymouth. Cavendish was in the Galleon Leicester as admiral. The vice-admiral was the Roebuck, captained by Cavendish's kinsman John Cocke. The Desire, rear-admiral, was captained by John Davis. The Dainty was captained by Randolph Cotton, a great friend of Davis. And finally there was the Black Pinnace, whose master was Tobias Paris or Parris. (Jane twice refers to a captain of the Pinnace, as well as the master, but he is a shadowy figure, if he existed).

The events of the voyage are the subject of the contemporary accounts which follow. Cavendish suffered delays in reaching the Brazilian coast and then spent an inexplicably long time occupying Santos. A terrible storm split the fleet on the way south and caused further delay. The Dainty detached herself to return to England, or was sunk, while her captain was aboard the Roebuck. It was already 20 March and the onset of winter before the four ships left the imperfect shelter of Port Desire to try to pass through the Magellan Straits. They were already weakened by the battering of the storms and shortage of food. In very bad conditions and intense cold they fought their way forward for thirteen days until 21 April, when they were forced to

FIG. 2. The Black Pinnace. This ship which sank with all hands during the Cavendish voyage is here pictured when she was bringing Sir Philip Sidney's body back to England from the Netherlands in 1586. The engraving, by Theodore de Bry, is from the frontispiece of Thomas Lant's *Sequitur celebritas et pompa funeris* [etc.], 1587. (Reproduced by permission of the British Library)

FIG. 3. A galleon. Engraving by Visscher of the Golden Lion; one of several representations of English ships which took part in the Armada battle of 1588. Frank Howard, in *Sailing Ships of War 1400–1860* (1979, p. 55), notes that the engravings were made well after the event and resemble Dutch ships of the period. Reproduced by permission of the National Maritime Museum, Greenwich)

anchor in a small cove near Cape Froward, which they named Tobias Bay (see Knivet, p. 89/15). They stayed put for three weeks, with men dying daily of the cold and scurvy, and with nothing to obtain ashore except mussels and weeds. Davis would have gone on, but Cavendish argued they should go back and try for the East Indies via the Cape of Good Hope. The prospect of the long haul across the South Atlantic with their perilous shortage of sails and tackle, and provisions, appalled his subordinates, and Cavendish was persuaded to return to the Brazilian coast to try to replenish stores and equipment there.

After leaving the eastern end of the Straits (20 May), the four ships lost touch during the night, 'in a fret of weather', Davis said. Cavendish, with the Leicester and the Roebuck, continued north; Davis, with the Desire and the Black Pinnace, waited for Cavendish at Port Desire. This was the second turning-point of the expedition. Cavendish (who never heard any more of the separated ships) was convinced that Davis had purposely deserted him. The intensity of his abounding anger in the narrative focuses on Davis's treachery, as he saw it, because the absence of the two smaller ships left him totally incapable of entering most of the harbours along the coast, whose entrances were too shallow for the Leicester and the Roebuck to negotiate. The thought that the two ships had made for Port Desire (see p. 62/9) must have occurred to him too late to act on it. His progress up the coast was utterly disastrous. In another terrible storm he lost touch with the Roebuck. Twenty-five men who went ashore at St Vincent were ambushed and killed by Portuguese and Indians. The Roebuck rejoined in a very battered state; Cavendish resolved to get rid of her, re-using what he could out of her, before making a fresh start for the Straits; but he dared not make his intention known. They went north to 'Spiritus Sanctus' (Vitória). A raid on two ships lying in the river went completely awry when two boats full of heavily armed men were ambushed from both sides of the river, causing severe casualties. On withdrawing, the Roebuck under cover of night detached herself and set course for England. Her sick captain, John Cocke, was aboard the Leicester. The Roebuck had on board the fleet's two surgeons, while the Leicester had the men wounded in the recent action.

The Leicester went south again, to the island of St Sebastian, which had been a haven for Cavendish on his circumnavigation. This was probably early October 1592 (see Cavendish's narrative, p. 74/5 and note). Cavendish went ashore to rebuild his boat, which took twelve days. He claims that an Irishman in his crew went over to the mainland

and betrayed his presence to the Portuguese. They came over anyway, and slaughtered many of those who in defiance of Cavendish's instructions were sleeping ashore.

In the face of the continuous hostility of his recalcitrant company, Cavendish at this point gave up all thought of returning to the Magellan Straits. He persuaded the crew to make for St Helena, there to mend or end. While he slept the course would be altered towards the north. They never reached St Helena. 'I was forced to go towards England.' John Cocke died, and we assume that soon afterwards Cavendish, having made his will and completed his narrative of the voyage, died also. If he died by his own hand there was a conspiracy of silence to conceal the fact. The Leicester was probably back in England by early February 1593 (see below, p. 49). She was certainly in Portsmouth, in company again with the Roebuck, in March.

What happened to Davis in the Desire is clearly and vividly described by John Jane. The Desire and the Black Pinnace remained at Port Desire from the end of May until early August, when they set sail for the Magellan Straits. They were still in poor condition, men and materials alike. After being beaten back twice, they eventually emerged into the Pacific, but into such a terrible storm that the Black Pinnace was lost with all hands. After nine days the Desire was forced to give up and put back through the straits to Port Desire yet again. They killed and salted penguins at Penguin Isle nearby, losing nine men to the Indians. They left on 22 December and made their way north in the teeth of scarcely credible adversities. Of the seventy-five men in the ship when they left England only sixteen survived, and of these only five men were fit enough to handle the ship as she came into Bearhaven in Ireland on 11 June 1593.

Meanwhile, a sealed package containing Cavendish's will and his account of the expedition had been duly delivered to its intended recipient, Tristram Gorges (Quinn 1975, p. 6). Gorges must have taken immediate steps to implement Cavendish's wishes about his effects. Letters of administration were granted to Cavendish's sister Anne on 14 March 1593, and the Privy Council wrote to the mayor of Portsmouth on 18 March asking the port to deliver the Leicester and the Roebuck 'with their lading' to Anne's husband Robert Dudley (*APC* 1592–3, p. 125). But counter-representations were made to the Privy Council by those who had returned in the Leicester, so the Council wrote to Gorges instructing him not to deny a proper share in the proceeds of the voyage to twelve 'soldiers', four of them being named as

John Theobald, Robert Russel, William Harrison, and Gabriel North (ibid., 232–3).

There was no protest, however, on Davis's behalf. Watch for his return (supposedly having made himself very rich in the South Sea!) was mounted by the Privy Council on 1 July 1593—by which time Davis and his one ruinous ship had actually reached Ireland. As soon as the Privy Council heard of Davis's arrival in Devon, they ordered him to be arrested and brought to London (ibid. 375, 435). He must have vindicated himself successfully, though there is no record of his interrogation. His public vindication appeared in the dedication to his book, *The Seaman's Secrets*, written in August 1594 and published in 1595, printed below, pp. 96–8.

Probate was eventually granted for Cavendish's estate on 4 February 1596. Gorges's legal representative added to the will a selection of passages of a testamentary character from Cavendish's narrative (Quinn 1975, pp. 41–3). To this remarkable narrative I now turn.

## 2. *Cavendish's Narrative*

Cavendish's own account of his final voyage was first printed by Samuel Purchas in *Hakluytus Posthumus or Purchas his Pilgrimes* (1625, vol. iv, bk. vi, pp. 1192–1201). Purchas's contents list indicates that he had the manuscript from Hakluyt, who presumably had decided not to print it in the 1598–1600 edition of his collection of voyages. Purchas discreetly omitted 'some passionate speeches of Master Candish against some private persons' (see p. 53/12). Either he or Hakluyt before him also smoothed and sophisticated the rough edges of Cavendish's impetuous discourse to a considerable degree. Three hundred and thirty years later, in 1956, a manuscript of the narrative (now in the possession of Paul Mellon) was shown to Professor David B. Quinn of Liverpool University, who produced an outstanding edition, with facsimile, transcript, and full introduction and commentary, in 1975.

It is hard to agree with David Quinn's contention that the manuscript was in fact written in Cavendish's own hand. The one letter of Cavendish's which survives (to Walsingham, 8 October 1588, reproduced by Quinn, p. 4) is in italic; it is a rounded italic, quite unlike the angular italic which occurs here and there in the narrative (which as a whole is in secretary hand). The signature at the end of the narrative is in the same angular italic, and is not at all like the recorded specimens of Cavendish's signature which Quinn reproduces (pp. 4, 5, 143). It is also spelt differently, 'Caundyshe', whereas all the others have double 's', 'Caundysshe' or 'Caundyssh'. Quinn also argued that Cavendish's will (which he reproduces in facsimile) is in his own hand. The will is certainly signed by Cavendish, but it looks very much as though the text itself is in the hand of the last witness, Robert Hues, the mathematician and geographer who accompanied Cavendish on both his voyages.

It seems most likely that the extant manuscript is an extremely careful and faithful scribal transcript of Cavendish's original manuscript. The firmness and regularity of the writing are quite at odds with the despairing, impatient staccato of the language. The many erasures never seem to be the false starts of an author; they are often erasures of the more normal and expected wording, which has been corrected to take account of an unorthodox or eccentric phrase. There is evidence of scribal puzzlement too, as when 'not' is corrected to 'but' and then returned to 'not' again (p. 65/9). Several times there are corrections of what one can only take to be initial misreadings. The impossible 'hurte' is corrected to 'shorte' (p. 62/14), and 'lacketh' is corrected to 'loveth' (p. 74/19). The obvious error 'quarter' is corrected to 'equator' (p. 78/1).

It would seem almost certain that the manuscript edited by Quinn was also the manuscript used as copy by Purchas's compositors in 1625. The unusual spelling 'the rune' for 'they run' (p. 79/29) appears in Purchas as 'the ruine'! On three occasions a smudge of ink in the manuscript has been taken for a deletion. In the phrase 'turne to windewarde' (p. 58/13) the word 'to' is blotched and does not appear in Purchas. There is a smudge over 'else' (p. 64/6) and the word is omitted in Purchas. Similarly the word 'of' in 'fote of water' (p. 65/6) is obscured by a blob of ink, and Purchas's compositor, again presumably understanding a deletion, prints 'foot water'. It is nevertheless puzzling that occasionally, when a word has been erased and changed in the manuscript, Purchas prints the old instead of the new reading (e.g. 'willingly' instead of 'wilfully' at p. 62/27).

If the manuscript is scribal rather than authorial, there is no doubt that the scribe has taken the greatest trouble to reproduce carefully the quirks and idiosyncracies in the wording of his original, restoring oddities where he had first written normalities, and preserving anomalies of grammar which are ruthlessly 'corrected' by Purchas. The disorder of the language leaves us in no doubt that we have an authentic reproduction of Cavendish's own account in his own hand, but I do not think we possess his original papers.

Cavendish presumably began to write his account when the Leicester had failed to find St Helena (thanks largely to the efforts of the crew) and he had given up hope of achieving any kind of success, however small. He was passively accepting the northward course which his men had been urging on him for weeks. The last recorded event in the narrative is that when he was 'eight degrees benorth the line' (i.e. about the latitude of the Orinoco) his dear kinsman and ally John Cocke died. It was at this time, I take it, that Cavendish made his will and began his narrative of self-justification, not expecting to live to report his own cause in England. The narrative is filled with the certainty of impending death. It is for the reader to judge whether the voice we hear in the narrative is the voice of a dying man or of a man determined to die. I consider the narrative to be the last act of defiance of a defeated leader before he took his own life.

The purpose of the narrative as I see it is threefold: to save his name from disgrace by demonstrating that the failure of the expedition was not his fault; to reach out and lay posthumous claim for his own nominees to whatever financial assets might be rescued and realized from the voyage; and, by stressing as he wrote that he was terminally ill, to avoid the inevitable forfeiture to the Crown of all his goods and chattels if it were known that he had committed suicide. All these objectives are evident in the opening pages. He stresses that he feels the hand of death on him; he harps on the possible return of ships that disappeared in the night, whose winnings will still be his; he objurgates Davis for 'running' from him and crippling the expedition; he belabours his mutinous and unruly ship's company; he dwells on the fury of the weather they encountered, 'such as worser might not be endured'.

As Cavendish describes the voyage, it was a continuous struggle against terrible weather and treasonable associates. Nothing whatever is said of the under-provisioning of the fleet, nor of the disastrously extended stay at Santos. Nothing whatever is said about exposing sick men to die on shore, once in the bitter cold of winter in the Magellan Straits and once in enemy territory in Brazil (see Jane, p. 101/5 and Knivet, p. 90/1 and p. 93/21). Nothing whatever is said about hanging the Portuguese pilot who overestimated the depth of water at the entrance to Spiritus Sanctus. But while he does not mention a number of exhibitions of personal violence described by Knivet, he is not reticent in his account of quelling a mutiny by half-strangling the ringleader (p. 75/26).

Cavendish writes at length about two major phases of the voyage: the decision to turn back when the ships were so very near to the Pacific, and the débâcle at Spiritus Sanctus (Vitória). Concerning the first, Cavendish expatiates on his inability to persuade his recalcitrant men to go for the Cape of Good Hope when all they wanted was the coast of Brazil 'which I so much hated'; but in the end, he says laconically, 'I was forced to take that way'. Concerning the raid on Spiritus Sanctus, Cavendish goes to extreme lengths to absolve himself of any responsibility for a disaster which he blamed entirely on the continued disobedience of headstrong men.

Towards the end of the narrative, Cavendish's burden is that in spite of all reversals, all losses, all desertions, he never intended to give up and return to England empty-handed and inglorious. Even after the disaster at Spiritus Sanctus and the desertion of the Roebuck, he says he was encouraging his men 'to perform or die' (p. 75/2). He states that he still intended to go for the Magellan Straits and the Pacific. 'These persuasions took no place with them.' With the further reverses at St Sebastian, a new note of refusal enters as he records his company's determination to return to England:

But in truth I desired nothing more than to attempt that course, rather desiring to die in going forward than basely [to live] in returning backward again. But God would not suffer me to die so happy a man, although I sought all the ways I could still to attempt to perform somewhat. ... I resolved them plainly that to England I would never give my consent to go, and that if they would not take such courses as I intended, that then I was determined that ship and all should sink in the seas together.   (p. 77)

So the intention was formed for St Helena, 'to make ourselves happy by mending or ending'. Perhaps they would find a carrack, and so wreak that revenge on the Portuguese which he had so vociferously promised (p. 64/25) and so ignominiously failed to effect. But the Leicester never reached St Helena.

As the histrionic self-justification nears its end and Cavendish nears *his* end, the narrative becomes very moving even in its continued extravagance.

And now by this, what with grief for him [John Cocke] and the continual trouble I endured amongst such hell-hounds, my spirit was clean spent, wishing myself upon any desert place in the world, there to die, rather than thus basely to return home again.   (p. 79)

How he died, no one has told us. With the making of his will, and the instructions to the master what to do with some of the ordnance when the ship returned, it is quite clear that those who were close to him knew that either through illness or determination he was very near death. But of the death itself there is no record. Death by violence or sickness was so much a matter of course on this expedition, from which two-thirds of those involved never returned (Quinn 1975, p. 38), that perhaps the silence is not so extraordinary. Of course, it could be suggested that he did *not* die at this time; that his nearness to death in the narrative was pretended and his subsequent death on board was faked; that he re-entered England to live under another name. But such a hoax imputes to the narrative a cunning which would need the temerity and mastery of Iago to contrive.

The language of Cavendish's narrative is remarkable. The elaborate syntax is in a perpetual state of defeat, which mirrors the continuous frustration he is describing. The trailing clauses of his labyrinthine sentences and the absence of main verbs are an index of Cavendish's paralysis, his indecision and his helplessness. It is not rapid writing alone that generates these continuously uncompleted sentences; the sudden switches from one grammatical construction to another, the insertion of parentheses which invade and take over the paragraph altogether, vividly suggest the turbulence of reliving his torments of indecision and vain resolution. The punctuation in this edition is entirely editorial; while it does less than Purchas's does to cool the fever of Cavendish's emotions, it still imposes on the narrative an order it does not possess (as can be seen from Quinn's transcript). It will be noticed that at times the confusion is caused by an attempt to be orderly, deliberate, and rational. Present participles show him weighing up the situation, I knowing this and finding that—but there the trouble starts; the considerations get more and more involved and a decisive main verb becomes less and less possible.

What may seem to the reader an occasional dramatic confusion of tenses is in fact an illusion, for example: 'The next morning I shot ordnance, yet I see no boat come' (p. 63/24). 'See' is Cavendish's normal form of the past tense (for 'saw'). But at the very beginning of the narrative there is a particularly dramatic use of an unexpected tense. 'I have appointed some of the most sensiblest men *that I left behind me . . .*', he tells Gorges. Even as he begins his narrative, he thinks of himself as dead.

## 3. *Antony Knivet*

Antony Knivet's narrative comes from Samuel Purchas's *Hakluytus Posthumus or Purchas his Pilgrimes* (1625, pt. iv, bk. vi, pp. 1201–42), where, as here, it immediately follows Cavendish's own account. Purchas's contents list marks it 'HP', indicating that he had the manuscript from Hakluyt but that he himself had supplemented it or edited it.

It was a full ten years after embarking with Cavendish in the Galleon Leicester at Plymouth in 1591 that Knivet got back to England. His story of his adventures, which one imagines was written up at Hakluyt's request, is an extraordinary narrative. The account of the voyage itself, which is all that is given in this book, is only the opening of a unique Elizabethan autobiography. When Cavendish reached St Sebastian in October 1592, still debating with himself what he could do to save his expedition from total failure, he put twenty sick men out of the Leicester and left them ashore to fend for themselves. (He does not tell us this in his narrative.) Knivet, seriously ill and disabled with the after-effects of frost-bite, was one of these. He survived, to be captured by the Portuguese; he again survived, escaping summary execution because he spoke Portuguese. He saw the Leicester sailing away into the distance and entered his years of hardship living with the Portuguese and the Indian tribes, always failing in his attempts to escape, eventually becoming accepted by his captors, until in 1599 he reached Lisbon and set up as an interpreter to English and Scottish merchants. On 27 September 1601 it was recorded that 'Antony Knyvett, an Englishman born in Wiltshire, who has been prisoner in Spain and Brazil these seven years' had landed at Portsmouth and was being sent by the mayor to see Sir Robert Cecil (*CSP Dom.*, 1601–3, p. 105).

Almost nothing is known about Antony Knivet, or Knyvet, apart from what he tells us himself. The Knyvets were an ancient Norfolk family, the main branch being at Buckenham, between Bury St Edmunds and Norwich. Antony belonged to the branch which settled at Charlton in Wiltshire during the sixteenth century. Many of the family achieved positions of note in Tudor and Stuart times. It is quite clear that the Antony we are concerned with was a gentleman. Purchas tells us so (see p. 54/18), and his fellow-survivor Henry Barrawell was shocked when on their first interrogation by Salvador Correia de Sá, governor of the Rio de Janeiro region, Knivet told him he was 'a poor ship boy'. Barrawell 'reproved' him, but Knivet, grimly realistic, retorted that 'he was no other' than a poor ship boy (Purchas, xvi. 196). Of one of the darkest periods of his time in Brazil, when he had been living for months with an Indian tribe, naked as they, he wrote: 'I began to curse the time that ever I heard the name of the sea, and grieved to think how fond I was to forsake my natural country where I wanted nothing' (ibid. 224). It was obviously not poverty that drove Knivet to join Cavendish but adventure. He was a young gentleman volunteer, looking for action and (no doubt) plunder. He was noticed by John Cocke, vice-admiral of the expedition and Cavendish's kinsman, who singled him out for favour (p. 84/27) and intervened to protect him (p. 90/8).

Knivet was an unusual young man. He had an extraordinary gift for languages. Presumably he acquired the knowledge of Portuguese that saved his life from the two Portuguese taken on board by Cavendish (who at different times hanged them both). The same facility enabled him to pick up the languages of the different tribes of Indians he came in contact with, especially the Puri and the Tamoios, and his value as an interpreter was fully recognized by Salvador Correia de Sá from the beginning. (On a voyage to Pernambuco, the governor's ship was wrecked. 'The Governor commanded me to be set on shore to talk with the wild people, and to know of them upon what coast we were' (Purchas, xvi. 239).)

Knivet seems to have had a delight in seeking out and befriending the stranger, the foreigner, the fugitive, even before he himself became a captive in a strange land. On the voyage out, Christopher the Japanese was for a time his particular friend. He took a great interest in the two Indians who fled from the Portuguese at Santos and were taken on board by Cavendish; without special intention his narrative keeps these two in view, as it does the Portuguese pilot Gaspar Jorge, captured at Cabo Frio, and it follows each of the three to his separate unhappy end. In Brazil, on one of his many attempts to escape, he came across a fugitive Indian slave and teamed up with him. 'Never man found truer friendship of any than I did of him' (Purchas, xvi. 203). Much later, when he was in much better circumstances, he befriended a 'mulatto slave', Domingos Gomez (ibid. 234, 244).

Although there are in the narrative occasional general comments on the faithlessness or brutality of the Portuguese or the Indians, Knivet is in the main concerned with people as individuals and there is remarkably little racism in his bestowal of praise and blame. He was betrayed, deceived, or badly let down by people of all nationalities, his Japanese friend, an English fellow-captive, an Indian chief, his Portuguese master. The brutality of Cavendish is recorded as impartially as that of the Portuguese governor. The Indians come off best, although Knivet had strong preferences among the tribes and although he records some very gruesome details of cannibalism. Being ordered by the Portuguese to go into very wild territory to find new slaves, he was reluctant to obey, but in the end 'I chose once again rather to stand to the heathen mercy of savage maneaters than at the bloody cruelty of Christian Portugals' (Purchas, xvi. 206).

We must now consider the very difficult matter of Knivet's accuracy and veracity. The circumstantial detail of the narrative is most striking, as in (let us say) Cavendish gambling just before the great storm (p. 86), or the Portuguese woman in the captured canoe who 'was going to be married that morning' (p. 84/6), or the all-important question of the whereabouts of the boats at the time of the massacre of Cavendish's men at Santos (pp. 91–2). These incidents, told as freshly as if they had happened yesterday, happened seven or eight years before the events at the end of the narrative.

It is impossible that Knivet should have kept a manuscript journal or record with him (as Dampier did years later). Disastrously, he lost all his possessions overboard before the Leicester reached the Straits. He lay helpless and ill for many weeks before being put ashore to die. He then endured a long period of degradation as a prisoner and a slave of the Portuguese. He spent many months as a runaway living with Indians. He could not have had writing materials with him during this long period of utter destitution. At the same time, we do not have to think that he wrote nothing down until he was home again in England and then began, perhaps at Hakluyt's instigation, to compose the narrative we have, which with its frequent 'I told you before of . . .' certainly suggests a unified reporting effort. After a year or two in Brazil he was in much better circumstances and was actually being paid for the work he was doing, and he could well have begun to set down the recollections which form the basis of the narrative. Again, he must have told his adventures to all sorts of companions from the beginning of his long land-service and in this way preserved the memories. Perhaps even more important as regards the minuteness of detail about the voyage itself is the fact that he several times mentions former shipmates *now living in England* who can corroborate his story. This applies particularly to an incident which Knivet clearly feels will not be credited, and which he relates twice, the occasion when the frost-bitten nose of Harris the goldsmith came away in his hand (p. 89). Knivet must have sought out the survivors of the

Leicester on his return, and his narrative way well have been reinforced by their joint recollections.

To feel that we can explain the phenomenal detail of the narrative is not to settle the larger question of Knivet's truthfulness. It is hard at first not to feel an amused scepticism about Knivet's adventures. Doesn't he say that he had seen a mermaid? (Purchas, xvi. 282.) I have become more and more convinced that Knivet's story is essentially true. What is really extraordinary about Knivet is not his inventive talent at all but his capacity for survival, his tenacious memory, and his passion for detail. This last eventually defeated Purchas, who at one point wrote in the margin, 'Dangers of the author which here followed, as in other places of the history, for brevity's sake are omitted' (ibid. 237).

It is probable that Purchas as well as Hakluyt knew Knivet and discussed his narrative with him (ibid. 212). They corroborated his story when they could. When Knivet mentions a Thomas Turner in Brazil, the marginal note reads, 'This Thomas Turner I was acquainted with, and received of him some notes, which follow after M. Knivet' (ibid. 243). But corroboration goes much further; for all the individuality of Knivet's recollections, the structure of the voyage as he relates it tallies perfectly with the other accounts, while for the years in Brazil the work of Francisco Carvalho Franco in measuring Portuguese records against Knivet's account has dramatically confirmed its veracity (see especially p. 136 of his 1947 edition). Modern ethnologists and anthropologists find his descriptions of the customs of the individual Indian tribes an important source of information. John Hemming made much use of Knivet in his comprehensive study, *Red Gold: The Conquest of the Brazilian Indians* (1978).

If Knivet's tale were a tissue of invention, he would be a greater story-teller than Defoe. Defoe's business was to mislead the public into accepting that Crusoe was a real person who had actually undergone the adventures described. Defoe was brilliant in creating the circumstantial details and the melancholy musings which gave the public the conviction that they had an authentic document before them. But not even Defoe can manufacture that genuineness which stamps Knivet's meeting with the leader of the Portuguese force on San Sebastian after his capture (p. 95):

This Canibal carried me along the shore, and when we came where any rocks reached into the sea, he would take me on his back and swim with me round about the rocks till we were free from the rocks. Thus we went almost all night, till at length we came by a great cliff that stood by the shore. Then the savage

whistled and another savage answered him from the cliff, whereupon five or six
Portugals came forth, and amongst them came the captain with a piece of bread
and marmalet in his hand. And as soon as he saw me he asked me what news. I
answered that I was very hungry and desired him that he would give me some
meat, and then I would tell him all the news that I could. With that all the
Portugals brake out in a laughter, and gave me bread and fish to eat.

However, with all this said, the Cavendish voyage as Knivet presents
it is the voyage as he experienced it and the voyage as he remembered it,
and the voyage as he chose to write it up and had the capacity to write it
up. It is what has stuck in his memory that counts (incidents often
unnoticed or ignored by others), and these memories have assumed a
patina through the lapse of time, through constant retelling, through the
operation of both voluntary and involuntary censorship, through the
shaping activity of language. Fading and distortion, addition and
omission, embroidery and smoothing there are bound to be. The
sequence of events in particular seems very muddled—self-evidently
muddled as well as by reference to known, datable events. But these
disorderings do not sabotage or disqualify what seems to be a
fundamental honesty in Knivet's story.

This honesty appears clearly and matters greatly in his presentation of
himself. Knivet is almost indifferent to the kind of figure he cuts in his
own story. Apart from the talent for self-exculpation ineradicable in
humanity, there is no attempt whatsoever to glorify or even dignify
himself. If he is pleased with himself at times, his long record of
vicissitudes is cast in a wholly unheroic mode. The question might arise,
is it then anti-heroic? A comparison with Thomas Nashe's unfortunate
traveller Jack Wilton, whose fictional adventures were published in
1954, is irresistible (see P. Edwards 1987). Here too is a young
gentleman getting into scrapes on a military expedition and eventually
finding himself on his own in extreme situations where the comedy of
his hair-raising escapes is more obvious to the reader than to the
participant. He is always the underdog, he always comes off worst, he
always survives. It is Antony Knivet who gets stuck under the boat's
thwarts and nearly suffocates (p. 83); Antony Knivet who gets tricked
out of his money by his best friend (p. 86); Antony Knivet whose feeble
voice tells the burying party that he is still alive (p. 90); Antony Knivet
who slides helplessly on a sea-chest from side to side of the deck during
a storm at night (p. 91); Antony Knivet whom the General strikes with a
rope's-end as he tries to chastise the top-of-yard men (p. 91). Knivet
certainly emphasizes that he is on the receiving end of Fortune's

buffeting, and it is sometimes difficult not to laugh at his misfortunes. His resemblance to a picaresque hero of fiction is at times startling, but here the 'I' of the story really is the author, and his sufferings were real. If his attitude towards himself sometimes seems to belong to a convention, that doesn't give him back his frost-bitten toes.

The great value of Knivet's ironic presentation of himself and of the whole voyage is in the splendid contrast which is established with Cavendish's grandiose, self-justifying, self-pitying account. Possibly some of Knivet's comments on the man who put him ashore to die were suppressed by Hakluyt and Purchas, but what did Purchas think he was achieving by printing Knivet's account immediately after Cavendish's? It is like Shakespeare's *Henry V*, when the rhetoric of the thieving Pistol guys and debunks the King's imperialist eloquence, or like Yeats's *On Baile's Strand*, in which the Fool's actions are a cynical and belittling mirror of Cuchulain's impulsive heroism. For in Knivet's narrative great endeavour is bathed in a different light; what we hear about is the bickering and quarrelling among the gentlemen soldiers, the perpetual hunger, and the 'sharking' for the food which they pillaged on shore. It is an anarchic, Hobbesian society that Knivet portrays, never reduced to order and submission by the cruel and unjust autocrat who led them. It is Knivet's tribute to Cavendish when his courage and his example inspired the company (p. 87/15) that makes his many examples of Cavendish's ruthlessness so telling, just as his occasional examples of affection and co-operation among individuals underline the centrifugal, disintegrating quality of the entire voyage.

The power of Knivet's narrative does not lie in literary artistry. I shall take one paragraph as an example. As he prepares to relate the traumatic event which was the turning-point of his whole life, being abandoned on St Sebastian (p. 93), there is a kind of pause, as it were a collection of himself to do justice to this dark moment, in its first sentence. 'Well, we came to San Sebastian Island.' He gathers pace only slowly, frequently repeating himself: 'I was not able to stir', 'I could not speak nor stir'. This halting simplicity is already creating the effect that he is manœuvring to achieve. When by the end of the paragraph he has obtained the confidence of a literary sententiousness most unusual in him, we admire it not for itself at all but as a token of the deep emotion with which he recollects a terrifying situation and which makes him try to invest it with an appropriate eloquence.

When I saw all these men dead I praised God that had rid them out of their miserable estate and cursed my hard fortune that death itself did refuse to end my tormented and most miserable life. I looked towards the shore and saw nothing but these pease, and if I did eat them I was sure of death; if I did not eat them I saw no remedy but to starve.

Knivet's eloquence works in ways he doesn't know about; by inadequacy and over-adequacy.

It is difficult to find a severance-point at which to conclude the 'Cavendish chapter' of Knivet's account. I have chosen the moment of a brief improvement in his fortunes after he had been brought before the Portuguese governor and assigned to work for the 'mestizo' who had saved him from the slaughter of the English on St Sebastian. Summarizing what happened to Knivet after this is not an easy matter, because of the multitude of incidents and because the sequence of these incidents is very unreliable.

It was presumably while he was working for the mestizo that the men from Davis's ship the Desire, putting in at Ilha Grande on their way north, were massacred by the Portuguese. Two survived and Knivet met them (see p. 90). One of them, a one-eyed surgeon called Andrew Towers, became revered by the Portuguese as a magus; later, he invented a diving-suit in order to retrieve some sunken Portuguese cannons, and Knivet, who was promised his freedom if he could get a line round these guns, nearly died in the futile experiment.

Knivet was taken away from the mestizo and forced to work in a sugar-mill. He got away and with help from the Indians lived rough for many months, until the governor found him again and put him to hard labour under a particularly malevolent factor at the mill. The governor's illegitimate son, Martim de Sá, then asked for Knivet and was granted him, and used him well for two years. Knivet describes in detail an expedition he was sent on to gather new slaves.

In 1593, Knivet heard that Richard Hawkins was off the coast in the Dainty. He made a bid to get to St Sebastian to try to find him. He said that he actually saw the ships, but his little boat came to grief and he was recaptured. He was condemned to death but the friars begged his life; he was publicly flogged and made to work in fetters at the mill. He was again so badly treated by the factor that he attacked him and left him for dead and ran away again. He came across another fugitive, an Indian, and after long travel they were adopted by the Puri tribe. Knivet tried to work them up against the Portuguese, but in the end they betrayed him to Martim de Sá. He was sent on another slave-gathering expedition, a very dangerous one, no doubt being regarded as entirely expendable.

In time Knivet became accepted by the governor and was actually paid for his work. The governor even looked favourably on Knivet's desire to get to Angola. (Knivet had a scheme for getting home via Turkey.) But he was conscripted onto a major punitive expedition, or bandeira, led by Martim de Sá against the Tamoio tribe. This was a very tough expedition; it took many weeks and in the end they could not find their enemy. In the wilderness Martim de Sá made all sorts of accusations against Knivet and condemned him to be hanged. The Portuguese refused to carry out the sentence and it was generally believed that Martim was looking for a way of getting rid of Knivet. This contretemps was the end of an expedition which in its mismanagement and fruitlessness rivalled Cavendish's. Rather than return with the main body, Knivet and twelve young Portuguese broke off to seek their fortunes 'rather than return without anything'. Their plan to make for the South Sea ended abruptly when they were captured by Tamoio Indians who ceremonially slew the twelve Portuguese, sparing Knivet because he swore he was a Frenchman! Knivet lived with them for many months, going naked as they, and (he claims) teaching them the art of warfare. 'By this means we had always the upper hand of our enemies, and I was held in great accompt amongst them. ... The Tamoyes offered me many wives, but I refused, saying it was not our custom to take wives out of our country' (Purchas, xvi. 223).

Knivet now made the serious error of persuading the Tamoios to migrate to the coast, with the hope of trading with the French. As they neared Santos, the Portuguese got wind of the migration and mounted an expedition which massacred a third of the tribe and took the remainder as slaves. According to John Hemming, who noted that Knivet expresses no regret for his action, the tribe has no further history (Hemming, pp. 138, 159).

In 1597 Knivet was smuggled aboard a ship and actually got across the South Atlantic to Angola. But mishaps protracted the voyage, and word of his defection had already reached Angola. He was quickly found and sent back in irons to Rio de Janeiro. The governor 'began to laugh and to jest with me, saying I was welcome out of England'. But he 'used me very well'. It must have been earlier than this (1595?), though Knivet says it was afterwards, that he had English companions who had deserted from Abraham Cocke's expedition to the River Plate. 'We were then nine Englishmen,' said Knivet. This presumably includes Henry Barrawell (who settled in Brazil) and Andrew Towers. They and three Dutchmen made a plan to get away but one of the Englishmen, Richard

Heixt ('they all said that he was a gentleman') informed on them to the governor, adding lurid emboidery to the scheme which only discredited him. The governor said 'that he never saw men of so perverse and vile condition as we were to seek the destruction of each other'.

In 1599 (one of three datings which he gives) Knivet went to Lisbon with the governor with whom he had been associated for so long, Salvador Correia de Sá. After a good nine months living in the governor's house and spending all his money, he fell seriously ill and was saved from dying by the good offices of an Englishwoman, Mistress Foster, who 'made her approbation' in a convent.

Knivet now found work as an interpreter to Scottish and English merchants and began to do well. But Salvador Correia de Sá, believing he had a right to his services, demanded his return. Knivet ignored him and so de Sá had him arrested in the street 'as if I had been some notorious villain'. He was put in prison, and he shouted through the bars for help. 'Many pitied me, but none could help me, &c.' And there, tantalizingly and mysteriously, the narrative breaks off. What follows is a voluminous but extremely interesting account by Knivet of 'the divers nations of savages in Brazil' and 'the description of divers rivers, ports, harbours, islands of Brazil'. What the rest of his Portuguese experiences were and how he got to England again is not known.

## 4. *John Davis*

John Davis, the man whom Cavendish recruited as third in command of his expedition and whom in the end he accused of betraying him and ruining the voyage, was without doubt one of the finest of all the Elizabethan seamen. And he was indeed a seaman, not an adventurer or a plunderer; a fine seaman, who made notable expeditions into northern waters, who wrote an important book on navigation, who was liberal, tolerant, and peaceable in his dealings with the men he commanded and with the inhabitants of the regions he explored. He was ten years older than Cavendish (born about 1550) and had much more experience in handling ships and exploring little-known seas.

He was a West Country man, closely associated with the Gilberts, especially Adrian. Humphrey Gilbert was an ardent believer in the existence of the north-west passage, and this route to China and the East became Davis's life-long obsession. Martin Frobisher had made three voyages in the 1570s, and in 1579, after the completion of the last of these, we find Davis with Adrian Gilbert in discussions with John

Dee, the savant of British imperialism who advised so many Elizabethan explorers on matters of mathematics and cosmography. In 1583 Gilbert and Davis were with Dee again, and this time no less a person than Sir Francis Walsingham, Secretary of State, joined them, and was made 'privy of the N.W. passage' (Markham, p. ix).

There followed in 1584 Letters Patent from the Queen, granting permission to a company presided over by Adrian Gilbert to search for a passage to China by north-west and north-east and north. Davis then made three major voyages, in 1585, 1586, and 1587, which were financed by a number of merchants, the most important of whom was William Sanderson. Sanderson's nephew and agent, John Jane or Janes, accompanied Davis and became his loyal associate and the historian of his voyages. Davis himself wrote up his second voyage, and gave a splendid, detailed account of the inhabitants of Greenland. But the passage was not found, and the merchants, apart from Sanderson, were unwilling to finance further efforts. As Davis himself put it with amusing frankness, they had this objection: 'Why hath not Davis discovered this passage being thrice that way employed?'

The possibility of exploring the China passage from its western end in the northern Pacific led Davis (he says) to accept Cavendish's invitation to accompany him on his attempt at a second circumnavigation. He brought with him the Dainty, which he co-owned with Adrian Gilbert, and it was captained by his friend Randolph Cotton. Davis himself was captain of the Desire, in which Cavendish had made his first world voyage. The behaviour of the Dainty is puzzling. Knivet says she was loaded with sugar and plunder from the Portuguese ships at Santos, and that then the captain, 'having made a good voyage', told Cavendish he was returning to England. Cavendish persuaded him to stay with the fleet until they reached the River Plate. The severe storm of 7 February put paid to any plans for a foray into the River Plate, and the ships were scattered. Knivet says that the Dainty never showed up at Port Desire; Jane says that she returned to England when her captain was aboard the Roebuck and had with him only 'the apparel that he wore'.

It is very unlikely that Knivet was correct in saying that Cotton was ready to give up the voyage at Santos. What then would Davis do when they reached California? If there was indeed a plan to return, for whatever reason, why did they turn back when the captain was temporarily out of the ship? It seems possible that the storm of 7 February blew up very suddenly and took Cotton by surprise when he was visiting the Roebuck (see note to Jane, p. 100/12). Either the Dainty sank in the storm, or, finding themselves on their own, her master and men decided they had had enough of Cavendish and made their way home. But once she was gone, Davis's plans to explore the north-west passage from its western exit must have changed radically. Whether, after losing touch with Cavendish and making a second attempt to get through the Magellan Straits with the Desire and the Black Pinnace, he was still thinking of going to the Arctic, it is impossible to say. His actions from the separation on 20 May 1592 until the dismal exhausted remnant brought the Desire into Bearhaven in June 1593 are discussed in the next section of this introduction.

Hurrying back to England from Bearhaven, Davis found himself faced with the dead Cavendish's accusations of desertion and treachery. Though he must have answered them successfully, their effect on him may be judged from the force of the public protest which he made in the dedication of his book, *The Seaman's Secrets*, dated August 1594. This protest is the only account of the voyage we have from Davis (if we exclude the high-flown speeches which Jane put into his mouth), and the relevant extracts are given on pp. 96–8. The book was entered for publication on 3 September 1594. Until recently the earliest known edition was that of 1607, which A. H. Markham reprinted in his Hakluyt Society volume of 1880, *The Voyages and Works of John Davis*. The text given here is from the British Library copy of the 1595 edition. There are numerous differences in the wording of the dedication between the two editions. I have paraphrased the introductory courtesies.

Davis's next book, *The World's Hydrographical Description*, is essentially an argument for the existence of the north-west passage, but Davis never put his beliefs to the test again. It is thought that he accompanied Essex in 1596 and 1597 to Cadiz and the Azores. In 1599 he acted as pilot for a Dutch expedition to the East Indies. His extremely interesting and well-written account of the voyage was printed by Purchas. He made two further voyages to the East, with James Lancaster for the new East-India Company in 1601–3, and finally with Sir Edward Michelborne in the Tiger. He was killed by Japanese pirates in the South China Sea in 1605. He was about 55, and a widower. He left three sons, and was engaged to be married on his return from the voyage to a second wife, Judith Havard.

## 5. *John Jane*

John Jane wrote his account of Cavendish's voyage in the full knowledge of the accusations made by Cavendish against Davis, and the whole narrative is shaped to demonstrate that Davis had no other end during the voyage than to serve Cavendish and further his interests. His account is a blend of punctilious detail recorded at the time and a forensic rhetoric to prove Davis's fidelity. Presumably the account was written soon after the voyage was over, and presumably it circulated in manuscript before being printed by Hakluyt in the third volume (1600) of the second edition of his *Principal Navigations* (1598–1600). Jane, as we have seen, was the nephew and agent of Davis's main financial backer, William Sanderson, and had accompanied him on each of his three previous voyages in search of the north-west passage.

The narrative is inimical to Cavendish, and to Cavendish's men, from the start. The foray against Santos was bungled by John Cocke, so that desperately needed supplies, easily available, were lost. Cavendish had named no rendezvous in case of separation by bad weather. (This statement is contrary to Knivet's evidence.) Cavendish disloyally slandered his own gentlemen in the Galleon. In the Straits, Cavendish put the sick men ashore to die in the freezing cold. Cavendish disregarded both the willingness of his company and the advice of Davis in deciding to turn back in the Straits in May 1592.

The thrust of the narrative, however, is not to denigrate Cavendish but to justify Davis in his every action from the moment that the fleet separated during the night of 20 May on the way back from the Straits. There is a prelude to this justification in Jane's account of the February storm on the way south from Santos, in which, describing how the Desire found the stricken Roebuck, Jane rather unctuously writes of Davis's concern in going aboard the Roebuck to speak to Cocke and ordering the master of the Desire to take especial care not to lose touch. Davis, it is implied, is not a man who abandons his colleagues.

Jane gives two versions of the events of 20 May, one in his main narrative and one in the 'testimonial' written at Port Desire to record and explain what had happened. In neither of these does he mention the 'fret of weather' which Davis in *The Seaman's Secrets* says was responsible for the separation. Apparently the wind was from NNE, that is, a direct headwind. The testimonial says that in the late afternoon they were lying NE (which is not possible) and then tacked SSE and sometimes SE (which is incomprehensible if their desired course was NE). The main narrative says that they were lying close-hauled 'to seaward', which with the wind at NNE implies an easterly course.

Anyway, in the morning the Desire found herself alone. She soon picked up the Black Pinnace, and both ships decided to head for Port Desire to wait for Cavendish. That the separation from the Galleon Leicester and the Roebuck was a deliberate plot by Davis is pretty well impossible to believe. He was in a ship whose company was largely made up of Cavendish's own men. He would need to have previously enlisted the Black Pinnace into his conspiracy. Above all, he would need the active assistance of the master of the Desire, a brilliant seaman (name unknown) who had accompanied Cavendish on the circumnavigation and who is referred to throughout as Cavendish's man. The master was sick at the time that they lost touch with the Galleon, and his mate was on watch (p. 110/19); if there was a plot, this was his prepared excuse.

The extreme tension between the General's men in the Desire and Davis with his few associates (including Jane and Cotton) is emphasized throughout Jane's account. The deep suspicion of Davis came to a head in Port Desire when Davis proposed to look for Cavendish in the Black Pinnace. In the belief that this was a plot to abandon them, there was a conspiracy to murder Davis, the master, Jane, 'and all those which they thought were their friends'. The conspiracy was betrayed by the boatswain. It is notable that the professional seamen, the master and the boatswain, stuck by Davis. It was the gentlemen adventurers (whose numbers Davis had complained of p. 101/36) who opposed him. And undoubtedly a number of them believed, as Cavendish did in his far-distant Galleon, that Davis had deliberately lost contact on the night of 20 May. His determination to get through the Straits and his conviction that Cavendish had made an utterly wrong decision were known to everyone. So it was that Knivet, a prisoner of the Portuguese, heard months later from two of the company of the Desire who survived the massacre on Ilha Grande that 'Davis, which was captain of the Desire, and Tobie, master of the Pinnace, did deceive us and went for the Straits' (Knivet, p. 90/26).

Everything that Davis now did is described by Jane as the most reasonable expedient to rejoin Cavendish. Extraordinary efforts were made to refit and re-equip the two ships in Port Desire; then in August, Cavendish not having turned up, they decided he would have gone for the Straits and they set out to find him. Jane describes their hardships on the way through the Straits with great vividness. Twice they emerged from the western end and twice they were driven back by storms. Morale was very bad; some were for going back to Port Desire, there to be put ashore and try their luck by land (p. 109/15). It is at this point that Jane gives Davis a formal oration to the master, which makes him rather glibly apologize for being so devoted to Cavendish's interests that he has brought this suffering on the ships' companies. He argues nevertheless that they should still keep trying to get through to the Pacific, and he urges the master to support him. The reply which Jane gives to the master opens up the promise of the abundance of the coast of Chile and Peru which he had found on the previous voyage.

But the third venture into the Pacific was a disaster. The Black Pinnace was lost with all hands, and on board the Desire there was little hope they could survive. Jane describes finding Davis sitting in the gallery, almost frozen to death, in utter dejection. There are no formal orations about abandoning the enterprise. Almost miraculously the seamanship of the master got them back into the comparative protection of the Straits.

The continuous misadventures of the return, with further rebellion, a mortal skirmish with Indians, a massacre by the Portuguese, wasting disease, and death, are too movingly told to retell here. It is quite extraordinary that the ship ever got back to home waters.

## 6. *Thomas Lodge*

The last of the Cavendish narratives is from the writer Thomas Lodge; it consists of a sonnet, and two extracts from the prefatory matter to his romance, *A Margarite of America*. These prefatory remarks state that the romance was written while Lodge was on the Cavendish expedition. There is no reason to believe that this is not at least partly true, though it has been disputed. It is possible that the sonnet was also written on the voyage.

Thomas Lodge (born about 1558) was the son of Sir Thomas Lodge, lord mayor of London, whose hopes for his son, whom he educated at Merchant Taylors School, Trinity College Oxford, and Lincoln's Inn, were most certainly not fulfilled. Lodge resisted the career and lost the estates intended for him; but that does not mean that he was the dissolute swaggerer he has been made out to be (though he was jailed once). Lodge was a serious-minded man: the extraordinary range of his reading (see Walker), his conversion to Catholicism, his decision in mid-life to train as a doctor, his formidable labours as translator of both Seneca and Josephus, are evidence enough of that. There were not many careers open to a gentleman graduate with tastes like his, and that is no doubt why in his early thirties he turned to the possible rewards of becoming a gentleman soldier on privateering voyages. The dedication to Lord Hunsdon of his most famous work, *Rosalynde: Euphues' Golden Legacy* (1590; the source of *As You Like It*) runs as follows:

Having with Captain Clarke made a voyage to the islands of Terceras and the Canaries, to beguile the time with labour I writ this book; rough, as hatched in the storms of the ocean, and feathered in the surges of many perilous seas.

This is followed by an address 'To the Gentlemen Readers', in which he says:

To be brief, gentlemen, room for a soldier and a sailor, that gives you the fruits of his labours that he wrote in the ocean, when every line was wet with a surge, and every humorous passion counterchecked with a storm.

The various attempts to identify this voyage (summarized by Cuvelier, pp. 97–103) have overlooked the most likely one. Clarke went on a privateering voyage in the Galleon Dudley in 1590 (see above, p. 23). This expedition was promoted by Cavendish. The Dudley was back in Southampton in July, with a prize (Andrews 1966, p. 263; Quinn 1975, p. 19). *Rosalynde* was entered for publication in the Stationers' Register on 6 October.

Next year, then, Lodge was ready to set out on another and much more ambitious Cavendish venture, a second circumnavigation, with the riches of the Orient in prospect. He no doubt expected to be away from England for at least the two and a quarter years of Cavendish's first circumnavigation, and he left behind him two works to be published in his absence, *Catharos* and *Euphues' Shadow*. Robert Greene saw the latter through the press:

Gentlemen ... I present you with *Euphues' Shadow*, in the behalf of my absent friend M. Thomas Lodge, who at his departure to sea upon a long voyage, was willing, as a general farewell to all courteous gentlemen, to leave this work to the view, which, if you grace with your favours ... what labours his sea studies affords, shall be, I dare promise, offered to your sight.

Greene knew what a compulsive writer Lodge was. In 1593, the year that he returned from his voyage, sooner than he expected and empty-handed, Lodge published *The Life and Death of William Longbeard*, a derivative medley, and the sonnet sequence *Phillis*. Both of these may well have been, in part at least, the 'sea studies' of which Greene speaks.

*Phillis* is largely translation work. The Induction begins, 'I that obscured have fled the scene of fame', and continues:

> Smile on these loves but lately hatched,
>> Who from the wrastling waves have made retreat,
>> To plead for life before thy judgement seat.

Sonnet ii, which is given in the narrative, is actually a translation from the *Rime volgari* (1549) of Lodovico Pascale (see Kastner). But Lodge cleverly adopts the sea imagary of the original to his own 'travel desolate and hellish' in 'this watery world where now I sail'.

The third work to come out of the Cavendish voyage was *A Margarite of America*, which was not published until 1596. Lodge says that he found the story which was the source of his romance in the library of the Jesuits at Santos—where Knivet was also billeted. This source has never been identified, and the statement has been challenged on the grounds that the influences on Lodge's tale are thoroughly Italian and not Spanish at all (see Pollack). But undoubtedly Lodge was busy in that library during the long stay at Santos which was so fatal to the expedition at large. He took away from the library (and thereby saved from destruction?) a manuscript embodying the Jesuits' attempts to present Christian doctrine to the native tribes in their own language, 'Doutrina Christana na lingua Brasilica'. This manuscript he kept safe with his own writings during all the tempestuous difficulties of the voyage, and eventually presented to the Bodleian Library, Oxford, where it remains, 'the only tangible relic of the voyage to survive', says Quinn (1975, p. 23), with the inscription 'Ex dono Thomae Lodge D.M. Oxoniensis, qui sua manu e brasilia deduxit'.

It was interestingly argued by Alice Walker that Lodge's adventitious encounter with Jesuit propaganda in the occupied college at Santos may have provided him with an introduction to the contemporary Spanish theological writing of Luis de Granada and Joseph Anglés. He made frequent use of these in his later writings, and Alice Walker believed they might have influenced his conversion to Catholicism. Perhaps, she suggested, he might have appropriated these volumes as well.

How big an impact these weeks at Santos had on Lodge is shown by a private letter that he wrote years later (1609) which he closed by taking leave of his correspondent 'as an old Genovese did of me of the noble house of the Adorni, when, after many kind offices done unto him on Mr. Caundish's expedition, I was to depart and ready to set sail: *Vale*, said he, *mi fili, Deus te salvum reducat in domum tuam*.' This Italian, 'Josef

Adorno' or 'Joffe Doro', owned a sugar plantation and refinery. His daughter had married the remarkable English merchant, John Whithall, who had opened up a sugar trade with London, which was brought to an end by the belligerence of earlier English expeditions, particularly Fenton's of 1582 (see George; Andrews 1984, pp. 160–5; Donno, pp. 34–8; Hakluyt, x. 26 ff.). It is not surprising that the civility and courtesy of this Italian amidst the ferocious bluster of Cavendish's attack so struck Lodge, who might have felt that he had enlisted under Attila. His complex loyalties led him in later years to become the medical officer of a regiment of Englishmen in service with the Spaniards in the Netherlands, and to leave the post in 1606 for one with an Irish regiment when he felt that his continuance was understood to imply disaffection towards king and country (George, pp. 93–4; Eccles, pp. 81–6)!

*A Margarite of America* was described by C. S. Lewis as the best of all Lodge's romances (Lewis, p. 424). It is certainly very well written. It concerns two emperors and their families, the emperor of Mosco and the emperor of Cusco. At the beginning of the tale they are fighting for the town of Mantinea (which is in Arcadia in central Greece). While Mosco is clearly enough Moscow, Cusco is clearly not Cuzco, the ancient Peruvian capital of the Incas—which might have given some point to the title, *A Margarite of America*. Cusco is only a few days' land travel from Mosco, and the emperor (who has read Plato and Plutarch) has in his court a Duke of Moravia, so presumably it is the ancient city Košice in Czechoslovakia, formerly Kaschau or Kassa. The heroine Margarita is the daughter of the Emperor of Mosco; she passionately loves but is scorned by the vicious and sadistic heir to the Cusco empire. She has nothing whatever to do with America, so the title must mean that this story about Margarita is a margarite or pearl from America— Lodge's South American journey. Perhaps the brutality and suffering on the voyage (which Lodge refers to in the preliminary matter) were partly responsible for the horrific violence of the story's incidents, but on the other hand it is difficult to believe that either Lodge's memory or the capacity of a shipboard library could have provided the extensive literary and historical allusions of the tale. C. J. Sisson's outright rejection of Lodge's statement that he wrote *A Margarite* at sea is quite unreasonable (Sisson, pp. 105–7), but it is more than likely that Lodge laid aside the manuscript with all the imperfections which the circumstances of writing would have produced, and took it up again later to amplify and revise.

On the question of which of the ships Lodge was in, E. A. Tenney was surely right that Lodge's words 'being at sea with M. Candish' mean what they say (Tenney, p. 115). He was in the Leicester with the man of whose memory, he said, 'if I repent not, I lament not' (that is, he is not sorry to have known him but cannot grieve for his death). Lodge has left us his brief testimony to the cold and discomfort of the attempted passage through the Magellan Straits, and the discord among the company, but he has said nothing about the disasters on the South American coast nor Cavendish's mysterious death. He was back in England, on a cross-country journey, in February 1593 (Sisson, p. 89). If he *was* in the Leicester, this is firm evidence of the date of the return of the galleon. Both the Leicester and the Roebuck are known to have been in Portsmouth in March. David Quinn, in view of Lodge's later profession, thought Lodge might have been one of the two surgeons, whose return in the Roebuck so upset Cavendish (see p. 73). But there is no evidence that Lodge had any interest or skill in medicine at this time. time.

# NARRATIVES

## 1. *The Circumnavigation, 1588*[1]

A letter of Master Thomas Candish to the Right Honourable the Lord
Chamberlain, one of her majesty's most honourable Privy Council,[2]
touching the success of his voyage about the world.

RIGHT Honourable, as your favour heretofore hath been most greatly
extended towards me, so I humbly desire a continuance thereof; and
though there be no means in me to deserve the same, yet the uttermost
of my services shall not be wanting whensoever it shall please your
honour to dispose thereof. I am humbly to desire your honour to make
known unto her majesty the desire I have had to do her majesty service in
the performance of this voyage. And as it hath pleased God to give her
the victory over part of her enemies, so I trust ere long to see her
overthrow them all. For the places of their wealth, whereby they have
maintained and made their wars, are now perfectly discovered; and if it    10
please her majesty, with a very small power she may take the spoil[3] of
them all.

It hath pleased the Almighty to suffer me to circumpass[4] the whole
globe of the world, entering in at the Strait of Magellan and returning by
the cape of Bona Sperança. In which voyage I have either discovered or
brought certain intelligence of all the rich places of the world that ever
were known or discovered by any Christian. I navigated alongst the coast
of Chile, Peru, and Nova Spagna,[5] where I made great spoils. I burnt
and sunk nineteen sails of ships small and great. All the villages and
towns that ever I landed at, I burnt and spoiled. And had I not been    20
discovered upon the coast, I had taken great quantity of treasure. The

---

[1] Text from Hakluyt 1589, p. 808. Quinn (1975, p. 16) notes its publication also in an
anonymous French pamphlet bearing the date 1588, *Advertisement certain contenant les
pertes advenues en l'armée d'Espagne.*

[2] Henry Carey, Lord Hunsdon, became Lord Chamberlain in 1585. He was a patron
of players, most famously of Shakespeare's company in 1594. His son George Carey, a
close friend and supporter of Cavendish (who refers to him several times in his narrative),
succeeded him as Lord Chamberlain in 1597.

[3] Booty.

[4] *OED* has no other example of this word.

[5] ('Nova Hispania' in the next paragraph) Mexico.

matter of most profit unto me was a great ship of the king's which I took at California;[6] which ship came from the Philippinas, being one of the richest of merchandise that ever passed those seas, as the king's register and merchants' accompts did show; for it did amount in value to * in Mexico to be sold.[7] Which goods (for that my ships were not able to contain the least part of them) I was enforced to set on fire.

From the cape of California, being the uttermost part of all Nova Hispania, I navigated to the islands of Philippinas, hard upon the coast of China; of which country I have brought such intelligence as hath not been heard of in these parts. The stateliness and riches of which country I fear to make report of, lest I should not be credited; for if I had not known sufficiently the incomparable wealth of that country, I should have been as incredulous thereof as others will be that have not had the like experience.

I sailed along the islands of the Malluccas,[8] where among some of the heathen people I was well entreated, where our countrymen may have trade as freely as the Portingals, if they will themselves. From thence I passed by the cape of Bona Sperança, and found out by the way homeward the island of Saint Helena, where the Portingals use to relieve themselves.[9] And from that island God hath suffered me to return into England.

All which services, with myself, I humbly prostrate at her majesty's feet, desiring the Almighty long to continue her reign amongst us; for at this day she is the most famous and victorious prince that liveth in the world.

Thus humbly desiring pardon of your honour for my tediousness, I leave your lordship to the tuition of the Almighty. Plymouth this ninth of September, 1588.

Your honour's most humble to command,<br>THOMAS CANDISH.

[6] The Santa Ana; see Introduction, p. 22.
[7] The asterisk presumably indicates that Hakluyt was printing from a draft in which the amount had not been entered.
[8] Moluccas or Spice Islands, between Borneo and New Guinea.
[9] Cavendish was the first English voyager to visit St Helena; Francis Pretty gives a lyrical account of it as an earthly paradise in his account of the voyage (Hakluyt, xi. 343–6).

## 2. *Samuel Purchas, 1625*[1]

### TO THE READER.

Here maist thou read that dismal and fatal voyage of Master Thomas Candish, in which he consummated his earthly peregrination. In the former voyage of his (which amongst our circumnavigations of the globe we have presented thee) thou findest a perpetual sunshine, no man ever having in near so little time compassed that huge circumference, or taken his choice of so much more wealth than he could bring home, or revisited his native soil with greater pomp and triumph.[2] The clearest day hath a night, nor doth summer last alway; the sea hath his ebbing as well as flowing; the air hath calms and storms; the moon hideth sometimes the sun's lustre from us by her interposition; sometimes is 10 herself merely darkened by the earth's shadow. And if the elements, seasons, and heaven's two eyes be subject to such vicissitudes, what is this little molehill of earth, this model of clay, this moveable circumference of constant inconstancy, immutable mutability, this vanishing centre of diversified vanity which we call man, that herein also he should not resemble this sampler[3] of the universe, as becometh a little map to be like that larger prototype? This we see all and feel daily in ourselves; this in Master Candish here, in Sir Francis Drake's before, the sea's two darlings, there and thence both living and dying, if dissolution of the body may be called a death, where the soul arriveth in heaven, the name 20 fills the earth, the deeds are precedents to posterity, and England their country hath the glory alone that she hath brought forth two illustrious captains and generals, which have fortunately embraced the round waist of their vast mother, without waste of life, reputation, and substance. Yea, victorious over elements and enemies, illustrious in wealth and honour, they have come home like the sun in a summer's day, seeming greatest nearest his evening home, the whole sky entertaining and welcoming him in festival scarlets and displayed colours of triumph.[4]

·    ·    ·    ·    ·

[1] Purchas wrote this preface for the first publication of the narratives of Cavendish and Knivet in *Hakluytus Posthumus or Purchas his Pilgrimes*, 1625.

[2] 'I have heard', says Purchas in the margin, 'that all his sails at his return in the river were silk.'

[3] Example.

[4] Some chauvinistic reflections and poor puns are here omitted.

But where it is said *ye are gods*, it is added *ye shall die like men.*[5] The sea is a waving, wavering foundation, the winds theatre both for comedies and tragedies. You have seen Drake acting both, and in both you here find Candish. Christ is yesterday, today, the same for ever; God is without shadow, without possibility[6] or possibility of change, a light in whom is no darkness. But sublunary things are like the moon their nearest planet, which never views the earth two days together with one face. God hath made our way to him so full of chances and changes that our unsteady, slippery way on this earth, and calm-storm voyage in these seas, may make us more to meditate, and thirst after that haven of instability[7] and heaven of eternity.

Some passionate speeches of Master Candish against some private persons not employed in this action, I have suppressed;[8] some others I have let pass, not that I charge Captain Davis or others, but that it may appear what the General thought of them. Master Hakluyt hath published Master Jane's report of this voyage, which makes more favourable on Captain Davis his side. If he did deal treacherously, treachery found him out, as in his last voyage before is declared.[9] If any think the Captain here to conceive amiss, I shall be willing to have the most charitable conceit, and therefore remit the reader to Master Hakluyt's relation aforesaid, for his apology.[10]

. . . . . .

But let us hear Master Candish himself more than acting his own part. *Discite justitiam moniti.*[11] Let not prosperity poison the soul with the sting of the old serpent, swelling in pride, ingratitude, or contempt of God or man. Let not any magnify himself in whatsoever exploits, or trust in uncertain riches, or promise to himself the perpetual smiles of the world. And then it shall seem no new thing nor cause of despair if she bites instead of kissing. She is a witch which transformeth men into swine with her Cyrcæan cups, if the mind learn not by religion to fasten itself to God, to account Him her treasure, and make herself the treasury, as a pilgrim pressing toward the prize of our high calling, that

[5] Psalm 82; 6–7.

[6] Susceptibility to external impression.

[7] Presumably he means a haven for those who suffer instability.

[8] e.g. the comments on Carew Ralegh and Henry Seckford on pp. 55–6. All these passages are of course given in this edition.

[9] A reference to the death of Davis in 1605 at the hands of some Japanese pirates who had been allowed aboard. Purchas printed the narrative of the voyage in his first volume.

[10] Purchas now summarizes Jane's narrative.

[11] having been warned, learn righteousness (Virgil, *Aeneid* vi. 620).

inheritance of the saints in light; for which robes, to be stripped of these
rags is a blessed purchase; meanwhile knowing that nothing doth, shall,
can happen but by His providence, which is a Father most wise, loving,
bountiful, and merciful, which already hath given us His Son, doth now
give His Spirit, and will give us Himself. No rocks can wrack that soul,
no storms oppress, no seas can sink, no fortunes can either puff up with
success, or sink and make to shrink in itself by any pressures to despair,
which hath thus made God her portion. Yea, the worst of adversities by a
holy *Antiperistasis*[12] do contract and more unite the soul's forces to
greater acts of fortitude in doing and suffering His will, to whose ours   10
ought alway to be subordinated. It is the voice of a pagan, but the virtue
of a Christian, *Omnia mea mecum porto*,[13] and with Job to say *The Lord
hath given, the Lord hath taken, blessed be the name of the Lord.*[14]

I have given Master Knivet's relation after this of Master Candish, as
before Peter Carder[15] after Sir Francis Drake; that as both served under
them in their discoveries, so they may in this our discovery of those
discoveries, as pages to those worthies; the one a mariner waiting on a
mariner, the other a gentleman following a gentleman; both unmatch-
able by any English for the rare adventures, disadventures, and manifold
successions of miseries in those wild countries, and with those wilder   20
countrymen, of Brasilia; especially Master Knivet, who betwixt the
Brazilian and Portugal as betwixt two millstones was almost ground to
powder; whom colds, sickness, famine, wanderings, calumnies, desertions, solitariness, deserts, woods, mountains, fens, rivers, seas, flights,
fights, wild beasts, wilder serpents, wildest men, and strait passages
beyond all names of wildness (those Magellan straits, succeeded by
drowning, fainting, freezing, betraying, beating, starving, hanging
straits) have in various successions made the subject of their working;
whom God yet delivered, that out of his manifold pains thou maist
gather this posy of pleasures, and learn to be thankful for thy native   30
sweets at home, even *delights in the multitude of peace.*

---

[12]  Contrary reaction.

[13]  All I have I carry with me (Cicero, *Paradoxes*, i; spoken by Bias, who was being urged
to carry his possessions with him after the sack of his native city).

[14]  Job 1: 21.

[15]  Purchas had placed Carder's adventures immediately before this. He was one of
Winter's crew in the Elizabeth, which left Drake and returned home via the Magellan
Straits. He was in a boat that lost the ship in bad weather, and it was nine years before he
got home again. Like Knivet he lived with Indians and learned their language, and became
a captive of the Portuguese. He had an audience of the Queen on his return.

## 3. *Cavendish's Narrative*

Master Thomas Candish his discourse of his fatal and disastrous voyage towards the South Sea, with his many disadventures in the Magellan Straits and other places; written with his own hand to Sir Tristram Gorges, his executor.[1]

Most loving friend, there is nothing in this world that makes a truer trial of friendship than at death to show mindfulness of love and friendship, which now you shall make a perfect experience[2] of, desiring you to hold my love as dear, dying poor, as if I had been most infinitely rich. The success of this most unfortunate action, the bitter torments thereof lie so heavy upon me as with much pain am I able to write these few lines, much less to make discourse unto you of all the adverse haps that hath befallen me in this voyage, the least whereof is my death. But because you shall not be ignorant of them, I have appointed some of the most sensiblest men that I left behind me to make discourse unto you of all these accidents. I have made a simple will wherein I have made you sole and only disposer of all such little which is left.[3]

The Roebuck left me in the most desolatest case that ever man was left in. What is become of her I can not imagine, but if she be returned into England it is a most admirable matter. But if she be at home, or any other of my goods whatsoever return into England, I have made you only possessor of them. And now to come to that villain that hath been the death of me and the decay of this whole action, I mean Davis, whose only[4] treachery in running from me hath been an utter ruin of all. If any good return by him, as ever you love me make such friends as he of all others may reap least gain. I assure myself you will be careful in all friendship of my last requests. My debts which be owing be not much.[5] There is 200 pounds upon a bond to Carew Ralegh,[6] which he will infinitely trouble you for. You know his humour, he only likes to bargain;

---

13 desolatest] desoluteste *MS, Quinn*; desolate *Purchas*    18 this whole] *MS, Purchas*; the whole *Quinn*    23 200 pounds] 200$^{li}$ (*here and elsewhere*)    bond] bande *MS, Quinn*    Carew Ralegh] Carewe Raleighe *MS, Quinn*

[1] This heading is taken from Purchas; it is not of course in the MS.
[2] Experiment, trial.
[3] Cavendish's will, undated but signed by him and witnessed is given in facsimile with transcript by Quinn 1975, pp. 138–43, 148–9.
[4] Unique, unsurpassable.
[5] Purchas omits the rest of the paragraph with the candid details of debts and persons.
[6] Sir Walter's elder brother, 'closely concerned with many ventures' (Andrews 1966, p. 98).

satisfy him in the same sort. There is due to two merchants in London upon a bill of adventure[7] which the ships are bound for, 250 pounds, which you may slightly[8] compound for. For other adventures whatsoever, they run in the victuals[9] as all other adventures doth. I pray you do this for me: Sir George Carey[10] hath a bill of an 150 pound venture which I gave him for four iron guns. Deliver him if the Roebuck be returned two demi-culverins[11] of brass with mine arms on them and his four iron pieces (they are to be known by his mark which is a swan). Sir Henry Palmer[12] adventured twenty pounds, I pray see him answered. For private debts I know of none, but it may be my untrusty servants have left some paltry sums unpaid; if you think they be mine I know you will use your good discretion in it. There is a bill of adventure to Henry Seckford[13] of 300 pounds. He is an hungry man and one that will seek much. Use your discretion with him; he can claim nothing but as a part victualler. If any such importunate men trouble you, comfort them with the return of the other ships, which truly there is some hope of. If ever they return they cannot but be rich.

But I, most unfortunate villain,[14] was matched with the most abject minded and mutinous company that ever was carried out of England by any man living. For I protest unto you that in going to the Straits of Magelanus, after I was passed to the southward of the River of Plate and had bidden[15] the fury of storms which indeed I think to be such as worser might not be endured, I never made my course to the Straitsward but I was in continual danger by my company, which never ceased to practise and mutiny against me. And having gotten the appointed

10

20

---

7 demi-culverins] demye culverin*es MS*              9 I pray see] I praie see *MS*; praie
seen *Quinn*          13 Seckford] Sakeforde *MS*

[7] Speculative advance of money. The merchants (one of whom, Quinn says, was Sir Thomas Middleton of Chirk) have put up money, with the ships as security, in exchange for a share in the profits of the expedition.

[8] Easily.

[9] Presumably the advance here was not of money but of supplies.

[10] Son of the Lord Chamberlain to whom Cavendish had written his letter in 1588. He was captain-general of the Isle of Wight and an enthusiastic promoter of overseas enterprises.

[11] Nine-pounder cannons.

[12] A Scotsman who was an important naval commander in Elizabeth's reign, playing a leading part in the Armada.

[13] Cavendish later calls him his cousin. He was Groom of the Chamber and Keeper of the Privy Purse, and one of the leading investors in privateering expeditions.

[14] i.e. wretch. Not commonly applied to oneself.

[15] Undergone.

place[16] called Port Desire I met with all my company, which had been there near twenty days before me. And had not my most true friends been there (whom to name my heart bleeds, I mean my cousin Cocke)[17] I had been constrained either to have suffered violence or some other most disordered mishap.

I came into this harbour with my boat, my ship[18] riding without at sea, where I found the Roebuck, the Desire, and the Pinnace, all which complained unto me that the tide ran so violently as they were not able to ride, but were driven aground; and wished me in any wise not to come in
10 with my ship, for that if she should come on ground she would be utterly cast away, which I knew to be most true. And finding it to be no place for so great a ship without her utter ruin, I forthwith commanded them to make themselves ready to depart, they being fresh and infinitely well relieved with seals and birds, which in that place did abound, my company being grown weak and feeble with continual watching, pumping, and bailing, for I must say truly unto you there were never men that endured more extremities of the seas than my poor company had done.[19] Such was the fury of the west-south-west and south-west winds[20] as we were driven from the shore 400 leagues[21] and constrained
20 to beat from 50 degrees to the southward into 40 to the northward again before we could recover near the shore, in which time we had a new shift of sails clean blown away, and our ship in danger to sink in the sea three times, which with extremity of men's labour we recovered.

In this weakness we departed for the Straits, being from that harbour

---

6 ship] Shippes *MS?*, *Quinn*; ships *Purchas*      22 sails] sailes *Purchas*; Seales *MS*

[16] John Jane complained that no emergency rendezvous had been appointed (p. 99/32), but according to Knivet (p. 88/2) Cavendish told the company of the Galleon at this time that all the ships had been instructed to make for Port Desire if separated. Port Desire (now Puerto Deseado, Argentina, 47° 45′ S.) played a very important part in this voyage, especially for John Davis.

[17] John Cocke, in command of the Roebuck. Purchas persistently and inexplicably calls him Locke. His death in the Leicester in mid-Atlantic soon before Cavendish began this narrative is recorded on p. 79.

[18] The Leicester. The Dainty had already parted company in the great storm of 7 Feb., and had possibly set course for England. The final 's' of the MS 'Shippes' is blurred as though deletion were intended.

[19] This is the same company he has just been abusing as abject-minded and mutinous.

[20] He is harking back to the storm that parted the ships earlier, before reaching Port Desire.

[21] A league was three sea-miles (6,000 yds. or 5.5 km.) but the term is used with great vagueness.

80 leagues, and in eighteen days we gate[22] the Straits, in which time the men in my ship were grown extremely weak. The other ships' company were in good case by reason of their late relief. And now we had been almost four months between the coast of Brazil and the Straits, being in distance not above 600 leagues, which is commonly run in twenty or thirty days. Such was the adverseness of our fortunes as in coming thither we spent the summer, and found in the Straits the beginning of a most extreme winter, not durable for Christians.[23]

In despite of all storms and tempest, so long as we had ground to anchor in and tides to help us we beat into the Straits some 50 leagues, 10 having for the most part the winds contrary. At length being forced by the extremity of storms and the narrowness of the strait, being not able to turn to windward[24] no longer, we got into a harbour[25] where we rid from the eighteenth day of April till the tenth of May, in all which time we never had other than most furious contrary winds, and after that the month of May was come in nothing but such flights of snow and extremity of frosts as in all the time of my life I never see none[26] to be compared with them. This extremity caused the weak men, in my ship only, to decay, for in seven or eight days in this extremity there died forty men and sickened seventy, so that there was not fifty men that were able 20 to stand upon the hatches.[27]

I finding this miserable calamity to fall upon me, and found that besides the decay of my men and expense of my victual, the snow and frost decayed our sails and tackle, and the contagiousness[28] of the place to be such, for extremity of frost and snow, as there was no long staying without the utter ruin of us all. What by these extremities and by the daily decay of my men, I was constrained forthwith to determine some course, and not (for[29] all this extremity of weather) to tarry there any longer.

 1  gate] *MS*; got *Purchas*              4  coast] *Purchas*; Coste *MS*; Costes *Quinn*
13  to windward] *MS*; windward *Purchas*      14  eighteenth] *Purchas*; 18 *MS*
14  tenth] *Purchas*; 10 *MS*

[22]  Got; that is, reached.
[23]  Cavendish never mentions the fatal delay at Santos; Introduction, p. 23.
[24]  'to' is blotched in the MS and Purchas's compositor evidently thought it had been deleted and left it out.
[25]  Near Cape Froward; Knivet, p. 88; Jane, p. 100.
[26]  'see' is Cavendish's normal form of the past tense (= saw). The form 'saw' appears only once in the entire narrative, and may be scribal.
[27]  Both Jane and Knivet say that Cavendish put sick men ashore and left them to die. He himself was at this time aboard the Desire with Davis; Jane, p. 101/9.
[28]  Not in the modern sense; he means the place bred pestilence.
[29]  Because of.

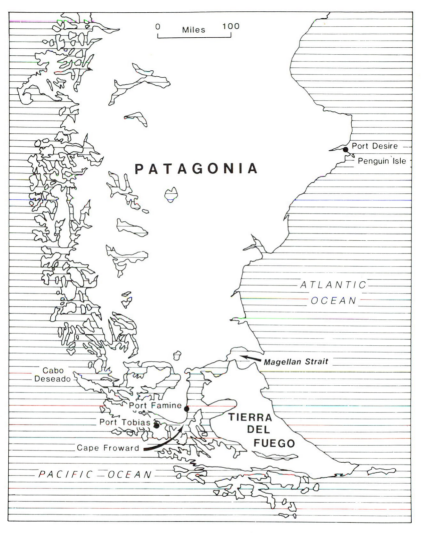

MAP I. The Magellan Strait

Upon this, I assembled my company together, and showed them that my intention was to go for China, and that there was two ways thither, the one through the Strait, the other by the way of *Caba bona spe*,[30] which course I showed them was as well known unto me as the way I had undertaken, and although that fortune had denied us this passage, yet I doubted not but soon to recover to this cape, where I showed them I made no doubt but we should relieve ourselves, and perform to their contents our intended voyage. These persuasions, with many others which I used, seemed to content them for the present. But they were no sooner gone from me but forthwith all manner of discontents were unripped amongst themselves, and to go that way they plainly and resolutely determined never to give their willing consents.

Some of the best and honestest sort, hearing this their resolution, wished them rather to put up a supplication to me than thus privately among themselves to mutine and murmur, which course might cause an utter ruin to fall upon them all, affirming that they knew me to be so reasonable as I would not refuse to hear their petition. Upon this, they framed a humble supplication unto me, as they termed it, the effect whereof was, that first they protested to spend their lives most willingly for my sake, and that their love was such to me as their chiefest care was for me, and they grieved very much to see me put on a resolution which, as they supposed, would be the end of myself, which was their greatest grief. And next their own lives would imminently follow, both by reason of the length of the course, all which they must perform without relief; and further we had not left four months victual, which might very well be spent in running a course not half so long. But if it would please me to return again for the coast of Brazil, where they know[31] my force being together was able to take any place there, we might both provide victual to return again, and furnish ourselves of all other such wants as these extremities had brought upon us, and at a seasonable time return again and so perform our first intention.

Now I, knowing their resolution, and finding that in some things their reasons were not vain, began more seriously to look into all my wants.

2 and that] *Purchas*; and that, that *MS*    15 mutine] muten *MS*; mutinie *Purchas*    22 self] *MS*; life *Purchas*    23 imminently] Iminentlie *MS*; immediately *Purchas*    27 know] knowe *MS*; knew *Purchas*

[30] The Cape of Good Hope, in no particular language; '*spe*' is probably an abbreviation for '*speranza*'.

[31] The present tense suggests that Cavendish had the original supplication in front of him as he wrote. Purchas gives the more grammatical 'knew'.

First, I found my greatest decay to be in ropes and sails, wherein (by means of such mighty extremities) I was utterly unfurnished, for I lost a new shift of sails coming thither, and further the Desire had bidden the like extremity, which I furnished, so as I had left no store at all, for no ships carrieth three new shifts of sails, all which had been little enough for me; and last of all our victuals to be most short, I was to fall into due consideration what to do. I knew well that the winds were such and so continually against us as by no means it was possible to pass through.[32] For the violent snows were such as in two days together we should not be able to see five hours, the place not a league over[33] in breadth, our ships not to be handled in such extremity of wind: no, nor canvas to hold the fury of the wind; our men so weak as of 150 men I had not in my ship in health 50. And this ship coming,[34] with all her company, was like three times to have been upon the shore by reason of her unyary[35] working. These causes made me utterly despair of any passage at this season. So I resolved the company, I would put out of the harbour and beat to get through so long as the furious and westerly winds would suffer us. But if they came upon us so as we could not hold it up, we would then bear up again and so, according unto their requests, go for the coast of Brazil, which they so much seemed to desire and I so much hated. But in truth I was forced to take that way, for that there was no place where this ship could come into to tarry out a winter. For Port Saint Julian[36] is a barred harbour over which two of my ships would not go, and Port Desire hath neither wood nor water, and besides that, the tide runneth so extremely as it is not possible for anchors to hold, the ground being so bad. But the last cause of all to be considered was the sickness of my men, having no clothes to defend them from the extreme cold. These causes, and their ardent desire of being out of the cold, moved me to go back again for that most wicked coast of Brazil, where I encountered all manner misfortunes, which as I have unripped these former, so I will briefly declare the latter.

We were beaten out of the Strait with a most monstrous storm at west-south-west, from which place we continued together till we came

17 furious] *Purchas*; furies *MS*   22 Port Saint Julian] *Porte Sa Iulian MS*
28 desire of] *MS*; desires of *Purchas*; desire to *Quinn*

[32] Davis disagreed (Davis, p. 97/28; Jane, p. 101/13); but Davis himself failed in his attempt in the following year.
[33] Across.
[34] i.e. on the way to this place.
[35] From the adjective 'yare' = easily manageable (of a ship). Not elsewhere recorded.
[36] About 140 miles S. of Port Desire, where Drake hanged Doughty.

in the latitude of 47. In which place Davis in the Desire, and my Pinnace, lost me in the night,[37] after which time I never heard of them; but as I since understood,[38] Davis his intention was ever to run away. This is God's will, that I should put him in trust that should be the end of my life, and the decay of the whole action. For had not these two small ships parted from us we could not have miscarried on the coast of Brazil, for the only decay of us was that we could not get into their barred harbours. What became of these small ships I am not able to judge, but sure it is most like they went back again for Port Desire, a place of relief for two so small ships, for they might lie on ground there without danger, 10 and being so few men they might relieve themselves with seals and birds, and so take a good time of year and pass the Straits. The men in these small ships were all lusty and in health, wherefore the likelier to hold out. The short of all is this: Davis his only intent was utterly to overthrow me, which he hath well performed.

These ships being parted from us, we little suspecting of any treachery, the Roebuck and myself held our course for Brazil, and kept together till we came in the latitude of 36, where we encountered the most grievous storm that ever any Christians endured upon the seas to live, in which storm we lost company. We with most extreme labour and 20 great danger got the coast of Brazil where we were fifteen days and never heard of the Roebuck. We came to an anchor in the bay of Saint Vincent,[39] and being at an anchor there, the gentlemen desired me to give them leave to go ashore to some of the Portingales' farmhouses to get some fresh victual, which I granted; willing them to make present return, knowing very well the whole country was not able to prejudice them if they wilfully would not endanger themselves. They went to a sugar-mill hard by me where I rode (for that was my special charge, that they should never go a mile from the ship) where they got some victual, and came aboard again very well. 30

The next day in the morning betimes, an Indian came unto me with

---

11  seals] sayles *MS*        12  of year] of yeare *MS*; of the yeere *Purchas*        18  in the] *MS*; *Purchas*; to the *Quinn*        23  gentlemen] *Purchas*; gent *MS*        25  make present] *MS*; *Purchas*; make a present *Quinn*        27  wilfully] willfully *MS* ('willinglie' *erased*); willingly *Purchas*

[37]  That Davis deliberately separated himself is very doubtful; see the discussion in the Introduction (p. 44). It is very strange that no proper contingency arrangements had been made for a rendezvous in a situation like this.

[38]  He must mean allegations made by the company in the Galleon.

[39]  Adjoining Santos; see Map 2 (*a*), p. 67. Cavendish burned it as he came south.

Captain Barker.[40] Which Indian ran from his master at my last being there; this savage knew all the country. He came unto me and said that beyond a point not a culverin shot off, there was a very rich farmhouse, and desired ten or twelve men to go thither. Captain Barker being one whom I most trusted in the conduction of men, and who ever was the most carefullest in such matters of service, I appointed him to go and to take some twenty or thirty men with him, and willed him, as he had any respect or regard of my commandment, not to stay but to come presently away, finding anything or nothing. He forthwith took twenty-five of the
10 most principal men in the ship, and then your cousin Stafford[41] would by no means be left behind. They departed by four of the clock in the morning, so as I did not see their company. But what should I write more than this unto you? that they were all such as neither respected me nor anything that I commanded. Away they went, and by one of the clock they sent my boat again with guinea wheat[42] and six hens and a small hog. I seeing no return again of the company, for they had sent away the boat only with men to row her aboard, I was very much grieved, and presently returned the boat again, with message that I much marvelled they would tarry at a place so long with so few men, and further that it
20 was not a hog and six hens could relieve us; and seeing there was no other relief to be had I charged them straightly to come aboard presently. Thus having despatched away my boat for them, I still expected their present coming aboard. All that night I heard nothing of them. The next morning I shot ordnance, yet I see no boat come. Then I weighed anchor and made aboard into the bay; yet for all this I heard nothing of them. Then I doubted with myself very greatly, knowing there was no means left to make any manifester signs to them to hasten away. All that day I heard nothing of them. In the evening I set sails again and ran into the shore so as I rode within musket shot of the shore. All
30 that night I heard no news of them.

The next morning I saw an Indian came down to the sea side and waved unto the ship. We being desirous to hear some news caused a raft to be made, for boat we had none, and sent it ashore and set the Indian

---

28 sails] *Purchas*; sail *Quinn* (*the final* 's' *in MS is overwritten*)     29 as ... shore] *MS*; *om. Purchas*

[40] Not positively identified; see Quinn 1975, p. 72.
[41] For the relationship, see Quinn 1975, p. 27. Edward Stafford was on Ralegh's 1585 Virginian expedition, remaining behind with Ralph Lane. He was also on the next venture (1587), possibly in command of the Lion; see Quinn 1955.
[42] Maize.

aboard. When we see him we found him to be our own Indian, which had escaped away, being sore hurt in three places. He told us that all the rest of our men were slain with[43] 300 Indians and 80 Portingales, which in the evening set upon them suddenly. Then I demanded why they came not aboard?[44] The Indian answered me that some were unwilling to come, and the rest did nothing else but eat hens and hogs, which they had there in abundance, and that they minded nothing to come aboard. I leave you to judge in what grief I was in, to see twenty-five of my principal men thus basely and wilfully cast away; but I leave you to enquire of others the practices[45] of these men, lest in writing unto you it should be thought I did it of malice, which I protest is far from me, they being now dead and myself looking imminently to follow them.

Thus I was left destitute of my principal men and a boat, and had I not by great hap the day afore taken an old boat from the Portingales, I had been utterly undone.[46] Which boat I sent to an island 15 leagues off to see if they could hear any news of the rest of my ships.[47] She returned within eight days, all which time I remained without a boat. Thus I was sixteen days before I heard news of any of my consorts.

The seventeenth day came in the Roebuck, having spent all her masts but their mizzen, their sails blown clean away, and in the most miserablest case that ever ship was in. All which mishaps falling upon me, and then missing my small ships wherein (upon that coast) consisted all my strength, having no pinnaces nor great boats left to land my men in, for they were all cast away going to the strait—I (notwithstanding the want of boats and pinnaces) determined rather and not[48] to be revenged of so base dogs, to venture the ships to go down the river afore their

---

2 the rest] *Purchas*; they reste *MS*        6 nothing else] *MS* ('else' *deleted*); nothing *Purchas*      25 rather and] *MS*; rather then *Purchas*

[43] i.e. slain by.

[44] i.e. why they had stayed ashore before the attack.

[45] Wrongdoings, malpractices.

[46] This presumably is the 'great bark' that Knivet says the shore-party captured and sent back, with food, to the ship. Knivet says that it was through the shore-party not having this boat with them that the massacre was so complete (Knivet, pp. 91/21–92/8). There is no way of squaring Cavendish's statement that he had no boat and had to make a raft with Knivet's statement not only that Cavendish had this captured boat but also that the wounded Indian swam to the ship with the help of a log. No doubt Cavendish was here concealing the fact that he had a boat available which he could have used at least to find out what was happening.

[47] Cavendish was hoping to see not only the Roebuck but also the Desire and the Black Pinnace.

[48] Is this a colloquialism or an error?

town, and to have beaten it to the ground; which forthwith I put in execution. And having gotten down half the way, we found the river so narrow by reason of a shoal as all the company affirmed plainly it was both desperate and most dangerous. For the river is all ooze, and if a ship come aground it is unpossible ever to get off, for there riseth not above a foot of water,[49] and no anchors will hold to hale off any my ship in so narrow a place as we were almost aground in wending. Seeing this apparent danger, I forthwith bare up out of the river, where we escaped no small danger to get well out, for we had not little[50] more water than we drew, and if she had come aground it had been unpossible ever to have gotten her off.

By this means of not passing the river, we were constrained to let our revenge pass, for our boats were so bad and small as we durst put no men in them. Notwithstanding, we landed, and did them much spoil upon their farmhouses and got some quantity of fresh victual. This place being not for us, considering our ships were not able to pass to their town, and farther our great wants did constrain us to seek some course of relief, which being not to be had there, both for that we had spoiled it a little before, and also for that we could not conveniently come to do them any prejudice without most lost to ourselves, I determined to part from thence and to go to a small island some 20 leagues off,[51] and there to have fitted all my necessaries and to have cast off the Roebuck, for that by no means her wants could by me be furnished, and so at a seasonable time to have gone for the Straits of Magelanus again.

Which intention, I must confess, I kept most secret for fear of some mutiny, but showed the whole company that I would go for Saint Elena, where we should meet with the carracks. Which course I well knew did not much please them, for they desired nothing more than returning home into England, and if I had but named the Straits they would forthwith have fallen into a most extreme mutiny. For such was the miseries and torments they had endured, as all the best sort had taken an oath upon a Bible to die rather than ever to yield their consents to go back that way again. I knowing this seemed to speak nothing of that course, but comforting their despairing minds as well as I might—.

---

6 foot of water] fote of water *MS* ('of' *smudged*); foot water *Purchas*      20 lost]
loste *MS*; losse *Purchas*

[49] Purchas's compositor mistook a smudged 'of' as a deletion; the inference that he was using this very manuscript is strong.

[50] Only a little.

[51] St Sebastian.

And[52] their greatest grief was for the want of the small ships, without which they all affirmed (and that truly) that we were able to do nothing, for the ports where their towns stand were all barred harbours, and that it was not possible to get any of these ships over them, whereby we could relieve ourselves of such wants as we were in. These things being alleged I seemed to pass over as slightly as might be, but yet comforted them that we would presently seek some place of relief with all speed.

There was a Portingale aboard me who took upon him to be a pilot.[53] He came unto me and told me upon his life that he would take upon him to carry both my ships over the bar at Spiritus Sanctus,[54] a place indeed of great relief and the only place in Brazil for victual and all other wants that we were in. I knowing very well that if I could bring my ships within shot of the town I should land my men, and farther it would not be in them to make resistance, the whole company desired this course, affirming that there was no way left to relieve all our wants but this, and that there they were in hope to find some ships, to repair the Roebuck again. I finding their willingness, and charging the Portingale upon his life to tell me truly whether the ships might pass over the bar without danger, he willed me to take his life if ever the ships came in less water than 5 fathom, with such constant affirmations as he desired not to live if he should not perform this. I considering the greatness of our wants, and knowing right well the place to be the only wished town on all the coast to relieve us, forthwith gave my consent, and thither we went, leaving all other intentions.

We anchored before the bar and sent my boat to sound the bar, and found the deepest water to be 16 and 17 foot, the Portingale himself going with them; all over the bar the most water to be but 3 fathom.[55] They coming aboard brought me word of the truth. I called for the Portingale and demanded of him why he had so lied unto me. He affirmed that he had never sounded the bar before, and that he had

---

1 And] *MS*; seeing *Purchas*

[52] Understandably trying to continue the previous incomplete sentence, Purchas substitutes 'seeing'; but Cavendish has interrupted his sentence with this long parenthesis, attacking Davis's desertion in the voice of his company, resuming with 'comforted' in l. 6.

[53] The luckless Jasper Jorge, captured at Cabo Frio in Dec. 1591; see Knivet, p. 82.

[54] Now Vitória, in the Bay of Espírito Santo; see Map 2 (c), p. 67.

[55] A note in Franco's edition of Knivet's narrative (p. 35) quotes an 1897 authority that there would have been 5 fathoms at high tide.

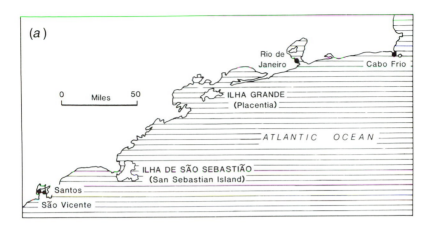

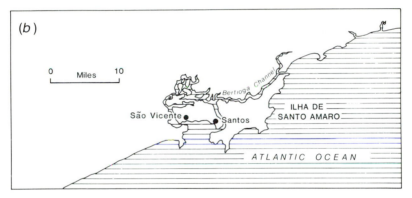

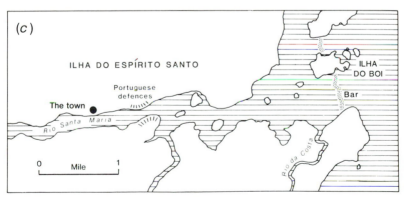

MAP 2. The Brazilian coast: (*a*) Santos to Cabo Frio; (*b*) Santos and São Vicente; (*c*) Vitória (Spiritus Sanctus)

brought in ships of an 100 tons, and that he made accompt there had not been less water than 5 fathom.[56]

This mishap was no small amazing to me and all the company, considering our distress for water and other necessaries, and that the road was so ill as we were scant able to ride there, so as we could neither take in water nor do no other business. In this meantime while we were scanning of these matters, the Roebuck's boat, rowing further into the bay, see where three ships were at an anchor not far from the town, and came aboard and brought me word thereof. At which news the company seemed much to rejoice, and all affirmed that they would go with our boats and bring them out of the harbour. I showed them how much the taking of them imported us, and told them that although the day was spent, yet I thought the night not to be altogether inconvenient, if they would put on mind to perform it resolutely. My reasons were these: first, they[57] were not so sufficiently provided to defend themselves at that instant as they would be in the morning, and further I told them that if they were not able to defend them, they would take the principal and best things out of them, being so near the shore. And that if they had wherewith to defend themselves, it would be less offensive to us in the night than in the day, and we in greatest security and more offensive to the enemy, especially this exploit being to be done on the water, not landing.

These persuasions seemed a little[58] to move them, for they all desired to stay till morning; yet some of them prepared themselves. Coming amongst them, I found them all, or for the most part, utterly unwilling to go that night. Upon which occasion I confess I was much moved and gave them some bitter words and showed them our case was not to make detractions[59] but to take that opportunity which was offered us, and not to fear a night more than a day, and told them plainly that in refusing of this I could stay there no longer, for over the bar we could not go, and the road so dangerous as never ships rid in a worse. And further we see all the country to be fired round about, and that to land we could not without utter spoil to us all, for our boats were naught, and further we could by no means be succoured by our ships. So as I intended to depart

---

3  amazing] a maseinge *MS*; amazement *Purchas*              18  so near] so neare *MS*;
so neere *Purchas*; neare *Quinn*

[56]  Having so built it up that the Portingale swore 'on his life' that the ships could clear the bar, Cavendish omits to say that at this point he had him hanged. See Knivet, p. 92/34.

[57]  i.e. the Portuguese.              [58]  i.e. only a little. They were not much moved.

[59]  Protractions, delays.

the next morning from that place. In the morning there was almost an uproar among them, the most of them swearing that if I would not give them leave they would take the boats and bring away these ships of themselves. I coming amongst them began to reprehend them for their rashness, and told them that now all opportunity was past, and that now they must be contented, for go they should not. They much importuned me and some of the chiefest of them desired me with tears in their eyes that they might go, affirming that there was no danger to be feared at all, for if they were not able to take them they would return again, and that to
10 depart without attempting to do this was a thing that most greatly grieved them.

I knowing right well that if they landed not, they could receive no prejudice, for if their ships had been able to have withstood them, it was in their power to go from them, being stark calm. And farther I knew that no ships useth Brazil that be able to defend themselves from a cock-boat, much less that they should be of force to offend these boats wherein there were so many musketeers as could sit one by one other. I seeing their great importunity was contented to give them leave to go. And this was my charge to Captain Morgan,[60] to whom at that present I
20 left my directions. That first, upon pain of his life he should not land at all, what opportunity soever there was offered; and that if he see any danger in coming to these ships that he should attempt no further, but return aboard again. But contrariwise, if he see that the place was such as we might land without too much disadvantage, and if that we might land on plain ground free from woods or bushes hard afore the town, that then he would presently repair unto me again, and I and so many as these bad boats would carry would presently land upon them.

Thus my boats departed from me, having some eighty men as well furnished with weapons as it is possible to sort such an number withal.
30 Now you shall understand that in the night the Portingales had haled their ships hard afore the town. The river where the town stood on was not above a bird-bolt shot[61] over, and half-a-mile from the town where the ships rode.[62] The night we came in, they had new cast up two small

---

3 these] *MS*; those *Purchas, Quinn*

[60] Unidentified.

[61] 'Bird-bolt shot was the distance a light arrow, or crossbow quarrel used for shooting birds, would travel. It was a comparatively short distance' (Quinn). From the Admiralty chart, the distance would appear to be about 275 yds.

[62] The river where the ships were riding was only a bird-bolt shot in width; the town was about half a mile from the river.

trenches, on each side the river one, where they had planted some two small bases apiece.[63] Upon a hill right over them was thick woods and great rocks, so that if any were possessed of them they might but tumble stones down and beat away a thousand men. The trench on the wester side of the river shoot at our boats once or twice. Upon that they began to bethink with themselves what to do. Captain Morgan, affirming the place to be very narrow and that they could not well pass it without danger considering the many men in their boats, and also the charge which I had given was such, as if they see any danger they should presently repair aboard and certify me, and not to pass any farther till 10 they had understood my farther determination—this Master Morgan made known amongst them. Upon this some of harebrain sailors began to swear that they never thought other than that he was a coward, and now he well showed it that durst not land upon a bauble ditch,[64] as they termed it. Upon this the gentleman was very much moved and answered them that they should find him to be none such as they accompted him, and that come what could happen him, he would land.

Upon this, in they put the boats between the two sconces.[65] That on the easter they had not seen, and the boats being hard upon it were shot at, and in the biggest boat they hurt two and killed one with that shot. 20 Upon this they determined that the smallest boat with their company should land on the wester side and the other to land on the easter side. The small boat landed first, and that place having but few in it, they being not able to defend themselves ran away, so that our men entered peaceable, without hurt of any.

The other boat, drawing much water, was aground before she came near the shore, so as they that landed were fain to wade above knee high in water. Now the place or sconce was in high some 10 foot, made of stone. Captain Morgan (more resolute than discreetly) scaled the wall and ten more with him which went out of the boat together. Then the 30 Indians and the Portingales showed themselves, and with great stones from over the trench[66] killed Morgan and five more, and the rest of them being sore hurt retired to the boat, which by this time was so filled with

  2 apiece. Upon a hill right] a peese upon a hill: right *MS*; a peece upon an hill. Right
  *Purchas*   12 some of] *MS*; some of the *Purchas*   14 well showed] well
shewed *MS*; will shew *Purchas*   14 bauble] bable *MS*, *Purchas*   21 smallest]
*Purchas*; smalest *MS*; smale *Quinn*

    63 Small cannons.
    64 A toy of a ditch, a childish ditch.
    65 Fortifications.
    66 i.e. from the rocks above the trench.

Indian arrows as of forty-five men being in the boat there escaped not eight of them unhurt, some having three arrows sticking in them, some two, and there was none which escaped with one wound.[67] The fury of those arrows coming so thick, and so many of them being spoiled, they put the boat from the shore, leaving the rest on land a spoil for the Indians.

By this time, there came two boats full of lusty Portingales and some Spaniards. They knowing the sconce on the wester side to be weakly manned came with their boats to the fort's side[68] where my men had entered, not knowing (as it should seem) that our men had taken it. They let them come with their boats hard to the fort's side. One of them run ashore which was fullest of men. Then our men let fly their muskets at them and spoiled and killed all that were in that boat. The other, seeing their fellows speeded so ill, rowed back again with all their force and got the town again.

In this meantime, the great boat being gotten off, they called to them in the sconce[69] and willed them to forsake the fort and to come and help them, for they told them that all their men were spoiled and slain. Upon this they straight came out of the sconce again and retired to their boat.[70] They rushing in all together into the boat, she came on ground, so that off they could not get her but some must go out of her again. Ten of the lustiest men went out again, and by that time the Indians were come down into the fort again, and shot at our men. They which were a-land perceiving the arrows fly among them, ran again at the fort side and shot in at the loop-hole with their muskets. By this the boat was got off, and one that was master of the Roebuck, a most cowardly villain that ever was born of a woman, he caused them in the boat to row away, and so left those brave men a spoil for the Portingales. Yet they waded up to the necks in the water to them, and yet these merciless villains in the boat would have no pity on them. Their excuse was that the boat was so full of water that had they come in she would have sunk with all them in her. Thus vilely were these poor men lost.

And by this time, they which were landed on the other side[71] (the

---

3 with one] w^th one *MS*; without *Purchas*     9 where my men ... fort's side]
*MS*; *omitted Purchas*     25 loop-hole] loope hole *MS*; lower hold *Purchas*

[67] Purchas, understandably puzzled, reads 'without wound'. Cavendish's account of the numbers wounded seems contradictory on either reading.

[68] Purchas omits $3\frac{1}{2}$ lines of MS. The compositor's eye jumped from the first 'fort's side' to the second two lines below.

[69] i.e. the victors on the western side.    [70] The smaller boat on the western side.

[71] The eastern side, where Morgan had been killed.

great boat not being able to row near the shore to relieve them) were killed with stones by the Indians; being thus wilfully and undiscreetly spoiled, which you may well perceive, if you look into their landing, especially in such a place as they could not escape killing with stones.

They returned aboard again, having lost twenty-five men, whereof ten of them were left ashore in such sort as I have showed you. When the boats came to the ship's side, there were not eight men in the biggest boat which were not most grievously wounded. I demanding of them the cause of all their mishaps, and how they durst land, considering my strait commandment to the contrary, they answered me that there was no fault in Captain Morgan, but the greatest occasion of all this spoil unto them happened upon a controversy between the captain and those soldiers that landed with him and were killed at the fort; for their ill speeches and urging of Captain Morgan was the cause that he landed contrary to my commandment, and upon such a place as they all confessed forty men were sufficient to spoil five hundred.

I leave it to yourself to judge of what a sight it was to me to see so many of my best men thus wilfully spoiled, having not left in my ship fifty sound men, so as we were no more than able to weigh our anchors, which we the next morning did. And finding it calm we were constrained to come to an anchor again, for my only intention was to get out of that bad road and to put off into the sea, and there to determine what to do, for that place was not for us to tarry in, for the road was so bad as we were not able to help ourselves with a boat's lading of fresh water, whereof we stood in no small want of.

In this day's stay in the road, I comforted these distressed poor men what I might, and I found most of their desires to return again into England. I let them understand how we would go back again to the island of Saint Sebastian, and there we would water and do our other necessary business, and there to make a resolute determination of the rest of our proceedings. This course seemed to like them all very well, but the company in the Roebuck instantly desired nothing more than to return home, all affirming that it was pity such a ship should be cast off. But in truth it was not of any care of the ship, but only of a most cowardly mind of the master and chiefest of the company to return home.

Now you shall understand that the captain[72] was very sick, and since the time that the ship lost her masts she became the most laboursome ship that ever did swim in the sea, so as he was not able to endure in her,

[72] John Cocke.

and at that present lay aboard my ship, so as there was none of any trust or accompt left in her. But such was the case of that ship, being without sails, masts, or any manner of tackle, as in the sense and judgement of any man living there did not live that desperate-minded men in the world which in that case she was then in would have ventured to have sailed in her half so far as England. And if she do return, it is in my opinion the most admirable return that ever ship made, being so far off and in her case.

These villains having left in my ship all their hurt men, and having aboard of them both the surgeons, I having not one in my own ship which did know how to lay a plaster to a wound, much less to cure any by salves; and further, they having in their ship three times the proportion of my victual, wherein consisted the only relief and comfort of all my company—these most hard-hearted villains determined that night amongst themselves to lose me at their next convenient time they could espy, and in this case to go for England, leaving us in the most greatest distress that ever one Christian left another in. For we had all her hurt men in us, and we had taken out of her the best part of her men not long before; so as in running from us they not only carried away our surgeons and all their provision, but also the victual wherein consisted all our relief and comfort; having in them at their departure but forty-six men carrying away with them the proportion for six months' victual for 120 men at large.

I leave you to consider of this part of theirs and the miserable case I was left in, with so many hurt men, so few victual, and my boat being so bad as six or seven men continually bailing water were scant able to keep her from sinking; and mend her we could by no means before we recovered some shore. For had not these villains in the Roebuck that night we rode in this bay suffered their boat to run ashore with Irish men, which went ashore to betray us, I had taken her boat and sunk this great naughty boat. Such was the greatness of our mishaps as we were not left with the comfort and hope of a boat to relieve ourselves withal; we not having left in the ship not three tuns of water for a hundred and forty men, the most whereof being hurt and sick. We putting out of the road the next day, they the same night in this case left us, and, as I suppose, they could not accompt otherwise than that we should never again be heard on.

The next morning, looking for the Roebuck, she could nowhere be

33 for a hundred and forty men] for a 140 men *MS*

seen. I leave to you to judge in what plight my company was in, being
now destitute of surgeons, victuals, and all other relief, which in truth
was so great a discomfort unto them as they held themselves as dead
men, as well whole as hurt. The scantness of water made us that we
could not seek after them, but were enforced to seek to this island[73] with
all possible speed, having to beat back again thither 200 leagues; which
place God suffered us to get with our last cask-water,[74] the poor men
being most extremely pinched by want thereof. Where, after we had a
little refreshed ourselves, we presently mended our boat in such sort as
with great labour and danger we brought 40 tuns of water aboard. And  10
in the meantime, searching our store of ropes, tackle, and sails, we found
ourselves utterly unfurnished both of ropes and sails; which accident
pleased the company not a little, for by these wants they assuredly
accompted to go home. Then making a survey of the victual, we found to
be remaining in the ship (according to the rate we then lived at) fourteen
weeks' victuals large.

   Having rigged our ships in such sort as our small store would furnish
us, which was most meanly, for we had but four sails, our spritsail and
foretopsail being wanting, which two the ship most principally loveth,
and those which we had (except her mainsail) were more than half  20
worn—In this poor case being furnished, and our water being taken in,
my company knowing my determination, which was to hale my boat
aground and build her new, they forthwith openly began to murmur and
mutine, affirming plainly that I need not mend the boat, for they would
go home, and then there should be no use of her. I hearing these
speeches thought it was now time to look amongst them, called them
together and telled them that although we had many mishaps fallen
upon us, yet I hoped that their minds would not in such sort be overcome
with any of these misfortunes that they would go about to undertake any
base or disordered course; but that they would cheerfully go forward to  30
attempt either to make themselves famous in resolutely dying, or in
living to perform that which will be to their perpetual reputations. And
telled them the more we attempted, being in so weak a case, the more (if
we performed) would be to our honours. But contrariwise, if we died in

18  meanly] meanely *Purchas*; maynelie *MS*

[73]  St Sebastian. Their arrival was probably early Oct. 1592, using Knivet's statement
that he was captured 3 months before the Desire's men were massacred at Ilha Grande;
see Knivet, p. 90/28 and note. Knivet was about a month on St Sebastian before he was
captured.
[74]  The last of our cask water, or water in cask.

attempting, we did but that which we came for, which was either to perform or die.

And then I showed them my determination to go again for the Straits of Magelanus; which words were no sooner uttered but forthwith they all with one consent affirmed plainly they would never go that way again, and that they would all rather stay ashore in that desert island than in such case to go for the Straits. I sought by peaceable means to persuade them, showing them that in going that way we should relieve our victuals by salting of seals and birds, which they did well know we might do in greater quantity than our ship could carry. And further, if we got through the strait, which we might now easily perform considering we had the chiefest part of summer before us, we could not but make a most rich voyage, and also meet again with the two small ships which were gone from us.[75] And that it was but 600 leagues thither, and to go into England they had 2000. And further that they should be most infamous to the world, that being within 600 leagues of the place which we so much desired, to return home again so far being most infamous and beggarly.

These persuasions took no place with them, but most boldly they all affirmed that they had sworn that they would never go again to the Straits, neither by no means would they. And one of the chiefest of their faction most proudly and stubbornly uttered these words to my face in presence of all the rest. Which I seeing, and finding my own faction to be so weak (for there were not any that favoured my part but my poor cousin Cocke and the master of the ship) I took this bold companion by the bosom, and with my own hands put a rope about his neck, meaning resolutely to strangle him, for weapon about me I had none. His companions seeing one of their chief champions in this case, and perceiving me to go roundly to work with him, they all came to the master and desired him to speak, affirming they would be ready to take any course that I should think good of. I hearing of this stayed myself, and let the fellow go. After which time I found them something conformable, at least in speeches; though among themselves they still murmured at my intentions.

Thus having something pacified them, and persuaded them that by no means I would take any other course than to go for the Straits, I took ashore with me thirty soldiers and my carpenters, carrying fourteen days

---

[75] About this time, early Oct. 1592, the Desire and the Pinnace, after waiting for Cavendish in the Straits, were trying to reach the Pacific, hoping to rendezvous at Santa Maria (Jane, pp. 108–11).

victuals with me for them. Thus going ashore, I haled up my boat to new build her in such sort as she might be able to abide the seas, leaving aboard all my sailors and the rest to rig the ship and mend sails and to do other business.

And now to let you know in what case I lay ashore among these base men, you shall understand that of these thirty there were very few of them which had not rather have gone to the Portingales than to have remained with me, for there were some which at my being ashore were making rafts to go over to the main, which was not a mile over, where the Portingales had continual watch of us, looking but for a fit opportunity to  10 set upon us. Being in this case, always expecting the coming of the Portingales, against whom I could have made small resistance, and further the treachery of some of my company, which desired nothing more than to steal over so to betray me, I protest I lived hourly as he that still expecteth death.

In this case, I made all the speed I could to make an end of my boat, that we might be able to row her aboard, which in twelve days we mainly finished; which being done, I came aboard, and found all my business in good forwardness. So I determined with all possible speed to dispatch and be gone for the Straits of Magellan. But or ever we could get in all  20 our water and timber-wood[76] and other necessaries, an Irishman, a noble villain, having made a raft, got over to the main and telled the Portingales, which were there watching nothing but an opportunity, that if they would go over in the night they should find most of our men ashore without weapon, and that they might do by them what they would. Upon this, they the next night came over, and having taken some of our men, they brought them where the rest lay, which they most cruelly killed, the most being sick men not being able to stir to help themselves. Those which were ashore more than[77] the sick men had stolen out of the ship, for it was all my care to keep them aboard,  30 knowing well that the Portingales sought to spoil us, the place being so fit for them, which was all overgrown with woods and bushes, as their Indians might go and spoil us with their arrows at their pleasure and we not be able to hurt one of them.

In the morning (perceiving their coming)[78] I sent my boat ashore and rescued all my healthful men but five, which they found out in the night

---

9 rafts] *Purchas*; Rafes *MS*               22 raft] *Purchas*; Rafe *MS*

[76] Wood for repairs and carpentry rather than for fuel.
[77] Over and above.
[78] i.e. perceiving that the Portuguese had come.

without weapons to defend them. Whereof, beside the loss of our men, we having but four sails lost one ashore, which was no small mishap among the rest. The Portingales went presently again over to the main, but left their Indians to keep in the bushes about the watering place. Our men going ashore were shot at and hurt, and could by no means come to hurt them again by reason of the wood and bushes. Wherefore finding my men hurt, and that by any means I could do nothing there without more loss of men, which I had no need of, for I had not left above ninety men or little over, I notwithstanding my wants of wood and water, and

10 my boat being not sufficiently mended was in no possibility to do me pleasure, in this case was I forced to depart, fortune never ceasing to lay her greatest adversities upon me.

But now I am grown so weak and faint as I am scarce able to hold the pen in my hand. Wherefore I must leave you to enquire of the rest of our most unhappy proceedings. But know this, that for the Straits I could by no means get my company to give their consents to go, for after this misfortune and the want of our sails, which was a chief matter, they alleged—and to tell you truth all the men left in the ship were no more than able to weigh our anchors—. But in truth I desired nothing more

20 than to attempt that course, rather desiring to die in going forward than basely in returning backward again. But God would not suffer me to die so happy a man, although I sought all the ways I could still to attempt to perform somewhat. For after that by no means I see they could be brought to go for the Straits, having so many reasonable occasions to allege against me as they had: first, having but three sails and the place subject to such furious storms and the loss of one of these was death; and further our boat was not sufficiently repaired to abide the seas; and last of all, the fewness and weakness of our company, wherein we had not left thirty sailors; these causes being alleged against me, I could not well

30 answer. But I resolved them plainly that to England I would never give my consent to go, and that if they would not take such courses as I intended, that then I was determined that ship and all should sink in the seas together.

Upon this they began to be more tractable, and then I showed them that I would beat for Saint Elena, and there either to make ourselves happy by mending or ending. This course in truth pleased none of them. And yet, seeing my determination and supposing it would be more danger to resist me than in seeming to be willing, they were at quiet until

28 weakness] wekenes *MS*; feeblenesse *Purchas*

I had beaten from 29 degrees to the southward of the equator to 20, at which time, I finding that I was too far northerly to have good wind, I called them to tack about the ship to the southward again. They all plainly made answer they would not, and that they had rather die there than be starved in seeking an island which they thought that way we should never get.

What means I used to stand again to the southward I leave you to enquire of themselves, but from the latitude of 20 I beat back again into 28, with such contrary winds as I suppose never man was troubled with the like so long a time together. Being in this latitude I found the wind favourable, and then I stood again to the northward, willing the master and his company to sail east-north-east; and they in the night (I being asleep) steered north-east and mere northerly.[79] Notwithstanding all this most vile usage, we got within 60 leagues[80] of the island, and had the wind favoured us so as that we might have stemmed from 18 degrees to 16 east-north-east, we had found the island. But it was not God's will so great a blessing should befall me. Being now in the latitude of the island, almost 80 leagues[80] to the westward of it, the wind being continually at east-south-east (the most contrariest wind that could blow), I presently made a survey of my victual, and found that according to that proportion of victual which we then lived at, there was not left in the ship eight weeks victual, which being so far from relief was as I suppose as small a portion as ever men were at in the seas.

Being so uncertain of relief, I demanded of them whether they would venture like good-minded men to beat to the southward again to get this island, where we should not only relieve ourselves but also be in full assurance either to sink or take a carrack; and that by this means we should have a sufficient revenge of the Portingales for all their villainies done unto us; or that they would pinch and bate half the allowance they had before, and so to go for England. They all answered me they would pinch to death rather than go again to the southward. I knowing their dispositions, and having lived amongst them in such continual torment and disquietness,—and now to tell you of my greatest grief, which was the sickness of my dear kinsman John Cocke, who by this time was grown in great weakness, by reason whereof he desired rather quietness

13  Notwithstanding] *Purchas*; notwthstand/ing *MS*; witwithstand/ing *Quinn*
14  60] *MS*; two *Purchas*        18  80] *MS*; eighteene *Purchas*
[79]  Even northerly.
[80]  Inexplicably, Purchas prints 'two' and 'eighteene'. Was he trying to make Cavendish seem nearer to St Helena?

and contentedness in our course than such continual disquietness which never ceased me. And now by this, what with grief for him and the continual trouble I endured amongst such hell-hounds, my spirit was clean spent, wishing myself upon any desert place in the world, there to die, rather than thus basely to return home again. Which course I had put in execution, had I found an island[81] which the carts[82] make to be in 8 degrees to the southward of the line. I swear to you I sought it with all diligence, meaning if I had found it to have there ended my unfortunate life. But God suffered no such happiness to light upon me, for I could by no means find it; so as I was forced to go towards England. And having gotten 8 degrees benorth[83] the line, I lost my most dearest cousin.

And now consider whether a heart made of flesh be able to endure so many misfortunes all falling upon me without intermission. I thank my God that in ending of me he hath pleased to rid me of all further trouble and mishaps. And now to return to our private matters, I have made a will wherein I have given special charge that all goods, whatsoever belongs to me, to be delivered into your hands. For God's sake refuse not to do this last request for me. I owe little that I know of, and therefore it will be the less trouble. But if there be any debt that of truth is owing by me, for God's sake see it paid. I have left a space in the will for another name, and if you think it good I pray take in my cousin Henry Seckford; he will ease you much in many businesses. Although he look for gain, you shall find him a very fit man in some respects to join with you. There is a bill of adventure to my cousin Richard Cocke;[84] if it happen the other ship return home with anything, as it is not impossible, I pray remember him, for he hath nothing to show for it. And likewise Master Eaton,[85] the customer of Hampton,[86] which is 50 pounds, and one Elliot[87] of Ratcliffe by London, which is 50 pounds more. The rest have all bills of adventure but they run in the victual, only two excepted, which I have written unto you. I have given Sir George Carey the Desire, if ever she return, for I always promised him her if she returned, and a little part of her getting. If any such thing happen, I pray you see it performed.

---

6  carts] Cartes *MS*; Cardes *Purchas*    11  benorth] benorthe *MS*; by North *Purchas*; beneathe *Quinn*    12  be able] *MS*, *Purchas*; to be able *Quinn*    22  Although ... with you] *MS*; omitted by *Purchas*    27  Hampton] *Purchas*; Hernton *MS*

[81] Ascension.    [82] Charts were regularly called 'carts' or 'cards'.
[83] To the north of.    [84] Younger brother of John Cocke (Quinn).
[85] Thomas Eaton (Quinn).    [86] Southampton.
[87] Unidentified.

To use compliments of love now at my last breath were frivolous, but know that I left none in England whom I loved half so well as yourself, which you in such sort deserved at my hands as I can by no means requite. I have left all that little remaining unto you not to be accomptable for anything. That which you will, if you find any overplus of remainder, yourself especially being satisfied to your own desire, give unto my sister Anne Candish. I have written to no man living but yourself, leaving all friends and kinsmen, only reputing you as dearest. Commend me to both your brothers, being glad that your brother Edward escaped so unfortunate a voyage. Pray give this copy of my unhappy proceedings to none but only to Sir George Carey, and tell him that if I had thought the letters of a dead man would have been acceptable, I would have written unto him. I have taken order with the master of my ship to see his pieces of ordnance to be delivered to him, for he knoweth them. And if the Roebuck be not returned, then I have appointed him to deliver him two brass pieces out of this ship, which I pray see performed.

I have now no more to say, but take this last farewell, that you have lost the lovingest friend that was lost by any. Commend me to your wife. No more; but as you love God do not refuse to undertake this last request of mine. I pray forget not Master Carey of Cockington;[88] gratify him with something, for he used me kindly at my departure. Bear with this scribbling, for I protest I am scant able to hold a pen in my hand.

I pray cause to be delivered unto the bearer hereof 40 pounds.

Th. Caundyshe.

By him that [most] loved you.

Thomas C[aundyshe]

## 4. *Antony Knivet*

The admirable adventures and strange fortunes of Master Antony Knivet, which went with Master Thomas Candish in his second voyage to the South Sea. 1591.

What befell in their voyage to the Straits, and after, till he was taken by the Portugals.

6 remainder] *Quinn*; remained *Purchas*; remaind *MS* (*torn*)    7 living] *Purchas*; *MS torn*    8 dearest] *Purchas*; *MS torn*    10 escaped] *Purchas; MS torn*

[88] Another George Carey (d. 1616); see Quinn.

We departed from Plymouth with five sail of ships, determining to go for the South Sea. The names of our ships were these: the Galleon Leicester, which was our Admiral; the Roebuck, Vice-Admiral; the Desire, the Dainty, and the Black Pinnace. Six or seven days after that we were departed from the coast of England, we met with nineteen sail of Flemings in the night. Not regarding what they were, our Vice-Admiral took one of them, and all the rest escaped. In the morning, the master of our Flemish prize was brought before the General, and of him we had news of a fleet of ships that was departed out of Lisbon for Brazil, the which news we were very glad of.[1] The Flemish ship was laden with salt, whereof the General took three tun[2] for his provision. This Fleming also showed us a licence that he had to pass the seas, under Her Majesty's hand and seal, the which as our General had seen he presently commanded that every man should return all such things as they had taken from the Fleming, and he himself paid for the salt that he had taken, and so we departed from them with a fair wind, holding our course from the coast of Portugal to the islands of Canary.

Thus in twenty days we had sight of the said islands, which when our General knew of truth to be the same, he commanded his two smallest ships, the Dainty and the Black Pinnace, to be sent along the shore to see if they could espy any carvels[3] fishing, or any ships between the islands; and not descrying anything, the next morning they returned back unto us.

Under the equinoctial line we lay seven and twenty days, driving to and fro without puff of wind. In which time most of our men fell sick of the scurvy by reason of the extreme heat of the sun and the vapours of the night. Notwithstanding, our great danger of sickness did not appause[4] the hardness of our hearts, being in as great extremity as ever men were. It happened that two men of Japon which the General had taken in his first voyage,[5] bearing envy to a poor Portugal that went with us from Plymouth, accused him to the General (having before conspired his death) in this sort. The General being at dinner, these two Japoners came to his cabin telling their tale so loud that everyone might hear the report, which was thus: that the Portugal of the ship was a traitor, and

---

[1] The fleet was carrying the new governor-general, Don Francisco de Sousa (Franco).

[2] Probably three casks; 'tun' and 'ton' were not at this time differentiated.

[3] Light, fast, three-masted ships.

[4] So Purchas, but *OED* does not know the word; it should presumably be 'appease' (= allay).

[5] These were two Japanese youths, Christopher (then aged 17) and Cosmus (13), who had been aboard the Santa Ana.

that he had often given them counsel to run away with him at Brazil; moreover, quoth he, if it so had pleased God we had taken the town of Santos as our General had pretended,[6] from thence that he would guide them to the South Sea,[7] where they should be well rewarded for their intelligence. Upon the which accusations, the poor Portugal was hanged. And as for his going from Santos by land through America to the South Sea, it had been a thing impossible, for the country is all wilderness and full of savages.[8]

After we had been so long becalmed under the line we had a fair north-west wind,[9] and in twenty days sail we had sight of land on the coast of Brazil, but no man knew certainly what part it should be. At length, coming near the shore, we espied two small ships; the one of them we took, the other escaped. That we took was laden with blackamoors,[10] and some merchandise; they came from Fernam-baquo[11] and were determined to have gone to the River of Plate. By the pilot of this ship we knew we were at Cape Frio, that is, Cold Cape.[12] This cape lieth twelve leagues from the river of Jenero,[13] and thirty leagues from Santos, which was the town we meant to take. In this ship we took a friar, that hid himself in a chest of meal.

The night following, by the directions of our new-taken pilot,[14] we came to a place called Ilha Grande,[15] twelve leagues from Santos. At this place we took five or six houses with Portugals and savages of the country. Here we had good store of potatoes and plantains,[16] divers kinds of good roots, with some hogs and hens, which was very good and comfortable for the refreshing of our men. Here we had such disorder

---

7 it had] had *Purchas*          23 plantains] Plantons *Purchas*

[6] Was intending.

[7] Pacific Ocean.

[8] *Experto crede*! Knivet is no doubt thinking of the time some years later when after the failure of a 'bandeiro' into the interior, he had it in mind to try to make this crossing. See Purchas, xvi. 219.

[9] He must mean north-east.

[10] African slaves.

[11] Pernambuco, now Recife, on the easterly hump of Brazil, 8° S. 35° W.

[12] Cabo Frio, 80 miles east of Rio de Janeiro. Knivet's distances are a long way out; Santos is 300 miles away, not 90 (30 leagues).

[13] Janeiro. Spellings vary considerably.

[14] This luckless man, whom Knivet calls Jasper Jorge (p. 84), was later ruthlessly hanged by Cavendish for supposedly misleading him about the depth of water at Spirito Santo (see pp. 66 and 92).

[15] Between Rio de Janeiro and St Sebastian island.

[16] The banana-like fruit of *musa paradisiaca*.

amongst ourselves that if the Portugals had been of any courage they might have killed many of us, for our men would fight for their victuals as if they had been no Christians but Jews; and they that got the best would get them into some hole, or into the wilderness under some tree, and there they would remain as long as they had meat. For mine own part, there was such sharking I could in that place get neither meat nor money, and pure hunger compelled me to go into the woods to see if we could kill anything with our pieces,[17] or if we could find some potatoes. And as we went, we encountered with seven or eight of our company that were together by the ears about a hog they had killed, and the strife was who should have the best share. We coming in that time when everyone used their fists stole away a quarter, and went a good way into the wilderness, where we were merry for that night. The next day we came back again with good store of potato roots, and going into the house where the General's musicians were,[18] we found them dressing of eight young whelps for their dinner; we giving them of our roots they were contented that we should dine with them.

In the afternoon we set fire on a new ship and burned all the houses. Leaving the merchant and all his moors ashore, we departed from thence, and having a fair wind, about six of the clock we came to the island of San Sebastian, where we anchored, being five leagues from Santos. As soon as the ships were in the harbour every master and captain came aboard of the General, to know how he pretended to take the town of Santos. And they all resolved that our longboat and our shallop only,[19] with one hundred men, was enough for the taking of it. For the Portugal pilot told us that it was of no strength.[20]

On Christmas Eve, about ten o'clock in the night, when the boats were to go ashore, there were so many that would have gone that we began to fight and cast one another overboard into the sea. But as soon as our General heard the noise, he commanded every man to come aboard the ship again. I fearing the General, and being desirous to go ashore with the first (for I had seen before that they which came last got nothing) crept under the seat of our shallop, where I was for the space of two hours, and the boat being full of men I could not get out, but there

[17] Guns.

[18] In strong contrast with their frequent employment on the circumnavigation (see p. 23), the musicians had little to do on this voyage, and are not mentioned elsewhere.

[19] Both the shallop and the longboat would be quite large ship's boats capable of carrying masts and sails.

[20] Steps had been taken to fortify Santos following Fenton's raid in 1583 (see Franco, pp. 19–20).

had been smothered, if it had not been for William Waldren that was our boatsman and steered the boat, who hearing me cry under him tore up the boards and saved my life.

About three o'clock in the morning we met with a canoa (which is a boat that they make of a whole tree)[21] in which we took four Portugals and two women. The one of them was going to be married that morning. After we had taken this boat we went close to the shore, and having tarried for our boat an hour we heard the Portugals ring a bell. Presently[22] Jasper Jorge the Portugal pilot told us that now was the time to land, for he knew by that bell that they were in the middle of their 10 mass, and at that instant the friar was holding up the bread of sacrament before the people to worship it.

He had no sooner spoke but we were all on shore. And so, marching to the church, we took every man's sword without resistance; and there we remained till it was seven of the clock for the coming of our longboat and the rest of our company, for we were but twenty-three in all and we durst not take sack of the town with so few. By that means some of the Portugals that were in their houses escaped with their persons and money. Here was good store of victual and great store of succats,[23] sugars and cassavi meal,[24] of the which we made very good bread. In the 20 church there were three hundred men beside women and children.

As soon as we had taken the sack of the town and placed all our men in order, word was sent to our general of all that had been done. After the General had sent answer again to the town, all the Portugals were set at liberty, and we fortified ourselves in the town, keeping only seven or eight of the chiefest and principal prisoners. Master Cocke, captain of the Vice-Admiral, went captain of all the company that went ashore. He favoured me very much, and commanded me to take a friar's cell to lodge in in the College of Jesus,[25] where he himself lodged with many captains and young gentlemen. It was my chance going up and down 30 from cell to cell that I looked under a bed standing in a dark hole, where I found a little chest fast nailed, and the seams thereof were white with wheat flour. I drew it forth, and finding it of great weight broke it in pieces, wherein I found 1700 rials of eight,[26] each whereof containeth

---

26 Cocke] Cooke *Purchas*

[21] This is the original meaning of the word 'canoe', and its original spelling.
[22] At once.                    [23] Succates or succades; preserved or candied fruits.
[24] Tapioca, prepared from the root of the manioc or mandioca plant.
[25] Founded in 1585 (Franco).
[26] Spanish or Portuguese silver coins (also called reals or pieces of eight).

four shillings English. This hole I took for my lodging, and no man knew of my good purchase. Cloth, shirts, blankets, and beds and such stuff no man regarded.

The next day following, being St. Stephen's day,[27] the Portugals gave us a false alarm. The General came also with all the ships into the road and presently landed with two hundred men and commanded all the outward part of the town to be burned. Then he gave order for the building of a pinnace to row with twenty oars, and commanded all the ships that were in the harbour to be set on fire. At this town we took an
10 Englishman, called John King, which had been there fifteen years.[28]

Our General lay in the College of Jesus all the time that we were at Santos. This college had many back ways to the sea-side, and it happened one night that two savages, being abused by the Portugals, ran away, and knowing the passages of the college, came in the night to the General's bedside, and brought with them turkeys and hens. The General being awaked by them cried out for help. One of them that could speak Portugal fell down on his knees and said that he came to crave his favour and not to offend him. The morning following the General had discourse with these two savages, and by them he knew of
20 what strength the Portugals' camp was, and how that at his going out of the town they were determined to give battle. Likewise they told him of three great bags of money and a jar that was hid under the root of a fig tree, and guided us where we had three hundred head of cattle, which served us all the time we were there.

The Dainty being a small ship made a good voyage to Santos, for she came in before any of our fleet, by the which means they laded her with sugar and good commodities of the Portugals' ships that were in the harbour. This ship went voluntarily with us, and having made a good voyage the captain[29] told the General that he would return for England.
30 The General answered that he was determined to send him into the River of Plate, and then with all his heart he should return.

We continued two months at Santos,[30] which was the overthrow of our voyage. In the time that we were there many Canibals[31] came unto

---

[27] 26 Dec.
[28] Not otherwise known. Presumably he was an associate of John Whithall (see p. 48), the English merchant who had set up his sugar trade here in 1578, 13 years earlier.
[29] Randolph Cotton.    [30] About five weeks in fact; Jane says they left on 22 Jan.
[31] Although Knivet reports the practice of man-eating among the tribes that he later associated with, he uses the word 'cannibal' quite generally to refer to Indians. I therefore preserve the capital and the spelling given in Purchas to show that Knivet is not referring specifically to man-eaters.

us, desiring the General that he would destroy the Portugals and keep the country to himself, protesting to be all on his side. The General thanked them for their kindness and told them that at that time he had a farther pretence. We found store of gold in this town that the Indians had brought from a place called by the Indians Mutinga,[32] and now the Portugals have mines there. Many of our company counselled the General to winter at this town but he would not by any means.

From our first setting forth from England till we came to Santos I had great love to Christopher the Japon, because I found his experience to be good in many things. This Indian and I grew into such friendship one with another that we had nothing betwixt us unknown together. I a long time having found him true, I told him of the money I had found under the friar's bed. With that he told me of some money that he had got, and we swore to part half from thenceforth whatsoever God should permit us to obtain. Some four days after that, when we were ready to depart, he told me that that time of the year was past,[33] wherefore it was best to hide our money in the ground and remain in the country. I believing his persuasions agreed to do what he thought best; thus we determined both that the same day we were to go a shipboard, that then he should take all the money in a canoa and hide it by a river side. In the morning I delivered all the money into his hands, and he swore that in less than two hours he would return, but I stayed above five hours, and might have tarried all my life, for he was gone aboard the ship. Afterward by good means I got my own again, and so our former friendship was parted.

Our men marched by land from Santos to another town called San Vincent, and in the way our men burned five ingenios,[34] or sugar-mills. The disorder of our men was such at their embarking that if the Portugals had been of any courage they might easily have cut our throats. The two Indians which came at night to the General's chamber went with us to the straits.

We departed from Santos with a fair wind for the Straits of Magellan. Fourteen days we had fair weather; the fifteenth day, all the masters and captains of the fleet coming aboard, the Admiral won a great sum of money. Two days after, we were becalmed, and the pilots taking their

27 ingenios] Engenios *Purchas*

[32] More usually Maetinga or Amaetinga (Franco).
[33] i.e. for going south to get round to the Pacific.
[34] The word commonly used by the English for sugar-factories in the Caribbean. Originally, *ingenio de azúcar* (Sp.).

height[35] found it to be in the altitude[36] with the River of Plate. And we being far from the shore did bear room[37] for land, determining to send the Dainty, the Black Pinnace, and the [Desire?][38] into the aforesaid River of Plate. But it was not the will of God that we should execute our pretence. For the same day we thought to have descried land, the wind began to blow south-west, and the seas were very dark, swelling in waves so high that we could not perceive any of our accompanied ships, although we were very near one to another. The seas brake over the poop of our ship and washed our men astonished with fear into the

10 scuppers. The Roebuck in this storm ran her [stem?] against our poop and brake down all our gallery.[39] All things were cast into the sea that stood above hatches. Here miserable Fortune began to frown on us all, especially on me, for all that I had, both in clothes and money, were cast into the sea. All our ship [was flooded?] with the seas that brake over her sides. Here our General showed himself to be of a noble courage, for he did nothing but run up and down encouraging his men, which were all amazed, thinking that to be their last hour. This storm continued three days, in which time we lost most of our sails, blown away from the yards. (In this storm the Crow, a small boat of twenty ton, sunk before our eyes,

20 with twelve men and a boy. The Roebuck lost her boat with two men, and we lost ours with three men. And at the Straits we took the Desire's longboat for the Admiral.)[40]

It was the will of God that after we had been three days in the storm the wind ceased, but the seas continued so great that we were not able to bear any sail. We lying thus tossed with seas without sight of any of our fleet, the company murmured and wished themselves again at Santos. And indeed we all thought that the rest of our company were driven back with the storm to the coast, thinking it best for us to return again. The General, hearing what speeches passed in the ship, came forth upon the

10 scuppers] skippers *Purchas*

[35] Taking the height of the sun with the cross-staff.

[36] The angle of the sun. The pilots knew that they were in the same latitude as the River Plate. For a contemporary's explanation of the difference between altitude and latitude, see John Davis's *Seaman's Secrets*, in Markham, pp. 260–2.

[37] Run to leeward.

[38] There are three gaps in Purchas in this paragraph, presumably indicating some damage to the edge of the MS.

[39] A walkway built at the stern of a ship as an extension of the captain's or the admiral's cabin.

[40] This bracketed passage is printed in the margin by Purchas. It presumably represents an afterthought of Knivet's. The Crow was the pinnace built at Santos, whose loss is also mentioned by Jane (p. 100/15).

half-deck and commanded all the company to come before him. And after he had heard them speak he answered that he had given directions to all the masters and captains of the fleet that what weather soever should part them, that they should use their endeavour to take Port Desire, and that they should tarry a fortnight, so if none of the company came they should leave some mark on the shore and go on their voyage.

With that every man was satisfied. The General promising twenty pounds to whomsoever could first spy a sail, we made our course to Port Desire, and in ten days we safely arrived at our desired port, where we found all our fleet but the Dainty, which was no little comfort to us all, 10 because the time of our year was almost past. We stayed here but two days, taking a few penguins from an island right before Port Desire.

When we came to the mouth of the Straits we found the wind contrary, and were forced to lie beating before the harbour of Port Famine three days ere we could double that cape, for many times we did cast anchor without the cape in twenty fathoms water, but on a sudden the current would carry away the ships with cables and anchors afloat in the night. In this current the Roebuck, driven with the current, fell cross over the hawse;[41] there we had no other remedy but were forced to cut our cables and so lose our anchors. In the end with much ado we 20 doubled the cape and got into Port Famine, where we lay a sevennight for want of wind and weather to go forward.

In the time that we were at Port Famine, every day our men went on shore to get mussels and fruits of the country to eat, and the bark of a tree that was like cinnamon. One day, the boat being ashore, there came to us above a thousand Canibals naked, with feathers in their hands, but they would not come so near us as we could touch them. If we offered them anything they would reach to us with a long pole, and whatsoever we gave them they would return us feathers for it. We made our signs to them for victuals, and they would show us by signs that they had none 30 but what they could kill with their darts.

I have told you how my chest and all my clothes were cast overboard. Now coming to this cold climates[42] and wanting clothes, my hope of life was little, for here men were well at morning and by night frozen to death. It was my fortune to go ashore to get some food, for the allowance

19  hawse] haze *Purchas*

[41] The Roebuck came right across her bow as she lay at anchor. The hawse is the space between a ship's head and her anchor as it lies on the sea-bed. 'Another vessel which crosses this space is said to cross the hawse' (Kemp).

[42] Regions (considered with regard to weather). 'this' for 'these' is quite common.

of our ship was little, and coming aboard again with my feet wet, and wanting shift of clothes, the next morning I was numbed, that I could not stir my legs, and pulling off my stockings my toes came with them, and all my feet were as black as soot, and I had no feeling of them.[43] Then was I not able to stir.

Thus I continued for the space of a fortnight, till we came into a fair bay where there were many fair islands, and on the rocks of some of these islands we found scouts[44] made of the barks of trees, and afterwards we found many Indians, but none of them would come to us. 10 On the south-west side of the main we found a river which we thought had gone to the South Sea. Our longboat was sent up this river and found it to be very straight and deep. On the sides thereof they found great mussels, and in them good store of pearls, and we named it the River of Pearls. The bay had the name of the master of our pinnace, because he first found it and did discover it, called it Tobias Bay.[45] From this place we went further into the Straits, having the wind against us, and with the cold there died every day out of our ship eight or nine men. Here one Harris a goldsmith lost his nose, for going to blow it with his fingers cast it into the fire.[46] This John Chambers,[47] Caesar Ricasen, 20 and many that are now in England can testify.

The General having experience that the wind would tarry at least two months, his men died so fast that he thought best to return for the coast of Brazil, and there to separate our fleet to the havens that lie on the coast, River of Jenuary, Spirito Santo, and Santos;[48] determining by this means to furnish himself with ropes, sails, and victuals of such prizes as he did not doubt but to take, and likewise determining to take Santos again.

The General came back with this pretence for Brazil, came to Port Famine, where we anchored two days, and there took a note of all his

24 and Santos] of Santos (*after* havens) *Purchas*

[43] Knivet later says, 'in one night that I lay moist of my feet, I lost three of my toes on one of my feet, and four of the tops of the other foot' (Purchas, xvi. 267).

[44] Flat-bottomed boats (from the Dutch).

[45] Tobias Paris or Parris had been mate of the Muscovy Company's ship Thomas Allen in an expedition returning in 1581 (Hakluyt, iii. 247), and then mate of the Edward Bonaventure on Fenton's unsuccessful voyage in the South Atlantic in 1582–3. He presumably went down with the Black Pinnace as it sank after entering the Pacific with the Desire in Oct. (Jane, p. 111).

[46] Knivet refers to this sad event again in a later part of his narrative (Purchas, xvi. 267).

[47] Cavendish's cook.

[48] See text note. It looks as though Knivet had written 'and Santos' as a superscript insertion and it was misread and misplaced.

men that were living, and finding some of them very sick commanded
them to be set on shore.[49] (I was so ill in the Straits that no man thought
I would have lived, and twice I was brought upon the hatches to be
cast into the sea. But it was the will of God that when they had said
prayers, as they accustomed when any man died, and that they laid
hands on me to cast me overboard, I spake, desiring them not to cast
me overboard till I was dead.) At this Port Famine coming back, the
General would have set me on shore, but Captain Cocke entreated for
me; so I remained in the ship. I had very sorry clothes, the toes of my
feet full of lice, that (God is my record) they lay in clusters within my    10
flesh, and of many more besides myself. I had no cabin, but lay upon a
chest.

Now we come out of the Straits with all our fleet but the Dainty that
lost us in the River of Plate in the storm that we had, and the Crow that
was sunk. After that we came out of the Straits, we came before Port
Desire again, and there our boats went to Penguin Island for penguins.
At this place the General took a chirurgion who cured with words.[50]
This man coming aboard our ship said some words over my feet, and I
had feeling in my legs and feet, which I had lost before for the space of a
fortnight. Many times before this man came I had hot irons laid to my    20
feet, but I had no feeling were they never so hot.

That day that we departed from Port Desire, the General sent for all
the masters of the ships, and commanded them that till midnight they
should keep their course with him, and that when he should show them
two lights, then they should cast about and bear in with the shore. But
Davis, which was captain of the Desire, and Tobie, master of the
Pinnace, did deceive us and went for the Straits, as I was informed
afterwards by some of their men that were taken at Brazil after that I was
taken.[51] Three or four days after this we had a great storm, in the which
the Roebuck lost her main mast, and we lost her. Now were we all alone    30
in a great ship, and we knew not what we were best to do, but in the end

---

[49] Knivet later says that seven men were thus abandoned (Purchas, xvi. 267).

[50] Contemporary accounts of the shaman or pagé, supposed to have supernatural
knowledge and power, are given in Hemming, pp. 60–4.

[51] This strange reunion with the survivors of the attack on Davis's men at Ilha Grande
on 6 Feb. 1593 (see Jane, p. 118) is referred to in a later part of Knivet's narrative
(Purchas, xvi. 229). There he mentions only the one survivor, the inventive one-eyed
surgeon, Andrew Towers (see p. 38). But Brazilian sources mention both the surgeon
(who was a Catholic) and a young nobleman (Franco, p. 33). Knivet remarks that Davis's
men were taken three months after he himself was captured; this would make his own
capture early Nov. 1592.

we determined to come for Santos, hoping there to find the rest of our company.

In this storm I sat on a chest and was not able to stir, for still as the ship seeled[52] on one side, the chest went from starboard to larboard, and it was the will of God that it fell between a piece of ordnance and the carpenter's cabin on the one side, and on the other side between another piece and the chirurgion's cabin. Thus all the night I lay very cold, and it was the will of God that the chest never turned over, for if it had, I could not have escaped death. The next day the storm ceased, and most of our young sailors, which we call men of top a yard,[53] being wearied with their night's work that was past, were under hatches asleep, and would not come up to do some business that was to be done. With that the General came down with the end of a rope as big as mine arm, and one of the sailors hid himself behind me. The General spying him struck at him and hit me on the side of the head; and half an hour after, finding me in the same case as the General had left me in, they took me and would have cast me out of one of the ports of the ship, but it was the will of God that I spake and was saved. Here one of the Indians that came to the General in the night at Santos fell overboard by a mischance and was drowned.

We with much ado in the end got to the harbour of Santos, where we found none of our company. We anchored right before a sugar-mill that stood hard by the sea side. The General asked if there were any that would go ashore; then Captain Stafford, Captain Southwell,[54] and Captain Barker offered themselves to go on shore, and twenty more with them. The boat that they went in was made of sugar-chests and barrel boards. They landed and took the sugar-mill, at the which they took a great bark and sent it laden with victuals aboard our ship, which was more welcome unto us than if it had been gold. Here we continued all that day, and the next day they sent the great boat again, laden with sugars and guinea wheat. Then the General sent them word that they should come away, but they sent him word again that they had more provision on shore, and before all was aboard they would not come. The third day that our men were on shore the Portugal set on them. They had the little boat ashore, but the wind being from shore, the great boat went

17 ports] parts *Purchas*

[52] Rolled violently, heeled over.

[53] The topmen would be the fittest and most agile men in the ship but it is hardly surprising that they were exhausted. Trust Cavendish to go for them with a rope's end.

[54] Not mentioned by Cavendish (p. 63).

not from the ship side that day. The next day that our men were slain,
our longboat went ashore and brought us news how the little boat was
broke and how all our men were gone. One of the Indians that I have told
you of landed here with our men, and having experience of the country,
when our men were in the hottest of their fight, ran away, having one
arrow shot through his neck and another in his mouth and out at his poll.
This Indian swam aboard unto us upon a log, and told us that all our
men were slain.[55]

The General thought good to go from hence to the island of San
Sebastian, and there if he did not meet with some of the ships, that then     10
he would return for England. The same day that we were to depart from
Santos, the Roebuck passed by the mouth of the River of Bertia[56] where
we were and shot a piece, and we answered with another, then the
Roebuck came into us with her masts broken. After the Roebuck came
to us we went nearer the town, determining to have beaten down the
town with our ordnance, but wanting water the Galleon Leicester
touched ground, and we had much ado to get her clear again. Then we
landed eighty of our men at a small river near the town, where we had
great store of mandioca roots, potatoes, plantains, and pineapples. The
Portugals seeing our men going into the river sent six canoas to meet     20
them. We seeing them made a shot at them with the chain of our pump.
With that they returned, and our boats came safely aboard with good
store of the aforenamed roots.

In our ship there was a Portugal whom we took in the ship taken at
Cape Frio. This Portugal went with us to the Straits of Magellanus, and
seeing of our overthrow told us of a town called Spirito Sancto. This
Portugal said that we might go before the town with our ships, and that
without danger we might take many sugar-mills and good store of cattle.
The words of this Portugal made us break off our pretence that we had
for San Sebastian, and we went to Spirito Sancto. In eight days we got     30
before the mouth of the harbour. At length we came to an anchor in the
road and presently we went our boats to sound the channel; and we
found not half the depth that the Portugal said we should find. The
General thinking that the Portugal would have betrayed us, without any
trial caused him to be hanged, the which was done in a trice.

Here all the gentlemen that were living desired that they might go

18  mandioca] Mandiora *Purchas*

[55]  Cavendish's account differs considerably about the availability of boats.

[56]  The Bertioga channel separates the island of Santo Amaro from the mainland. It
joins the open sea 12 miles north-east of Santos.

ashore to take the town. The General was very unwilling, and told them
of divers inconveniences, but all would not suffice them. They were so
importunate that the General chose out one hundred and twenty men,
of the best that were in both the ships, and sent Captain Morgan, a
singular good land soldier, and Lieutenant Royden[57] for choice commanders in this action. They landed before a small fort with one of the
boats and drave the Portugals out of it. The other boat went higher,
when they had a very hot skirmish, and their lives were quickly
shortened, for they landed on a rock that stood before the fort; as they
10 leaped out of the boat they slid all armed into the sea, and so most of
them were drowned. To be short, we lost eighty men at this place, and of
the forty that returned there came not one without an arrow or two in his
body, and some had five or six.

When we saw we could do no good at this place, we determined to
come again for the island of San Sebastian, and there we meant to burn
one of our ships, and from thence we determined to go for the Straits
again. The company that was in the Roebuck, hearing of it, in the night
run away from us, and we were left alone again.

Well, we came to San Sebastian Island. All this while I lay under
20 hatches, lame, sick, and almost starved; I was not able to stir, I was so
weak. After we came to this island, the first thing that was done the sick
men were set on shore to shift for themselves. Twenty of us were set on
shore. All were able to go up and down, although very weakly, but I
(alas!) my toes were raw, my body was black, I could not speak nor stir. In
this case I was laid by the shore side, and thus I remained from five of the
clock in the morning till it was between eleven and twelve of the clock,
that the sun came to his highest, and the extreme heat of the sun pierced
through my body, whereby I came to my self as a man awaked from
sleep. And I saw them that were set on shore with me lie dead and a-
30 dying round about me. These men had eaten a kind of pease that did
grow by the sea side which did poison them. When I saw all these men
dead I praised God that had rid them out of their miserable estate and
cursed my hard fortune that death itself did refuse to end my tormented
and most miserable life. I looked towards the shore and saw nothing but
these pease, and if I did eat them I was sure of death; if I did not eat them
I saw no remedy but to starve.

Seeing in this manner, I looked towards the ship to see if the boat
came ashore, but alas, all my hopes were with speed to end my life, but

[57] Not mentioned by Cavendish.

that it was the will of God I saw things stir by the sea side, and it was a great ebb. Then I went creeping on my hands and my feet like a child, and when I had gotten to the sea side I saw many crabs lie in the holes of the mud. I pulled off one of my stockings and filled it with crabs, and as well as I could I carried them to a hollow fig tree, where I found a great fire made. So casting them on the coals I did eat them, and so I lay down to sleep till the next day; and then I watched for the ebb to get some more meat.

Thus I lived eight or nine days without sight of any man. The stink of some of the dead men that the sea came not to was so noisome that I was fain to remove from that place, and as I went along the shore to seek some place to abide in, I passed by a fair river that went into the sea, where I thought it good to make my abode because of the fresh water. I had not been there scarce the space of half a quarter of an hour but I saw a great thing come out of the water, with great scales on the back, with great ugly claws and a long tail.[58] This beast came towards me, and I had not the power to shun it, but as it came towards me I went and met it. When I came near it I stood still, amazed to see so monstrous a thing before me. Hereupon this beast stood still and opened his mouth and thrust out a long tongue like a harping iron. I commended myself to God and thought there to have been torn in pieces, but this beast turned again and went into the river, and I followed to the river's side.

The next day I went farther into the island, fearing to tarry in this place, and I found a great whale lying on the shore like a ship with the keel upwards, all covered with a kind of short moss with the long-lying there. At this place I made a little house, and fed on the whale for the space of a fortnight.[59] In this time the General set forty men more ashore at the place where I was set first on land. Likewise the General trimmed his boat at this place, and had a net continually a-fishing, of which John Chambers his cook had charge, who is this day living in London. After that these men came ashore, I left the place where I was with the whale and came to our men and lived with them, being at this time reasonable well, and able to go very well, for the use of going into the sea did heal my toes.

After these men had been on shore seven or eight days [and] we had

---

[58] This beast must have been a large alligator. But as Knivet became well acquainted with alligators up to 30 ft. long (see Purchas, xvi. 252) it is surprising that when writing this incident up he did not say that he later came to know what the monster was.

[59] It is hardly likely that Knivet could have eaten the flesh of a long-dead whale (Franco, p. 30).

taken wood and water for the ship, the Portugals of the River of January
landed on the north point of the island hard by the whale. They took two
of our men and one escaped, who came to us in the night and told us that
the Portugals and the savages were landed. That day we had taken a
great tortoise ashore, and we did bid the sailor to be of good cheer, for if
it were true it was the better for us, for we were sure that the General
would not take us again into the ship. With that we all commended
ourselves to God and drank to our friends in fair water. And so we
determined to march along the shore with a white shirt instead of a flag
10 of truce, but the sea was so high that we could not. Then we determined
to watch quarterly[60] till such times as we could espy them.

I had the first watch, and watched till I was weary, so called one of my
fellows to watch, and he answered angerly, 'Tut, 'tis a lie.' With that I lay
down by the fire as well as the rest. Before I was asleep the Portugals
were at our door; then I started up, and one of them took me by the leg.
Presently we were all led to the shore side. There all that were taken with
me were knocked on the heads with firebrands. The Indian that had
hold of me struck twice or thrice at me with a short bill, but I striving
cried out in Portugal that if they would save me I would tell them news.
20 With that a Portugal passed by and I caught hold of him. So well as I
could I told him a tale which saved my life at that time. This Portugal
gave me again to a savage, and I cried to him that I would go wheresoever
he went. Then he bid me not fear, that savage was his slave, and that he
would carry me to the captain. So I was content perforce to go I knew not
whither.

This Canibal carried me along the shore, and when we came where
any rocks reached into the sea, he would take me on his back and swim
with me round about the rocks till we were free from the rocks. Thus we
went almost all night, till at length we came by a great cliff that stood by
30 the shore. Then the savage whistled and another savage answered him
from the cliff, whereupon five or six Portugals came forth, and amongst
them came the captain with a piece of bread and marmalet[61] in his hand.
And as soon as he saw me he asked me what news. I answered that I was
very hungry and desired him that he would give me some meat, and then
I would tell him all the news that I could. With that all the Portugals
brake out in a laughter, and gave me bread and fish to eat. After I had
eaten that which they had given me, I told them the truth of all that they
asked me.

[60] In four shifts (as it might be, one hour on duty with three hours' rest).
[61] A normal spelling. Marmalade could be any kind of jam or preserve.

Here they killed eight and twenty of our men, and saved only myself and Henry Barrawell, who was saved by my means.[62]

The next day our ship weighed anchor, and whither she went I knew not. We were carried by the Portugals to the River of Janero. I went with a mestizo, which is half a Portugal and half a savage, that saved my life in the night when I was taken. When we came to the city of San Sebastian in the River of Janero, the Portugals in the canoas made such a noise with pipes and drums that all the people of the city came to shore to see us. With that, the canoas going round as if they were in fight, two Portugals took me and cast me towards the shore, saying, 'Here is our prize!' The tide being strong carried me to the main, where I had been drowned had it not been for a woman who, seeing the tide carry me away, sent two or three slaves, and they saved me. When I came ashore, all the Portugals were at the Church of Our Lady, and I would have gone into the church, but the Portugals would not let me, saying that I was not a Christian. Then I was brought before the Governor,[63] and he gave me to the man that had saved me, and I was very well contented, for he used me very kindly as I came with him from the island of San Sebastian.

For the space of three months that I was with this man I kept a house, and went to the sea side with his hogs, and there I every day brought him home a basket of great crabs that lie in the holes of the mud, as deep as you can thrust in your arm. This was a good life; my master called me son, and I dined and supped with him. Also I had a hanging net to lie in, and lay in the same room which he lay in.[64]

## 5. *John Davis*[1]

[*The readiness of the nobility to encourage 'speculative and mechanical' practices*] emboldeneth me to present unto your most honourable favour this small treatise of navigation, being a brief collection of such practices

---

[62] Barrawell figures a good deal in the later parts of the narrative. He had lost his hair in the intense cold of the Magellan Straits (or would it have been scurvy?). Franco says that he never returned to England, but married and settled in Brazil (p. 40).

[63] Salvador Correia de Sá, who with his illegitimate son Martim was to dominate Knivet's life for years to come.

[64] Knivet's good fortune did not last long. The further story of his extraordinary adventures during the next few years has no connection with Cavendish's voyage. See the Introduction.

[1] From the dedication of *The Seaman's Secrets* (1595) to Lord Howard of Effingham, Lord High Admiral. The text is from the British Library copy of the 1595 edition, C.54.bb.33.

as in my several voyages I have from experience collected. Among which are my three several attempts for the discovery of the Northwest Passage, thereby to find a short and navigable course unto the rich and famous countries of Cathayo, China, Pegu,[2] the isles of Molucan and Philippina, that thereby, to the great and inestimable benefit of our country, there might be a rich and plentiful trade procured between us and the said nations, in short time to be performed and with great safety in regard of the course.

. . . . .

10   Undoubtedly there is a passage navigable and easy to be performed by that course (whensoever it shall please God to reveal the same), by invincible reasons and sufficient experience to be proved. And although before I entered into that discovery I was sufficiently persuaded of the certainty thereof, by historical relation substantially confirmed, whereof to the adventurers I made sufficient proof ... yet I thank God that of late it hath been my very good chance to receive better assurance than ever before of the certainty of that passage; and such was my vehement desire for the performance thereof, that thereby I was only induced to go with M. Candish in his second attempt for the South Seas upon his constant 20   promise unto me, that when we came to the California I should there have his pinnace with my own bark[3] (which for that purpose went with me to my great charges) to search that northwest discovery upon those back parts of America.

But God hath otherwise disposed our purposes in his divine judgements; for M. Candish, being half-way through the straits of Magellan, and impatient of the tempestuous furiousness of that place, having all his ships and company with him, returned for Brazil, by the authority of his command; when with a leading wind we might have passed the same. And returning more than 80 leagues toward Brazil, myself being in his 30   ship named the Desire (without boat, oars, sails, cables, cordage, victuals, or health of my company sufficient for that attempt) was separated in a fret of weather, and forced to seek the next shore for my relief; and recovering a harbour by us named Port Desire (being in the latitude of 48 degrees) did there repair my most miserable wants. And there staying four months in most lamentable distress did again conclude with my company to give another attempt to pass the straits, as my

2 are] in *1595, 1607*

2   The capital of the Burmese empire in the 16th century.
3   The Dainty, which in the event turned back early in the voyage.

best mean to gain relief. And three times I was in the South Seas, but still by furious weather forced back again. Yet notwithstanding all this my labour to perform the voyage for his profit, and to save myself (for I did adventure, and my good friends for my sake, 1100 pounds in the action) M. Candish was content to account me to be the author of his overthrow, and to write with his dying hand that I ran from him, when as his own ship was returned many months before me.

I am bold to make this relation unto your lordship only to satisfy your honour of my conversation; for were I faulty of so foul a crime, I were worthy of ten thousand torments in presuming to present this treatise to your honourable lordship. And now referring my cause to your lordship's consideration, I will again return to my purpose.

# 6. *John Jane*[1]

The last voyage of the worshipful M. Thomas Candish esquire, intended for the South Sea, the Philippinas, and the coast of China, with three tall ships and two barks. Written by M. John Jane, a man of good observation, employed in the same and many other voyages.

The 26 of August 1591 we departed from Plymouth with three tall ships and two barks, the Galleon, wherein M. Candish went himself, being Admiral, the Roebuck Vice-Admiral, whereof M. Cocke was captain, the Desire Rear-Admiral, whereof was captain M. John Davis (with whom and for whose sake I went this voyage), the Black Pinnace, and a bark of M. Adrian Gilbert,[2] whereof M. Randolph Cotton was captain.

The 29 of November we fell with the bay of Salvador upon the coast of Brazil, twelve leagues on this side Cabo Frio, where we were becalmed until the second of December; at which time we took a small bark bound for the River of Plate with sugar, haberdash wares, and negroes. The master of this bark brought us unto an isle called Placencia,[3] thirty leagues west from Cabo Frio, where we arrived the fifth of December and rifled six or seven houses inhabited by Portugales. The 11 we departed from this place, and the fourteenth we arrived at the isle of San Sebastian, from whence M. Cocke and Captain Davis presently departed with the Desire and the Black Pinnace for the taking of the town of Santos. The 15 at evening we anchored at the bar

---

[1]  The text is from Hakluyt 1598–1600, iii. 842–52 (Hakluyt, xi. 389–416).
[2]  The Dainty.
[3]  Ilha Grande, 50 miles west of Rio de Janeiro.

of Santos, from whence we departed with our boats to the town; and the next morning about nine of the clock we came to Santos where, being discovered, we were enforced to land with twenty-four gentlemen, our longboat being far astern; by which expedition we took all the people of the town at mass, both men and women, whom we kept all that day in the church as prisoners.

The cause why M. Candish desired to take this town was to supply his great wants, for being in Santos and having it in quiet possession we stood in assurance to supply all our needs in great abundance. But such was the negligence of our governor Master Cocke that the Indians were suffered to carry out of the town whatsoever they would in open view, and no man did control them; and the next day after we had won the town our prisoners were all set at liberty; only four poor old men were kept as pawns to supply our wants. Thus in three days the town that was able to furnish such another fleet with all kind of necessaries was left unto us nakedly bare, without people and provision.

Eight or ten days after, Master Candish himself came thither, where he remained until the 22 of January, seeking by entreaty to have that whereof we were once possessed. But in conclusion we departed out of the town through extreme want of victual, not being able any longer to live there, and were glad to receive a few canisters[4] or baskets of cassavi meal.[5] So that in every condition we went worse furnished from the town than when we came unto it. The 22 of January we departed from Santos, and burned St. Vincent to the ground. The 24 we set sail, shaping our course for the Straits of Magellan.

The seventh of February we had a very great storm, and the eighth our fleet was separated by the fury of the tempest. Then our captain called unto him the master of our ship, whom he found to be a very honest and sufficient man,[6] and conferring with him he concluded to go for Port Desire, which is in the southerly latitude of 48 degrees, hoping that the General would come thither, because that in his first voyage he had found great relief there. For our captain could never get any direction what course to take in any such extremities, though many times he had entreated for it, as often I have heard him with grief report.[7] In sailing to this port, by good chance we met with the Roebuck, wherein

---

[4] The *OED* has no example of this word as early as this.

[5] Cassava or manioc is the root from which tapioca is prepared.

[6] Jane never gives his name, though he plays a very important part in his story. He had accompanied Cavendish on his circumnavigation.

[7] Knivet's evidence is quite to the contrary. See p. 88.

Master Cocke had endured great extremities and had lost his boat, and therefore desired our captain to keep him company, for he was in very desperate case. Our captain hoised[8] out his boat and went aboard him to know his estate, and returning told us the hardness thereof, and desired the master and all the company to be careful in all their watches not to lose the Roebuck, and so we both arrived in Port Desire the sixth of March.

The 16 of March the Black Pinnace came unto us, but Master Gilbert's bark came not, but returned home to England, having their captain aboard the Roebuck without any provision more than the apparel that he wore; who came from thence aboard our ship to remain with our captain, by reason of the great friendship between them.[9]

The 18, the Galleon came into the road, and Master Candish came into the harbour in a boat which he had made at sea; for his longboat and light-horseman[10] were lost at sea, as also a pinnace which he had built at Santos.[11] And being aboard the Desire he told our captain of all his extremities, and spake most hardly of his company and of divers gentlemen that were with him, purposing no more to go aboard his own ship but to stay in the Desire. We all sorrowed to hear such hard speeches of our good friends, but having spoken with the gentlemen of the Galleon we found them faithful, honest, and resolute in proceeding, although it pleased our General otherwise to conceive of them.

The 20 of March we departed from Port Desire, Master Candish being in the Desire with us. The eighth of April 1592 we fell with the Straits of Magellan, enduring many furious storms between Port Desire and the strait. The 14 we passed through the first strait. The 16 we passed the second strait, being ten leagues distant from the first. The 18 we doubled Cape Froward, which cape lieth in 53 degrees and ½. The 21 we were enforced by the fury of the weather to put into a small cove with our ships, four leagues from the said cape upon the south shore, where

[8] i.e. hoist; 'hoise' is the original word; the form for the past tense ('hoised' or 'hoist') was later used for the present as well.

[9] The fact that the Dainty turned back when her captain was it seems visiting the Roebuck is surprising in view of Knivet's statement that Cotton had discussed with Cavendish the question of when she was to return. Knivet's narrative indicates that captains were visiting each other's ships during a calm off the River Plate immediately before the great storm of 7 Feb. It seems very likely that the storm took Cotton unawares when he was out of the Dainty. It is grimly possible that the captainless Dainty was lost in the storm, and did not return to England. But presumably Jane, writing this account after his return to England, would have known if she had never got back.

[10] A light narrow ship's boat or gig.

[11] Knivet names this as the Crow.

we remained until the 15 of May. In the which time we endured extreme storms, with perpetual snow, where many of our men died with cursed famine and miserable cold, not having wherewith to cover their bodies nor to fill their bellies, but living by mussels, water, and weeds of the sea, with a small relief of the ship's store in meal sometimes. And all the sick men in the Galleon were most uncharitably put ashore into the woods in the snow, rain, and cold, when men of good health could scarcely endure it, where they ended their lives in the highest degree of misery; Master Candish all this while being aboard the Desire.

10 In these great extremities of snow and cold, doubting what the end would be, he asked our captain's opinion, because he was a man that had good experience of the North-west parts in his three several discoveries that way, employed by the merchants of London. Our captain told him that this snow was a matter of no long continuance, and gave him sufficient reason for it, and that thereby he could not much be prejudiced or hindered in his proceeding. Notwithstanding, he called together all the company and told them that he purposed not to stay in the Straits but to depart upon some other voyage, or else to return again for Brazil. But his resolution was to go for the Cape of Buena Esperanza.

20 The company answered that if it pleased him they did desire to stay God's favour for a wind, and to endure all hardness whatsoever rather than to give over the voyage. Considering they had been here but a small time, and because they were within forty leagues of the South Sea, it grieved them now to return. Notwithstanding, what he purposed that they would perform. So he concluded to go for the Cape of Buena Esperanza, and to give over this voyage.

Then our captain, after Master Candish was come aboard the Desire from talking with the company, told him that if it pleased him to consider the great extremity of his estate, the slenderness of his provisions, with 30 the weakness of his men, it was no course for him to proceed in that new enterprise. 'For if the rest of your ships,' said he, 'be furnished answerable to this, it is impossible to perform your determination. For we have no more sails than masts, no victuals, no ground-tackling,[12] no cordage more than is overhead, and among seventy and five persons there is but the Master alone that can order the ship, and but fourteen sailors. The rest are gentlemen, servingmen, and artificers. Therefore it will be a desperate case to take so hard an enterprise in hand.' These persuasions did our captain not only use to Master Candish but also to

[12] The gear wherewith to anchor or moor the ship.

Master Cocke. In fine, upon a petition delivered in writing by the chief of the whole company,[13] the General determined to depart out of the Straits of Magellan, and to return again for Santos in Brazil.

So the 15 of May we set sail, the General then being in the Galleon. The eighteenth we were free of the Straits, but at Cape Froward it was our hard hap to have our boat sunk at our stern in the night, and to be split and sore spoilt, and to lose all our oars.

The twentieth of May, being thwart of[14] Port Desire, in the night the General altered his course as we suppose, by which occasion we lost him. For in the evening he stood close by a wind to seaward,[15] having the wind at north-north-east; and we, standing the same way, the wind not altering, could not the next day see him. So that we then persuaded ourselves that he was gone for Port Desire to relieve himself, or that he had sustained some mischance at sea and was gone thither to remedy it. Whereupon our captain called the General's men unto him, with the rest, and asked their opinion what was to be done. Everyone said that they thought that the General was gone for Port Desire. Then the master, being the General's man and careful of his master's service, as also of good judgement in sea-matters, told the company how dangerous it was to go for Port Desire, if we should there miss the General. 'For,' said he, 'we have no boat to land ourselves, nor any cables nor anchors that I dare trust in so quick streams as are there.' Yet in all likelihood concluding that the General was gone thither, we stayed our course[16] for Port Desire, and by chance met with the Black Pinnace, which had likewise lost the fleet, being in very miserable case. So we both concluded to seek the General at Port Desire.

The six and twentieth day of May we came to Port Desire where, not finding our General as we hoped, being most slenderly victualled, without sails, boat, oars, nails, cordage, and all other necessaries for our relief, we were strucken into a deadly sorrow. But referring all to the providence and fatherly protection of the Almighty, we entered the harbour and by God's favour found a place of quiet road, which before we knew not. Having moored our ship with the Pinnace's boat, we landed upon the south shore, where we found a standing pool of fresh

---

[13] This is the 'humble supplication' which Cavendish spoke of (p. 60/18).

[14] Over against, in the parallel of.

[15] He was close-hauled, sailing as much into the wind as possible, which for a square-rigged vessel with the wind at NNE would be due east, if she was standing 'to seaward'. A less simple version of their course is given below in the 'testimonial' (p. 105/18–20).

[16] i.e. altered course.

water which by estimation might hold some ten tuns, whereby we were greatly comforted. From this pool we fet[17] more than forty tuns of water, and yet we left the pool as full as we found it. And because at our first being in this harbour we were at this place and found no water, we persuaded ourselves that God had sent it for our relief. Also there were such extraordinary low ebbs as we had never seen, whereby we got mussels in great plenty. Likewise God sent about our ships great abundance of smelts, so that with hooks made of pins every man caught as many as he could eat; by which means we preserved our ship's victuals, and spent not any during the time of our abode here.

Our captain and master, falling into the consideration of our estate and dispatch[18] to go to the General, found our wants so great as that in a month we could not fit our ship to set sail. For we must needs set up a smith's forge to make bolts, spikes and nails, besides the repairing of our other wants. Whereupon they concluded it to be their best course to take the Pinnace and to furnish her with the best of the company and to go to the General with all expedition, leaving the ship and the rest of the company until the General's return; for he had vowed to our captain that he would return again for the Straits, as he had told us. The captain and master of the Pinnace,[19] being the General's men, were well contented with the motion.

But the General having in our ship two most pestilent fellows, when they heard of this determination they utterly misliked it, and in secret dealt with the company of both ships, vehemently persuading them that our captain and master would leave them in the country to be devoured of the Canibals, and that they were merciless and without charity. Whereupon the whole company joined in secret with them in a night to murder our captain and master, with myself and all those which they thought were their friends. There were marks taken in his cabin how to kill him with muskets through the ship's side,[20] and bullets made of silver[21] for their execution if their other purposes should fail. All agreed hereunto except it were the boatswain of our ship, who when he knew the matter, and the slender ground thereof, revealed it unto our master, and so to the captain. Then the matter being called in question, those

[17] Fetched.    [18] Readiness.

[19] Jane twice refers to the captain of the Pinnace. We know that the master was Tobias Paris, but the captain's name is not known.

[20] This is not clear. A mark is an aiming-mark. Presumably they were intending to fire into the cabin through the ports.

[21] Supposed to be of special efficacy.

two most murderous fellows were found out, whose names were Charles Parker and Edward Smith.

The captain being thus hardly beset, in peril of famine and in danger of murdering, was constrained to use lenity, and by courteous means to pacify this fury; showing that to do the General service, unto whom he had vowed faith in this action, was the cause why he purposed to go unto him in the Pinnace, considering that the Pinnace was so necessary a thing for him as that he could not be without her, because he was fearful of the shore in so great ships. Whereupon all cried out with cursing and swearing that the Pinnace should not go unless the ship went. Then the captain desired them to show themselves Christians, and not so blasphemously to behave themselves, without regard or thanksgiving to God for their great deliverance and present sustenance bestowed upon them, alleging many examples of God's sharp punishment for such ingratitude; and withal promised to do anything that might stand with their good liking. By which gentle speeches the matter was pacified, and the captain and master at the request of the company were content to forgive this great treachery of Parker and Smith, who[22] after many admonitions concluded in these words, 'The Lord judge between you and me;' which[23] after came to a most sharp revenge even by the punishment of the Almighty.

Thus by a general consent it was concluded not to depart, but there to stay for the General's return. Then our captain and master, seeing that they could not do the General that service which they desired, made a motion to the company that they would lay down under their hands the losing of the General, with the extremities wherein we then stood. Whereunto they consented, and wrote under their hands as followeth.

The testimonial of the company of the Desire touching their losing of their General, which appeareth to have been utterly against their meanings.[24]

The 26 of August 1591, we whose names be hereunder written[25] with divers others departed from Plymouth under M. Thomas Candish our General, with four ships of his,[26] to wit, the Galleon, the Roebuck, the Desire, and the Black

---

[22] i.e. Davis.          [23] i.e. which affair.

[24] This title is obviously Hakluyt's, not Jane's. The relative clause means: 'which it is clear was completely unintentional'.

[25] There are 40 names out of a complement of 75 or 76, if we allow 'The Boatswain' and 'The Boatswain's mate' as names, and if we suppose that there were two men called William Maber. It must be an oversight that John Jane, who probably drafted the document, did not sign.

[26] Adrian Gilbert's ship, the Dainty, is not mentioned.

Pinnace, for the performance of a voyage into the South Sea. The 19 of November we fell with the Bay of Salvador in Brazil. The 16 of December we took the town of Santos, hoping there to revictual ourselves, but it fell not out to our contentment. The 24 of January we set sail from Santos, shaping our course for the Straits of Magellan. The 8 of February by violent storms the said fleet was parted. The Roebuck and the Desire arrived in Port Desire the 6 of March. The 16 of March the Black Pinnace arrived there also, and the 18 of the same our Admiral came into the road; with whom we departed the 20 of March in poor and weak estate.

10     The 8 of April 1592 we entered the Straits of Magellan. The 21 of April we anchored beyond Cape Froward, within 40 leagues of the South Sea, where we rode until the 15 of May. In which time we had great store of snow, with some gusty weather, the wind continuing still at west-north-west against us. In this time we were enforced, for the preserving of our victuals, to live the most part upon mussels, our provision was so slender. So that many of our men died in this hard extremity. Then our General returned for Brazil, there to winter and to procure victuals for this voyage against the next year. So we departed the Straits the 15 of May.

    The 21, being thwart of Port Desire, thirty leagues off the shore, the wind then at north-east and by north, at five of the clock at night lying north-east, we
20  suddenly cast about, lying south-east and by south, and sometimes south-east.[27] The whole fleet following the admiral, our ship coming under his lee shot ahead him, and so framed sail fit to keep company. This night we were severed, by what occasion we protest we know not, whether we lost them or they us. In the morning we only saw the Black Pinnace. Then, supposing that the Admiral had overshot us, all this day we stood to the eastwards hoping to find him, because it was not likely that he would stand to the shore again so suddenly. But missing him, towards night we stood to the shoreward, hoping by that course to find him.

    The 22 of May at night we had a violent storm, with the wind at north-west,
30  and we were enforced to hull,[28] not being able to bear sail. And in this night we perished[29] our main tressel-trees,[30] so that we could no more use our main topsail, lying most dangerously in the sea. The Pinnace likewise received a great leak, so that we were enforced to seek the next shore for our relief. And because famine was like to be the best end, we desired to go for Port Desire, hoping with seals and penguins to relieve ourselves, and so to make shift to follow the

[27] Davis's biographer and editor, Captain Markham, could make no sense of this account. If the wind was NNE they could not possibly be sailing NE. Then to have gone onto the other tack and sailed SE would make them head right away from their destination. He thought they might have been sailing NW and tacked towards the east to avoid getting too near the land during the night.

[28] Drift without sails set, the helm lashed a-lee.

[29] i.e. we lost through decay.

[30] (or trestle-trees): two short stout pieces of wood fixed to the mainmast to support the topmast.

General, or there to stay his coming from Brazil. The 24 of May we had much wind at north. The 25 was calm and the sea very lofty, so that our ship had dangerous foul weather. The 26 our fore-shrouds brake, so that if we had not been near the shore it had been impossible for us to get out of the sea.

And now being here moored in Port Desire, our shrouds are all rotten, not having a running rope whereto we may trust, and being provided only of one shift of sails all worn, our topsails not being able to abide any stress of weather, neither have we any pitch, tar, or nails, nor any store for the supplying of these wants; and we live only upon seals and mussels, having but five hogsheads of pork within board, and meal three ounces for a man a day, with water for to 10 drink.

And forasmuch as it hath pleased God to separate our fleet and to bring us into such hard extremities, that only now by His mere mercy we expect relief, though otherwise we are hopeless of comfort, yet because the wonderful works of God in His exceeding great favour toward us His creatures are far beyond the scope of man's capacity, therefore by Him we hope to have deliverance in this our deep distress. Also, forasmuch as those upon whom God will bestow the favour of life, with return home to their country, may not only themselves remain blameless, but also manifest the truth of our actions, we have thought good in Christian charity to lay down under our hands the truth of all our proceedings 20 even till the time of this our distress.

Given in Port Desire the 2 of June 1592. Beseeching the Almighty God of His mercy to deliver us from this misery, how or when it shall please His divine majesty.

| | |
|---|---|
| John Davis Captain | Thomas Watkins |
| Randolph Cotton | George Cunington |
| John Pery | John Whiting |
| William Maber gunner | James Ling |
| Charles Parker | The Boatswain |
| Rowland Miller | Francis Smith |
| Edward Smith | John Layes |
| Thomas Purpet | The Boatswain's mate |
| Matthew Stubbes | Fisher |
| John Jenkinson | John Austin |
| Thomas Edwards | Francis Copstone |
| Edward Granger | Richard Garet |
| John Lewis | James Eversby |
| William Hayman | Nicolas Parker |
| George Straker | Leonard |
| Thomas Walbie | John Pick |
| William Wyeth | Benjamin |
| Richard Alard | William Maber |
| Stephan Popham | James Not |
| Alexander Cole | Christopher Hauser |

After they had delivered this relation unto our captain under their hands, then we began to travail for our lives, and we built up a smith's forge, and made a coalpit and burned coals,[31] and there we made nails, bolts, and spikes; others made ropes of a piece of our cable, and the rest gathered mussels and took smelts for the whole company. Three leagues from this harbour there is an isle with four small isles about it, where there are great abundance of seals, and at the time of the year the penguins come thither in great plenty to breed. We concluded with the Pinnace that she should sometimes go thither to fetch seals for us, upon
10  which condition we would share our victuals with her man for man; whereunto the whole company agreed. So we parted[32] our poor store, and she laboured to fetch us seals to eat, wherewith we lived when smelts and mussels failed, for in the neap streams we could get no mussels.

Thus in most miserable calamity we remained until the sixth of August, still keeping watch upon the hills to look for our General, and so great was our vexation and anguish of soul as I think never flesh and blood endured more. Thus, our misery daily increasing, time passing, and our hope of the General being very cold, our captain and master were fully persuaded that the General might perhaps go directly for the
20  Straits and not come to this harbour. Whereupon they thought no course more convenient than to go presently for the Straits and there to stay his coming, for in that place he could not pass but of force we must see him. Whereunto the company most willingly consented, as also the captain and master of the Pinnace. So that upon this determination we made all possible speed to depart.

The sixth of August we set sail and went to Penguin Isle, and the next day we salted twenty hogsheads of seals, which was as much as our salt could possibly do, and so we departed for the Straits the poorest wretches that ever were created. The seventh of August toward night we
30  departed from Penguin Isle, shaping our course for the Straits, where we had full confidence to meet with our General. The ninth we had a sore storm, so that we were constrained to hull, for our sails were not to endure any force. The 14 we were driven in among certain isles never before discovered by any known relation, lying fifty leagues or better from the shore, east and northerly from the Straits;[33] in which place, unless it had pleased God of His wonderful mercy to have ceased the

---

[31] i.e. charcoal.

[32] Divided.

[33] These are assumed to be the Falkland Islands. In spite of Jane's statement, earlier maps suggest that this was not the first sighting. (See Markham; also R. V. Tooley, 'The Early Mapping of the Falkland Islands', *The Map Collector*, 20, Sept. 1982.)

wind, we must of necessity have perished. But the wind shifting to the
east, we directed our course for the Straits, and the 18 of August we fell
with the cape in a very thick fog, and the same night we anchored ten
leagues within the cape.

The 19 day we passed the first and the second straits. The 21 we
doubled Cape Froward. The 22 we anchored in Salvage Cove, so
named because we found many salvages there. Notwithstanding the
extreme cold of this place, yet do all these wild people go naked, and live
in the wood like satyrs, painted and disguised, and fly from you like wild
deer. They are very strong, and threw stones at us of three or four pound
weight an incredible distance. The 24 in the morning we departed from
this cove, and the same day we came into the north-west reach, which is
the last reach of the straits. The 25 we anchored in a good cove, within
fourteen leagues of the South Sea. In this place we purposed to stay for
the General, for the strait in this place is scarce three miles broad, so that
he could not pass but we must see him. After we had stayed here a
fortnight in the deep of winter, our victuals consuming (for our seals
stunk most vilely, and our men died pitifully through cold and famine,
for the greatest part of them had not clothes to defend the extremity of
the winter's cold), being in this heavy distress, our captain and master
thought it the best course to depart from the Straits into the South Sea,
and to go for the Isle of Santa Maria,[34] which is to the northward of
Baldivia[35] in 37 degrees and a quarter, where we might have relief, and
be in a temperate clime, and there stay for the General, for of necessity
he must come by that isle.

So we departed the 13 of September and came in sight of the South
Sea. The 14 we were forced back again, and recovered a cove three
leagues within the Straits from the South Sea. Again we put forth, and
being eight or ten leagues free of the land, the wind rising furiously at
west-north-west, we were enforced again into the Straits only for want
of sails, for we never durst bear sail in any stress of weather, they were so
weak. So again we recovered the cove three leagues within the straits,
where we endured most furious weather, so that one of our two cables
brake, whereby we were hopeless of life. Yet it pleased God to calm the
storm, and we unrived[36] our sheets, tacks, halliers,[37] and other ropes,

---

[34] Off Concepción, Chile. Cavendish reached it on 15 Mar. 1587 during his circumnavigation, and found not only a rich storehouse of food but friendly Indians.

[35] Valdivia, Chile.

[36] Unrove. They had to unreeve or dismantle the running rigging in order to moor the
ship.                                                                [37] Halyards.

and moored our ship to the trees close by the rocks. We laboured to recover our anchor again, but could not by any means, it lay so deep in the water, and as we think clean covered with ooze. Now had we but one anchor, which had but one whole fluke, a cable spliced in two places, and a piece of an old cable.

In the midst of these our troubles it pleased God that the wind came fair the first of October, whereupon with all expedition we loosed our moorings and weighed our anchor, and so towed off into the channel, for we had mended our boat in Port Desire, and had five oars of the Pinnace. When we had weighed our anchor, we found our cable broken; only one strand held.[38] Then we praised God, for we saw apparently His mercies in preserving us. Being in the channel, we rived our ropes and again rigged our ship. No man's hand was idle, but all laboured even for the last gasp of life. Here our company was divided; some desired to go again for Port Desire, and there to be set on shore, where they might travel for their lives,[39] and some stood with the captain and master to proceed.

Whereupon the captain said to the master: 'Master, you see the wonderful extremity of our estate, and the great doubts among our company of the truth of your reports as touching relief to be had in the South Sea. Some say in secret, as I am informed, that we undertake these desperate attempts through blind affection that we bear to the General. For mine own part, I plainly make known unto you that the love which I bare to the General caused me first to enter into this action, whereby I have not only heaped upon my head this bitter calamity now present, but also have in some sort procured the dislike of my best friends in England, as it is not unknown to some in this company. But now being thus entangled by the providence of God for my former offences (no doubt), I desire that it may please His Divine Majesty to show us such merciful favour that we may rather proceed than otherwise. Or if it be His will that our mortal being shall now take an end, I rather desire that it may be in proceeding than in returning.

'And because I see in reason that the limits of our time are now drawing to an end, I do in Christian charity entreat you all, first to forgive me in whatsoever I have been grievous unto you; secondly, that you will

---

[38] A cable is made of 3 strands.

[39] There is an awkward uncertainty here. 'travel' can mean either travel or travail. At p. 107/2, the phrase 'travel for our lives' obviously means travail or work for our lives. The context here suggests that some of the men simply wanted to get out of the ship and try their luck by land, but it may be they were only proposing to go back and refit the ship.

rather pray for our General than use hard speeches of him. And let us be fully persuaded that not for his cause and negligence but for our own offences against the Divine Majesty we are presently punished. Lastly, let us forgive one another and be reconciled as children in love and charity, and not think upon the vanities of this life; so shall we in leaving this life live with our glorious redeemer, or abiding in this life find favour with God.

'And now (good master), forasmuch as you have been in this voyage once before with your master the General, satisfy the company of such truths as are to you best known. And you, the rest of the General's men, which likewise have been with him in his first voyage, if you hear anything contrary to the truth, spare not to reprove it I pray you. And so I beseech the Lord to bestow His mercy upon us.'

Then the master began in these speeches: 'Captain, your request is very reasonable, and I refer to your judgement my honest care and great pains taken in the General's service, my love towards him, and in what sort I have discharged my duty from the first day to this hour. I was commanded by the General to follow your directions, which hitherto I have performed. You all know that, when I was extremely sick, the General was lost in my mate's watch, as you have well examined. Sithens[40] which time, in what anguish and grief of mind I have lived, God only knoweth, and you are in some part a witness. And now if you think good to return, I will not gainsay it; but this I assure you, if life may be preserved by any means, it is in proceeding. For at the Isle of Santa Maria I do assure you of wheat, pork and roots enough. Also I will bring you to an isle where pelicans be in great abundance, and at Santos[41] we shall have meal in great plenty, besides all our possibility of intercepting some ships upon the coast of Chile and Peru. But if we return there is nothing but death to be hoped for. Therefore do as you like; I am ready, but my desire is to proceed.'

These his speeches being confirmed by others that were in the former voyage, there was a general consent of proceeding. And so, the second of October we put into the South Sea, and were free of all land. This night the wind began to blow very much at west-north-west, and still increased in fury, so that we were in great doubt what course to take. To put into the Straits we durst not, for lack of ground tackle; to bear sail we doubted, the tempest was so furious and our sails so bad. The Pinnace come room with us,[42] and told us that she had received many grievous

---

[40] Since.   [41] Santa, near Chimbote, Peru, 9° 0′ S.
[42] 'To *come, or bear room* means to run down to a vessel to leeward' (Markham).

seas, and that her ropes did every hour fail her, so as they could not tell what shift to make. We being unable in any sort to help them, stood under our courses[43] in view of the lee-shore, still expecting our ruinous end.

The fourth of October, the storm growing beyond all reason furious, the Pinnace being in the wind of us, strake suddenly a-hull,[44] so that we thought she had received some grievous sea or sprung a leak, or that her sails failed her, because she came not with us. But we durst not hull in that unmerciful storm, but sometimes tried[45] under our main course, sometime with a haddock[46] of our sail, for our ship was very leeward and most laboursome in the sea. This night we lost the Pinnace, and never saw her again.

The fifth, our foresail was split and all to torn.[47] Then our master took the mizzen and brought it to the foremast to make our ship work, and with our spritsail we mended our foresail, the storm continuing without all reason in fury, with hail, snow, rain and wind such and so mighty as that in nature it could not possibly be more, the seas such and so lofty, with continual breach, that many times we were doubtful whether our ship did sink or swim.

The tenth of October, being by the accompt of our captain and master very near the shore, the weather dark, the storm furious, and most of our men having given over to travail,[48] we yielded ourselves to death, without further hope of succour. Our captain sitting in the gallery very pensive, I came and brought him some rosa solis[49] to comfort him, for he was so cold that he was scarce able to move a joint. After he had drunk, and was comforted in heart, he began for the ease of his conscience to make a large repetition of his forepassed time, and with many grievous sighs he concluded in these words: 'O most glorious God, with whose power the mightiest things among men are matters of no moment, I most humbly beseech thee that the intolerable burden of my sins may through the blood of Jesus Christ be taken from me; and end our days with speed, or show us some merciful sign of thy love and our preservation.'

Having thus ended, he desired me not to make known to any of the company his intolerable grief and anguish of mind, because they should

---

[43] Lower sails.
[44] She had taken in all sail; see note to p. 105/29.
[45] Lay-to.
[46] This term is not otherwise known; it obviously refers to a form of reefing.
[47] Completely torn, torn to pieces (see *OED*, *all*, C.14).
[48] Given up working (as being useless).
[49] Spiced brandy, a form of punch.

not thereby be dismayed. And so, suddenly, before I went from him, the sun shined clear, so that he and the master both observed the true elevation of the Pole,[50] whereby they knew by what course to recover the Straits.[51] Wherewithal our captain and master were so revived, and gave such comfortable speeches to the company that every man rejoiced as though we had received a present deliverance.

The next day, being the 11 of October, we saw Cabo Deseado, being the cape on the south shore. (The north shore is nothing but a company of dangerous rocks, isles and shoals.) This cape being within two leagues to leeward of us, our master greatly doubted that we could not 10 double the same; whereupon the captain told him: 'You see there is no remedy. Either we must double it or before noon we must die. Therefore loose your sails, and let us put it to God's mercy.' The master being a man of good spirit resolutely made quick despatch and set sails. Our sails had not been half an hour aboard but the footrope of our foresail brake, so that nothing held but the oylet holes.[52] The seas continually brake over the ship's poop, and flew into the sails with such violence that we still expected the tearing of our sails or oversetting of the ship; and withal, to our utter discomfort, we perceived that we fell still more and more to leeward, so that we could not double the cape. 20 We were now come within half a mile of the cape, and so near the shore that the counter-suff[53] of the sea would rebound against the ship's side, so that we were much dismayed with the horror of our present end.

Being thus at the very pinch of death, the wind and seas raging beyond measure, our master veered some of the main sheet.[54] And whether it was by that occasion, or by some current, or by the wonderful power of God, as we verily think it was, the ship quickened her way and shot past that rock where we thought she would have shored.[55] Then between the cape and the point there was a little bay, so that we were somewhat 30 farther from the shore; and when we were come so far as the cape we yielded to death, yet our good God the father of all mercies delivered us,

---

[50] i.e. the zenith, the imaginary point overhead, the angle between which and the sun would give the latitude of the ship.

[51] In striking contrast to the space given for the arguments for proceeding to the Pacific, absolutely nothing has been said about the decision to abandon the enterprise.

[52] 'Oylet' (or 'oillet') is an earlier form of 'eyelet'.

[53] The 'suff' is the inrush of the sea towards the shore, and the 'counter-suff' its rebound.

[54] i.e. he trimmed the mainsail by easing the sheet or line attached to its lower corner.

[55] Struck.

and we doubled the cape about the length of our ship, or very little more. Being shot past the cape, we presently took in our sails, which only God had preserved unto us; and when we were shot in between the high lands, the wind blowing trade,[56] without any inch of sail we spooned[57] before the sea, three men being not able to guide the helm, and in six hours we were put five and twenty leagues within the Straits, where we found a sea answerable to the ocean.

In this time we freed our ship from water, and after we had rested a little our men were not able to move; their sinews were stiff and their flesh dead, and many of them (which is most lamentable to be reported) were so eaten with lice as that in their flesh did lie clusters of lice as big as peason,[58] yea and some as big as beans. Being in this misery we were constrained to put into a cove for the refreshing our men. Our master, knowing the shore and every cove very perfectly, put in with the shore and moored to the trees, as beforetime we had done, laying our anchor to the seaward. Here we continued until the twentieth of October, but not being able any longer to stay through extremity of famine, the one and twentieth we put off into the channel, the weather being reasonable calm; but before night it blew most extremely at west-north-west. The storm growing outrageous, our men could scarcely stand by their labour; and the straits being full of turning reaches, we were constrained by discretion of the captain and master in their accounts to guide the ship in the hell-dark night,[59] when we could not see any shore, the channel being in some places scarce three miles broad. But our captain, as we first passed through the Straits, drew such an exquisite plat[60] of the same as I am assured it cannot in any sort be bettered. Which plat he and the master so often perused and so carefully regarded as that in memory they had every turning and creek; and in the deep dark night without any doubting they conveyed the ship through that crooked channel. So that I conclude the world hath not any so skilful pilots for that place as they are; for otherwise we could never have passed in such sort as we did.

The 25 we came to an island in the Straits named Penguin Isle, whither we sent our boat to seek relief, for there were great abundance

[56] Blowing steadily and strongly from the same direction. This is the earliest recorded use of the phrase from which 'trade wind' comes, an expression which originally had nothing to do with commerce.

[57] Scudded under bare poles.

[58] Peas.

[59] i.e. we were forced to rely on the good judgement of the captain and master in their reckoning of our position in order to navigate the ship.

[60] Chart.

of birds and the weather was very calm; so we came to an anchor by the
island in seven fathoms. While our boat was at shore, and we had great
store of penguins, there arose a sudden storm, so that our ship did drive
over a breach and our boat sank at the shore. Captain Cotton and the
Lieutenant being on shore leapt in the boat and freed the same, and
threw away all the birds, and with great difficulty recovered the ship.
Myself also was in the boat the same time, where for my life I laboured
to the best of my power. The ship all this while driving upon the lee
shore, when we came aboard we helped to set sail, and weighed the
anchor, for before our coming they could scarce hoise up their yards; yet
with much ado they set their fore-course. Thus in a mighty fret of
weather, the seven and twentieth day of October, we were free of the
Straits, and the thirtieth of October we came to Penguin Isle, being
three leagues from Port Desire, the place which we purposed to seek for
our relief.

When we were come to this isle we sent our boat on shore, which
returned laden with birds and eggs; and our men said that the penguins
were so thick upon the isle that ships might be laden with them, for they
could not go without treading upon the birds; whereat we greatly
rejoiced. Then the captain appointed Charles Parker and Edward
Smith, with twenty others, to go on shore and to stay upon the isle for the
killing and drying of those penguins, and promised after the ship was in
harbour to send the rest, not only for expedition but also to save the
small store of victuals in the ship. But Parker, Smith, and the rest of their
faction suspected that this was a device of the captain to leave his men on
shore, that by these means there might be victuals for the rest to recover
their country. And when they remembered that this was the place where
they would have slain their captain and master, 'surely,' thought they,
'for revenge hereof will they leave us on shore.'

Which when our captain understood, he used these speeches unto
them: 'I understand that you are doubtful of your security, through the
perverseness of your own guilty consciences. It is an extreme grief unto
me that you should judge me bloodthirsty, in whom you have seen
nothing but kind conversation. If you have found otherwise, speak boldy
and accuse me of the wrongs that I have done; if not, why do you then
measure me by your own uncharitable consciences? All the company
knoweth, indeed, that in this place you practised to the utmost of your
powers to murder me and the master, causeless, as God knoweth; which
evil in this place we did remit you. And now I may conceive, without
doing you wrong, that you again purpose some evil in bringing these

matters to repetition. But God has so shortened[61] your confederacy as that I nothing doubt you.[62] It is for your master's sake[63] that I have forborne you in your unchristian practices, and here I protest before God that for his sake alone I will yet endure this injury, and you shall in no sort be prejudiced, or in any thing be by me commanded, but when we come into England (if God so favour us) your master shall know your honesties. In the mean space be void of these suspicions, for, God I call to witness, revenge is no part of my thought.'

They gave him thanks, desiring to go into the harbour with the ship, which he granted. So there were ten left upon the isle, and the last of October we entered the harbour. Our master at our last being here having taken careful notice of every creek in the river, in a very convenient place, upon sandy ooze, ran the ship on ground, laying our anchors to seaward; and with our running ropes moored her to stakes upon the shore which he had fastened for that purpose; where the ship remained till our departure.

The third of November, our boat, with water, wood, and as many as she could carry, went for the Isle of Penguins; but being deep she durst not proceed,[64] but returned again the same night. Then Parker, Smith, Townsend, Purpet, with five others, desired that they might go by land, and that the boat might fetch them when they were against the isle, it being scarce a mile from the shore.[65] The captain bade them do what they thought best, advising them to take weapons with them, 'for,' said he, 'although we have not at any time seen people in this place, yet in the country there may be salvages.' They answered that here were great store of deer and ostriches, but if there were salvages, they would devour them. Notwithstanding, the captain caused them to carry weapons: calivers,[66] swords, and targets. So the sixth of November they departed by land, and the boat by sea; but from that day to this day we never heard of our men.

The 11, while most of our men were at the isle, only the captain and the master with six others being left in the ship, there came a great multitude of salvages to the ship, throwing dust in the air, leaping and running like brute beasts, having vizards on their faces like dogs' faces,

---

[61] Rendered ineffectual.
[62] Fear you.        [63] Cavendish.
[64] She found herself too low in the water to risk going the whole way.
[65] They would make their way to the point of the mainland which was nearest to the island, where the channel was about a mile wide.
[66] Light muskets.

or else their faces are dogs' faces indeed. We greatly feared lest they would set our ship on fire, for they would suddenly make fire, whereat we much marvelled. They came to windward of our ship and set the bushes on fire, so that we were in a very stinking smoke. But as soon as they came within our shot we shot at them, and striking one of them in the thigh, they all presently fled, so that we never heard nor saw more of them. Hereby we judged that these Canibals had slain our nine men. When we considered what they were that thus were slain, and found that they were the principal men that would have murdered our captain and master, with the rest of their friends, we saw the just judgement of God, and make supplication to His Divine Majesty to be merciful unto us.

While we were in this harbour, our captain and master went with the boat to discover how far this river did run, that if need should enforce us to leave our ship, we might know how far we might go by water. So they found that farther than twenty miles they could not go with the boat. At their return they sent the boat to the Isle of Penguins; whereby we understood that the penguins dried to our hearts' content, and that the multitude of them was infinite. This penguin hath the shape of a bird but hath no wings, only two stumps in the place of wings, by which he swimmeth under water with as great swiftness as any fish. They live upon smelts, whereof there is great abundance upon this coast. In eating, they be neither fish nor flesh; they lay great eggs, and the bird is of a reasonable bigness, very near twice so big as a duck. All the time that we were in this place, we fared passing well with eggs, penguins, young seals, young gulls, besides other birds such as I know not; of all which we had great abundance. In this place we found an herb called scurvy-grass,[67] which we fried with eggs, using train oil[68] instead of butter. This herb did so purge ye blood that it took away all kind of swellings (of which many died), and restored us to perfect health of body, so that we were in as good case as when we came first out of England. We stayed in this harbour until the 22 of December, in which time we had dried 20,000 penguins; and the captain, the master, and myself had made some salt by laying salt water upon the rocks in holes, which in six days would be kerned.[69] Thus God did feed us even as it were with manna from heaven.

The 22 of December we departed with our ship for the isle, where with great difficulty, by the skilful industry of our master, we got 14,000 of our birds, and had almost lost our captain in labouring to bring the

---

[67] *Cochlearia officinalis.*        [68] Whale or seal oil.        [69] Granulated.

birds aboard. And had not our master been very expert in the set of those
wicked tides, which run after many fashions, we had also lost our ship in
the same place; but God of His goodness hath in all our extremities been
our protector.

So, the 22 at night we departed with 14,000 dried penguins, not being
able to fetch the rest, and shaped our course for Brazil. Now our captain
rated[70] our victuals, and brought us to such allowance as that our
victuals might last six months; for our hope was that within six months
we might recover our country, though our sails were very bad. So the
10 allowance was two ounces and a half of meal for a man a day, and to have
so twice a week, so that five ounces did serve for a week. Three days a
week we had oil, three spoonfuls for a man a day; and two days in a week
peason, a pint between four men a day; and every day five penguins for
four men; and six quarts of water for four men a day. This was our
allowance; wherewith (we praise God) we lived, though weakly, and very
feeble.

The 30 of January we arrived at the Isle of Placencia[71] in Brazil, the
first place that outward bound we were at, and having made the shoal,
our ship lying off at sea, the captain with twenty-four of the company
20 went with the boat on shore, being a whole night before they could
recover it. The last of January at sun-rising they suddenly landed,
hoping to take the Portugales in their houses, and by that means to
recover some cassavi meal or other victuals for our relief. But when they
came to the houses, they were all razed and burnt to the ground, so that
we thought no man had remained on the island. Then the captain went
to the gardens and brought from thence fruits and roots for the
company, and came aboard the ship, and brought her into a fine creek
which he had found out, where we might moor her by the trees, and
where there was water, and hoops to trim our cask.[72] Our case being
30 very desperate, we presently laboured for dispatch away. Some cut
hoops, which the coopers made, others laboured upon the sails and ship,
every man travailing for his life, and still a guard was kept on shore to
defend those that laboured, every man having his weapon likewise by
him.

The 3 of February our men with 23 shot went again to the gardens,
being three miles from us upon the north shore, and fetched cassavi
roots out of the ground, to relieve our company instead of bread; for we
spent not of our meal while we stayed there. The 5 of February, being

[70] Allotted, appointed.     [71] Ilha Grande.     [72] Repair the casks.

Monday, our captain and master hasted the company to their labour; so some went with the coopers to gather hoops and the rest laboured aboard. This night many of our men in the ship dreamed of murder and slaughter. In the morning they reported their dreams, one saying to another, 'this night I dreamed that thou wert slain'; another answered, 'and I dreamed that thou wert slain'; and this was general through the ship. The captain hearing this, who likewise had dreamed very strangely himself, gave very strait charge that those which went on shore should take weapons with them, and saw them himself delivered into the boat, and sent some of purpose to guard the labourers.                    10

All the forenoon they laboured in quietness, and when it was ten of the clock, the heat being extreme, they came to a rock near the wood's side (for all this country is nothing but thick woods) and there they boiled cassavi roots and dined. After dinner some slept, some washed themselves in the sea, all being stripped to their shirts and no man keeping watch, no match[73] lighted, not a piece[74] charged. Suddenly, as they were thus sleeping and sporting, having gotten themselves into a corner out of sight of the ship, there came a multitude of Indians and Portugales upon them, and slew them sleeping. Only two escaped, one very sore hurt, the other not touched, by whom we understood of this    20 miserable massacre. With all speed we manned our boat and landed to succour our men. But we found them slain and laid naked on a rank one by another, with their faces upward, and a cross set by them. And withal we saw two very great pinnaces come from the River of Jenero very full of men, whom we mistrusted came from thence to take us, because there came from Jenero soldiers to Santos when the General had taken the town and was strong in it.

Of seventy-six persons which departed in our ship out of England, we were now left but twenty-seven, having lost thirteen in this place, with their chief furniture, as muskets, calivers, powder and shot. Our cask    30 was all in decay, so that we could not take in more water than was in our ship for want of cask, and that which we had was marvellous ill-conditioned. And being there moored by trees for want of cables and anchors, we still expected the cutting of our moorings, to be beaten from our decks with our own furniture,[75] and to be assailed by them of Jenero. What distress we were now driven into I am not able to express. To depart with eight tuns of water in such bad cask was to starve at sea, and

[73] The wick or rope used for igniting the powder in the muskets.
[74] Gun.
[75] The weapons just captured by the Portuguese.

in staying our case was ruinous. These were hard choices; but being thus perplexed, we made choice rather to fall into the hands of the Lord than into the hands of men; for His exceeding mercies we had tasted, and of the others' cruelty we were not ignorant.

So, concluding to depart, the 6 of February we were off in the channel, with our ordnance and small shot in a readiness for any assault that should come; and having a small gale of wind, we recovered the sea in most deep distress. Then, bemoaning our estate one to another and recounting over all our extremities, nothing grieved us more than the loss of our men twice, first by the slaughter of the Canibals at Port Desire, and at this Isle of Placencia by the Indians and Portugals. And considering what they were that were lost, we found that all those that conspired the murdering of our captain and master were now slain by salvages, the gunner only excepted. Being thus at sea, when we came to Cape Frio the wind was contrary, so that three weeks we were grievously vexed with cross winds, and our water consuming, our hope of life was very small. Some desired to go to Baya[76] and submit themselves to the Portugales rather than to die for thirst; but the captain with fair persuasions altered their purpose of yielding to the Portugales.

In this distress it pleased God to send us rain in such plenty as that we were well watered, and in good comfort to return. But after we came near unto the sun,[77] our dried penguins began to corrupt, and there bred in them a most loathsome and ugly worm of an inch long. This worm did so mightily increase and devour our victuals that there was in reason no hope how we should avoid famine, but be devoured of these wicked creatures. There was nothing that they did not devour, only iron excepted; our clothes, boots, shoes, hats, shirts, stockings; and for the ship, they did so eat the timbers as that we greatly feared they would undo us by gnawing through the ship's side. Great was the care and diligence of our captain, master, and company to consume these vermin, but the more we laboured to kill them the more they increased, so that at the last we could not sleep for them, but they would eat our flesh and bite like mosquitoes.

In this woeful case, after we had passed the equinoctial[78] toward the north, our men began to fall sick of such a monstrous disease as I think the like was never heard of. For in their ankles it began to swell; from thence in two days it would be in their breasts, so that they could not draw their breath; and then fell into their cods,[79] and their cods and

---

[76] Bahia (now Salvador), the main seat of government, several hundred miles north.
[77] The Equator.　　　　[78] The Equator.　　　　[79] Testicles.

yards did swell most grievously, and most dreadfully to behold, so that they could neither stand, lie, nor go. Whereupon our men grew mad with grief. Our captain with extreme anguish of his soul was in such woeful case that he desired only a speedy end, and though he were scarce able to speak for sorrow, yet he persuaded them to patience, and to give God thanks, and like dutiful children to accept of His chastisement. For all this, divers grew raging mad, and some died in most loathsome and furious pain.

It were incredible to write our misery as it was. There was no man in perfect health but the captain and one boy. The master, being a man of good spirit, with extreme labour bore out his grief so that it grew not upon him. To be short, all our men died except sixteen, of which there were but five able to move. The captain was in good health, the master indifferent, Captain Cotton and myself swollen and short-winded yet better than the rest that were sick, and one boy in health. Upon us five only, the labour of the ship did stand. The captain and master, as occasion served, would take in and heave out the topsails, the master only attended on the spritsail, and all of us at the capstan without sheets and tacks.[80] In fine, our misery and weakness was so great that we could not take in or heave out a sail, so our topsail and spritsails were torn all in pieces by the weather. The master and captain, taking their turns at the helm, were mightily distressed and monstrously grieved with the most woeful lamentation of our sick men.

Thus, as lost wanderers upon the sea, the 11 of June 1593, it pleased God that we arrived at Bearhaven in Ireland and there ran the ship on shore; where the Irishmen helped us to take in our sails and to moor our ship for floating; which slender pains of theirs cost the captain some ten pounds before he could have the ship in safety. Thus, without victuals, sails, men, or any furniture, God only guided us into Ireland, where the captain left the master and three or four of the company to keep the ship. And within five days after, he and certain others had passage in an English fisher-boat to Padstow in Cornwall. In this manner our small remnant by God's only mercy were preserved and restored to our country, to whom be all honour and glory world without end.

[80] It is hard to know what is meant by 'without'. The sheets and tacks are the lines attached to the lower corners of the sails in order to trim them. I suspect the proper reading is 'with the sheets and tacks'.

## 7. *Thomas Lodge*

(*a*) 'PHILLIS', Sonnet II

You sacred sea-nymphs pleasantly disporting
Amidst this watery world where now I sail,
If ever love or lovers' sad reporting
Had power sweet tears from your fair eyes to hale,
   And you, more gentle-hearted than the rest,
Under the northern noonstead sweetly streaming,
Lend those moist riches of your crystal crest
To quench the flames from my heart's Etna steaming,
   And thou, kind Triton, in thy trumpet relish
The ruthful accents of my discontent,
That midst this travel desolate and hellish,
Some gentle wind that listens my lament
     May prattle in the north in Phillis' ears,
     'Where Phillis wants, Damon consumes in tears.'

(*b*) A MARGARITE OF AMERICA

*To the noble, learned and virtuous lady,*
*the lady Russell, T.L. wisheth affluence*
*on earth, and felicity in heaven.*[1]

Madam, your deep and considerate judgement, your admired honour
and happy readings, have drawn me to present this labour of mine to
your gracious hands and favourable patronage; wherein, though you
shall find nothing to admire, yet doubt I not but you may meet many
things that deserve cherishing.

.    .    .    .    .

Touching the place where I wrote this, it was in those straits christened
by Magellan; in which place to the southward, many wondrous isles,
many strange fishes, many monstrous Patagons,[2] withdrew my senses.
Briefly, many bitter and extreme frosts at midsummer continually clothe

Patagons] Patagōnes *1596*

[1] Lady Elizabeth Russell (1528–1609) was the widow of Sir Thomas Hoby, the
translator of Castiglione. She married John, Lord Russell in 1574 (he died in 1584).

[2] From Spanish *patagón*. Members of the Indian tribe of this area: hence the name
Patagonia. Legend had it that they were giants; they were fearsome enough in reality; see
Jane, p. 115/32.

and clad the discomfortable mountains; so that as there was great wonder in the place wherein I writ this, so likewise it might be marvelled that in such scanty fare, such causes of fear, so mighty discouragements, and many crosses, I should deserve or eternize anything. Yet what I have done (good madam) judge and hope this felicity from my pen, that whilst the memory thereof shall live in any age, your charity, learning, nobility and virtues shall be eternized.

.        .        .        .        .

Thus hoping your ladyship will supply my boldness with your bounty and affability, I humbly kiss your most delicate hands, shutting up my English duty under an Italian copy of humanity and courtesy.

From my house this 4. of May 1596.

Your honour's in all zeal,

T. LODGE.

¶ *To the Gentlemen Readers.*

Gentlemen, I am prevented in mine own hopes; in seconding thrifts forward desires. Some four years since, being at sea with M. Candish (whose memory if I repent not, I lament not), it was my chance in the library of the Jesuits in Sanctum to find this history in the Spanish tongue, which as I read delighted me, and delighting me won me, and winning me, made me write it. The place where I began my work was a ship, where many soldiers of good reckoning finding disturbed stomachs, it cannot but stand with your discretions to pardon an undiscreet and unstayed pen; for hands may vary where stomachs miscarry. The time I wrote in was when I had rather will to get my dinner than to win my fame. The order I wrote in was past order, where I rather observed men's hands lest they should strike me, than curious reason of men to condemn me. In a word, I wrote under hope rather the fish should eat both me writing and my paper written, than fame should know me, hope should acquaint her with me, or any but misery should hear mine ending. For those faults (gentlemen) escaped by the printer, in not being acquainted with my hand, and the book printed in my absence, I must crave you with favour to judge of, and with your wonted courtesies to correct...

Yours   T. Lodge.

# II

# *The Last Voyage of*
# *Henry Hudson,*
# *1610–1611*

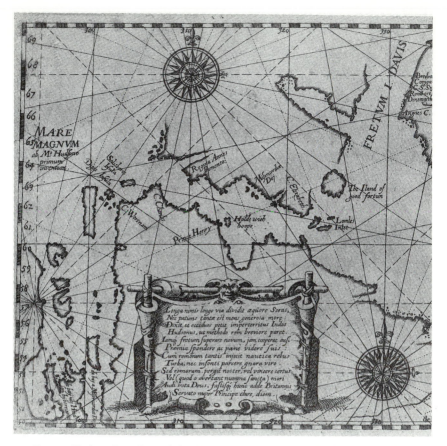

FIG. 4. Hudson Bay. Part of the *Tabula Nautica* published by Hessel Gerritz in Amsterdam in 1612 to illustrate and commemorate Hudson's final voyage of discovery. The map was probably based on Hudson's own chart (see p. 129). (Reproduced by permission of the British Library)

# INTRODUCTION

WHAT is essential for a tragic hero is presence, and presence is what, for us, Henry Hudson notably lacks. Very little is known about his personal life; little of his personality emanates from the matter-of-fact account he wrote of his 1608 voyage, and even less from what remains of his notes for the 1607 and 1610–11 voyages. Something of his determination and his obstinacy, his uncertain judgement, his distrust of his subordinates, comes through in what he has written and in what his contemporaries wrote about him; but by and large, compared with the other two leaders in this volume, he has left behind him little mark of his personality.

By the time of what we generally call his first voyage he was of course a much-experienced seaman—but nothing is known of how that experience was gathered. In 1607 he was a married man with three sons, Oliver, John, and Richard; and Richard was old enough to present him with a grandchild in 1608 (Powys, p. 61). On this 'first' voyage of 1607, he was sent by the Muscovy Company 'to discover a passage by the North Pole to Japan and China'. The crew of twelve in the Hopewell included his son John, 'a boy'. He followed the east coast of Greenland until he was halted by the ice between Greenland and Spitzbergen possibly as far north as 80°. The Muscovy Company sent him out a second time in the following year, 1608, and this time the crew contained, beside John Hudson, four men who went with him on his final voyage, Robert Juet as mate, Michael Perce, Arnold Lodlo (or Ludlow), and the faithful illiterate carpenter, Philip Staffe. They were to search for the north-east passage to the Far East between Spitzbergen and Novaya Zemlya. But they could find no way through the ice.

The final paragraph of Hudson's account of this second voyage says that he then 'resolved to use all means I could to sail to the north-west ... and to make trial of that place called Lumley's Inlet, and the furious overfall, by Captain Davis, hoping to run into it an hundred leagues and to return as God should enable me' (Purchas, xiii. 332). The 'furious overfall'—the tide rip at the entrance to the Hudson Strait—was not so described in Davis's written account, but this name is to be found on Emery Molyneux's globe (1592) with whose construction Davis had assisted (Markham, p. xxxvi; Wallis 1951, pp. 275–90; 1955, pp. 204–11). Lumley's Inlet is the passage between Resolution and Meta Incognita by which Hudson first tried to enter the Strait in 1610.

Hudson then said that he thought it his 'duty' to return home 'and not by foolish rashness ... to lay more charge upon the action than necessity should compel'. This is palpably disingenuous. For at the beginning of this final paragraph he wrote: 'I gave my company a certificate under my hand, of my free and willing return, without persuasion or force of any one of them.' The implication is that the crew refused to accept the 'foolish rashness' of extending 'the action' by a late bid for the Hudson Strait, that Hudson yielded, and that he further agreed to certify that his decision to turn for home was not made under duress or the threat of mutiny. (It looks as though at a critical point in his last voyage Hudson had to issue a similar certificate; see p. 156). Robert Juet wrote his own account of this voyage, which Purchas, regrettably, 'for brevity omitted'.

Hudson's services were now sought by the Dutch. He went to the Netherlands and in April 1609 the Dutch East India Company sent him out in the Half Moon to try for the north-east passage again. The account of the third voyage which Purchas prints is by Robert Juet; there are also Dutch records which indicate that Hudson again had trouble with his men as they pushed into the ice (Asher, p. 148). There were apparently 'quarrels among the crew', and Hudson laid before them two alternative ventures as substitutes for the original plan: either to make for Davis Strait (and the furious overfall) or to try to find a channel to the Pacific reputed to exist in the latitude of 40°. The latter was chosen, and Hudson went on to make his exploration of New York Harbour and the Hudson River.

Hudson's willingness to serve the Dutch was not well received in England, and soon after his return a group of promoters got together to finance another expedition. The chief of these were men of the City, Sir Thomas Smith and John Wolstenholme, with the energetic young diplomat and politician Sir Dudley Digges. There were many influential supporters, including the Earl of Salisbury, and possibly Prince Henry himself (see the note to Pricket's narrative, p. 154). The toughest of ships, the Discovery, in which George Waymouth had explored north-ern waters in 1602, was fitted out, and she sailed from St Katharine's Pool by the Tower of London in April 1610. We know the names of all twenty-three who sailed in her, and to a large extent the story of this voyage is the story of the relationship of these men, as well as of their struggle with the ice and the unknown.

Although it is not the purpose of this book to try to reconstruct the detail of the voyages it deals with, but rather to display the contemporary writings about these voyages, it is essential to go rather fully into some aspects of Hudson's last voyage if we are to make anything of the major surviving narrative, by Abacuck Pricket. I give first a brief outline of the whole voyage.

The Discovery went north up the east coast of Britain to Iceland and Greenland, and entered the Hudson Strait about the end of June. Hudson hugged the Labrador shore, looking for his passage to the Pacific, and, much troubled by ice, found himself 'embayed' in Ungava Bay. There was some disaffection in the ship's company. After a second attempt to find a southern outlet in Ungava Bay, Hudson groped his way through Hudson Strait proper into Hudson Bay through the narrow passage between the promontories he named Cape Digges and Cape Wolstenholme. He kept to the eastern shore southward until he was once more 'embayed', in James Bay. It was now September. For a long time he struggled to find a way south, and once again there was trouble on board, which Hudson tried to defuse by deposing both the mate, Juet, and the boatswain. Eventually it was necessary to find somewhere to winter. The place chosen was perhaps in Rupert Bay in the south of James Bay. One man, the gunner, had died on the voyage out; the remaining twenty-two managed to survive the privations of the winter, though many were lamed by frostbite.

The coming of spring brought very serious food problems. The ship had been provisioned for only six months (one witness says eight). Hudson hoped to make contact with the Eskimos, or Inuits, to secure supplies, but he failed. He made ready to return to England, but some of the company were suspicious that he still wanted to continue his exploration.

There were rows about sharing the exiguous supplies remaining. Then the mutiny. In June, with the ship still deep in James Bay, Hudson was seized and forced into the shallop (one of the ship's boats). The sick men were forced out too, plus others chosen by the mutineers, including Hudson's son; nine men in all. The shallop was cut adrift and the Discovery, sailing north, soon outdistanced her. Neither the shallop nor the nine men were ever seen again.

The Discovery made her uncertain way back to the western entrance to Hudson Strait between the two capes. The remaining crew met and fraternized with some of the native people, but at a second meeting the boat party was set upon without warning. Four men died of the wounds they received, including the two reputed ringleaders of the mutiny. The remaining eight men (four of them not mariners at all) brought the ship back to Ireland, one of them, the old mate Juet, dying on the way. This was September 1611. With extra help the ship was brought back to the Thames.

The surviving records of Hudson's last voyage are as follows:

1. The Trinity House examination of the survivors, October 1611. (Christy, pp. 629–34; with extracts in Quinn 1979, pp. 293–4.)
2. The High Court of Admiralty examinations, 1612, 1617–18. (Public Record Office; partially transcribed in Ewen 1938 and Powys, pp. 190–8, with photographs; extracts in Quinn 1979, pp. 294–6.)
3. Hessel Gerritz map, with a brief narrative account, published in 1612. (Asher, pp. 181–3; Quinn 1979, pp. 296–7.)
4. Henry Hudson's log; a fragment. (Purchas 1625, pt. 3, bk. iii, ch. 17, pp. 596–7.)
5. Abacuck Pricket's narrative. (Purchas 1625, as above, pp. 597–608.)
6. Thomas Woodhouse's notes. (Purchas 1625, as above, pp. 609–10.)
7. Robert Billet's log; a fragment. (Christy, pp. 632–3.)
8. Samuel Purchas's summary of Pricket. (*Purchas His Pilgrimage*, 1617; Asher, pp. 139–46.)
9. Luke Fox's summary of Pricket. (*North-West Fox*, 1635; Christy, pp. 120–60.)

Abacuck Pricket was a protégé of Sir Dudley Digges; we should not misunderstand Purchas calling him Digges's 'servant'. He was or had been a merchant; at the Admiralty trial he was called a haberdasher. Presumably he was a young man making his way in a City merchant-house who came to the notice of Digges as a suitable person to accompany Hudson; 'a landman put in by the adventurers', as the Trinity House examination put it. When the Discovery got back to London he went straight to Sir Thomas Smith, with Billet, to report on the disastrous outcome of the venture. His long narrative must be the formal written account which he then submitted to his employers, though he may have had a wider audience in mind as well. (He writes of his wish for a certain explanation to be 'set down to the view of all' (159/ 11).) Edward Wilson, the ship's surgeon, had read it; at the 1617 Admiralty examination he spoke of 'the book of the voyage in Sir Thomas Smith's power'. Purchas got the manuscript which he printed from Sir Dudley Digges, by way of Hakluyt (Asher, pp. 139–40).

Pricket's narrative has to be read as primarily his own apologia. Everything looks forward or back to the moment on 22 June 1611 when the Discovery pulled away from the shallop, with Pricket in the Discovery. His story is governed by his need to vindicate himself and to protect himself and his friends against charges of inciting the mutiny or collaborating with the mutineers. But Pricket also wrote to encourage the hopes of the adventurers (no difficult task, it would seem) that Hudson had actually located the north-west passage. And consequently the narrative was also designed to serve as a navigational aid to those who would be following Hudson.

What Pricket wrote must have been edited by the adventurers before being given to the public via Hakluyt and Purchas. It is notable that a passage in the 'book' to which Edward Wilson refers (about the sale of the clothes of the men who had been forced into the shallop) does not appear in the published version. It also looks as though Purchas may have tinkered with the manuscript (see note to p. 166/33).

Pricket and Billet also brought back Hudson's chart and his log, and Billet's own log. The chart, or much more likely a copy of it, came quickly into the hands of the Dutch map-maker and publisher Hessel Gerritz, who published it in 1612 with a brief note about the voyage. He had obtained the chart from the Belgian Peter Plancius, who presumably had it from Hakluyt (Abbe and Gillis, pp. 91–2).

Hudson's log is a problem. What Purchas printed he called an 'abstract'. It is in fact a mere fragment, with every item of interest carefully removed. It is natural to think that the leaders of the mutiny, especially Robert Juet, would have deleted or torn out references in the log to the troubles in Ungava Bay in July 1610 and in James Bay in September. But Pricket tells us that Henry Greene gave him the key to the master's chest after the mutiny and it is difficult to believe that Pricket himself would have mutilated the log, even if he had a motive for doing so. He would not have dared to present to the owners the derisory scrap which remains. We can in fact prove that what he gave the owners was more extensive than what has survived in print. For he wrote in the narrative (p. 152/22) about the reward that Hudson offered for killing 'beast, fish or fowl' to help the ship's provisions, 'as in his journal you have seen'. There is nothing about this in the log as we have it. So the skimpy few pages printed by Purchas may possibly represent all that the owners were prepared to release from what may have been a far too revealing document. Presumably, if they were prepared to release the chart and Pricket's account, they were not concerned to safeguard the navigational information in the log.

Thomas Woodhouse's note on the 'trial' of Juet in James Bay in September 1610 is invaluable, and it makes very clear important matters which Pricket leaves obscure. Who found the note in the desk of the 'student in the mathematics', and when, it is impossible to say.

A further corrective to Pricket's narrative is the testimony of the survivors, including Pricket himself, in the examinations at Trinity House and by the High Court of Admiralty.

The company of the Discovery was as follows:

Henry Hudson, master.
—— Coleburne or Colbert, put in by the adventurers as Hudson's assistant, but almost at once sent back by Hudson.
Robert Juet, mate. Demoted by Hudson in Hudson Bay on 10 September 1610.
Robert Billet (or Bylot). Appointed mate to replace Juet, but displaced by Hudson after the wintering.
Philip Staffe, carpenter. Appointed mate to replace Billet in May/ June 1611.
Francis Clements, boatswain. Demoted by Hudson, 10 September 1610.
William Wilson. Appointed boatswain in Clements's place.
John King, quartermaster.
Edward Wilson, surgeon.
Abacuck Pricket, agent of the adventurers.
Thomas Woodhouse (or Wydhouse), 'student in the mathematics'.
Henry Greene, protégé of Hudson.
John Williams, gunner.
Silvanus Bond, cooper.
Bennet Mathews, cook and trumpeter
John Hudson (Hudson's son), mariner.
Arnold Lodlo (or Ludlow), mariner.
Michael Bute (or Butt), mariner.
Syrack Faner, mariner.
Adam Moore, mariner.
Adrian Moter, mariner.
Michael Perce, mariner.
John Thomas, mariner.
Nicholas Sims, boy.

At the very beginning of the voyage there were two dramatic changes in personnel. The first was the 'putting out' of 'Master Coleburne', or Colbert as Pricket calls him, when the ship was off the Isle of Sheppey only fifteen days after leaving London. Some years later (1635) the northern voyager Luke Fox wrote that 'Master Coolbrand' was 'every way held to be a better man' than Hudson; he was 'put in by the adventurers' as Hudson's assistant but Hudson would have none of it; 'who, envying the same, (he having the command in his own hands) devised this course to send himself the same way, though in a far worse place' (Christy, p. 115). The implication is that by objecting to sharing his command Hudson in the end lost his command—in a far worse place, James Bay. It was suggested by Christy that this Coleburne/Colbert/Coolbrand might have been William Cobreth (or Cabreth!) who had been master of the Discovery under Waymouth in 1602 (see also Andrews 1984, p. 347). Whether or not this identification is correct, it is a shrewd surmise by Fox that it was the absence of an adviser on his own level that brought disaster to Hudson.

The second change was to bring in Henry Greene, who came on board at Gravesend—just before Coleburne was put out. Greene was Hudson's protégé, a young man who lived in his house, 'a serviceable man every way for manhood', wrote Pricket, who said that Hudson wanted him on the voyage 'because he could write well'. Pricket made Greene the arch-villain of his drama. As he was killed by the Inuits at Cape Digges he was not able to repudiate the role. There can be little doubt, however, that even if Pricket's account of him is prejudiced and over-drawn, Greene led the mutiny and with William Wilson was chiefly responsible for the callous brutality with which it was carried out. Pricket says nothing about Greene's arrival on board until he reaches the account of the wintering, when like an accomplished story-teller he backtracks to the beginning of the voyage in order to introduce his villain. Pricket's story of Greene and of his relationship with the patron whom he so contemptuously sent to his death is the most interesting feature of his narrative. Greene appears as a Marlovian character, quick to flame up and violent in his quarrels, with 'one Wilkinson' ashore at Harwich and with the surgeon in Iceland; one who was 'clean paper' as regards religion, who exploited his position as Hudson's favourite and then schemed to destroy him, and who at the very end, already seriously wounded, shouted 'Coragio!' as he fended off the Inuits from the boat before being killed by an arrow from the shore.

Pricket makes Hudson jealously possessive of his protégé, whom he had promised a place in Prince Henry's guard on their return. This is amusingly described in the scene of Hudson's fury when Greene went ashore with the carpenter with whom Hudson had just quarrelled (p. 154/10). Comedy changes to something near classic tragedy with the *anagnorisis* of the morning of 22 June, when the pinioned Hudson shouted through the 'horn' of Pricket's cabin, 'Juet will overthrow us all!'; ' "Nay," said I, "it is that villain Henry Greene." And I spoke it not softly.'

Indeed he did not speak it softly. Pricket surely underplays the role of Juet in the mutiny. It is from Woodhouse's account of the 'trial' on 10 September that we understand how the surliness and scepticism of the old mariner became an increasing threat to the morale of the company and even to the continuance of the voyage (Woodhouse, p. 173/17–24. Possibly he was drinking too much (Pricket, p. 153/15). Woodhouse makes it clear that it was Juet's disaffection which brought about the crisis when, with the ship in deep difficulty with the ice in Ungava Bay, Hudson 'brought forth his card' (i.e. chart) and put it to the vote whether they were to proceed with the voyage or not. It has to be remembered that if Juet the mate was dubious that they were ever going to get out, so also, in secret, was Hudson (Pricket, p. 145/24).

Matters between Juet and Hudson finally came to a head on 10 September after many weeks of fruitless search for the magic passage in James Bay. Pricket's narrative in no way conveys the gravity of the assembly which Hudson called. Juet insisted on bringing the company together, Woodhouse wrote, in order to redress 'some abuses and slanders, as he called them' against himself; that is, presumably, to challenge Hudson for what he was saying about him. But Hudson turned the tables. The whole record of Juet's mutterings and head-shakings and moanings about impending trouble, violence, and failure was established against him; above all, that in the present 'embayment' Juet was terrifying the company with the vision of having to winter in the frozen north and 'jesting at our master's hope to see Bantam by Candlemas' (i.e. be in Java by February).

The experienced and cynical seaman was quite correct in his appraisal of the situation and Hudson was quite wrong. But obviously Hudson could not continue to brook Juet's insubordination, and he removed him from his position as mate together with Clements from his position as boatswain, replacing them with Robert Billet and William Wilson.

Juet had the whole of the terrible wintering period in which to nurse

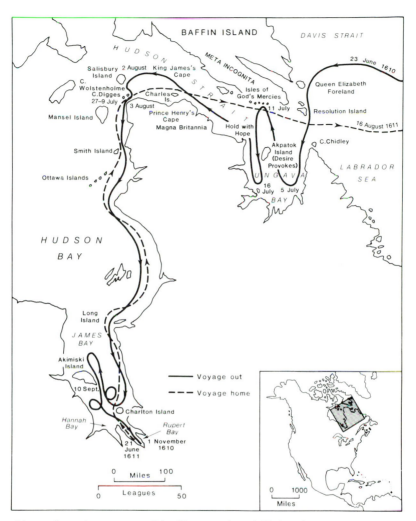

MAP 3. Approximate course of the Discovery through Hudson Strait to Hudson Bay, 1610, and the return in 1611

and brood over his wrongs. But those months must have changed everyone's personality. Hudson in particular seems to have become increasingly paranoid as the ship moved out of the ice into the bay and the great question arose of the next step to be taken. For no reason that Pricket gives, Hudson deposed his new mate, the excellent seaman Robert Billet, and replaced him by the carpenter, Philip Staffe. It is true that this level-headed, loyal, and ever-cheerful man was more than a very good carpenter. Pricket records his unheeded warning to Hudson that he was putting the ship on to the rocks (p. 151/23). But the crew's objection to a mate who could neither read nor write has some force. They thought that by this appointment Hudson had made himself the only person who knew where the ship was and therefore how to get her home. Pricket says Staffe told him that Hudson believed no one else could navigate the ship home and that he, Staffe, believed it too. For this reason Staffe was much less concerned than he should have been about going into the shallop, being confident that the mutineers would have to get Hudson back on board to take them home. Pricket also says that to achieve this security which he sought from the ignorance of others, Hudson had forbidden anyone to keep a log or a reckoning of the ship's course and had confiscated 'whatsoever served for that purpose'.

It is a fair inference that Hudson had hopes of revictualling the ship with the assistance of the native people, whose presence some way off was known from the burning of woodland. The shallop was 'set up', and he went off, probably towards Hannah Bay, to try to make contact. In the meantime the ship was to be got ready for departure. Hudson failed to get in touch with the Inuits and returned to the ship. Pricket says that now 'he fitted all things for his return', but that sounds too smooth, for he says as well that Hudson 'delivered also a bill of return' for the company to show when they got home. 'And he wept when he gave it unto them' (p. 156/20). This seems ominously like the occasion in Hudson's second voyage (see p. 126), when he gave the crew a certificate that he came home of his own free will and not under duress. It seems quite possible that when Hudson got back to the Discovery the company insisted not only that they should set sail for England, but that Hudson should indemnify them against possible charges of coercing him to return.

It is evident that this bill of return did not convince everyone that Hudson had in fact given up the search which so obsessed him. Pricket says that one of the chief grievances expressed by Wilson and Greene was 'the master not caring to go one way or other'. The other chief grievance was food. The men were very hungry, food was very short, and there was wide suspicion that Hudson was not dealing it out fairly. In both the Trinity House examination of 1611 and the Admiralty examinations of 1612 and 1617, the survivors constantly said that the cause of the mutiny was 'want of victual'. It was fear of starvation and suspicion of Hudson that drove the mutineers to put Hudson and the sick men into the shallop, so that they could head for home and have a better chance of surviving on the remaining food.

But who were the mutineers? Pricket names William Wilson and Henry Greene as the instigators. 'They and the rest of their associates would shift [*divide*] the company'; they could not delay 'lest their party should fail them.' Who were 'their associates', 'their party'?

Having examined all the survivors except the boy Sims, the Trinity House authorities concluded that 'the plot was begun by Henry Greene and William Wilson and that by the privity of Juet whom they presumed on for their best guide' (Christy, p. 631; Quinn reads 'presurved on'). The sentence is clumsy, but it would seem that Wilson and Greene had made Juet privy to their plot because they thought he could get the ship home. But Trinity House was also convinced that the eviction of Hudson was carried out 'by consent of all such as are come home and then were in health', and that even some of those who were finally put into the shallop had approved, Michael Bute or Butt in particular. As a result, the High Court of Admiralty eventually issued a bill of indictment for murder against all eight survivors, including Sims (Ewen, p. 3).

The question is what, given the circumstances in James Bay on the night of Saturday, 21 June 1611, and the following Sunday morning, we mean by 'consent'.

There is no reason to doubt the general truth of Pricket's story that Wilson and Greene came to him in his cabin where he lay disabled to try to get him to join their conspiracy, and that later in the night Juet came as well to add his persuasion. The importance of Pricket to them, Purchas argued (Woodhouse, p. 174/5), was that he was the owner's man and could help them when they faced the inevitable enquiry. Pricket's story is that he found them obdurate and unyielding to his attempts to dissuade them, and so he temporized with them. If we put the best light on his proceeding, he decided he could do more for Hudson that way. He managed to persuade them not to include the carpenter among their victims. Pricket wanted Staffe as an ally who might, if the eviction was actually carried out, convince Greene, Wilson, and Juet of their folly and take Hudson back into the ship. This part of his plan was of course defeated by Staffe's heroic refusal to desert Hudson.

Secondly, Pricket seems to have been playing for time during the night in the hope that someone might sneak aft to warn Hudson, which he could not do himself because of his lameness. His third and riskiest stratagem was the oath (p. 159). It is very strange that the oath is never mentioned in all the examinations and depositions, and yet Pricket said, 'I am much condemned for this oath.' Pricket's own allusions to it are contradictory. It looks as though he eventually agreed to co-operate with Wilson, Greene, and Juet, and hit on the idea of limiting the damage by binding the conspirators to swear truth to God, prince, and country, and *to harm no man*. It surely was an immense risk for Pricket to take. If it was an attempt to make the best of a bad job it failed, because many were irretrievably harmed.

The complicity of the others who remained in the Discovery is very hard to assess. Robert Billet was certainly in the plot because, in spite of his transparent efforts to protect him, Pricket inadvertently lets out that Billet's job was to keep the quartermaster, John King, occupied and out of the way (p. 160/25). But how far the 'consent' of Billet and others meant the intention to go as far as in the end the mutiny went is another matter. Edward Wilson the surgeon said that some of those who went into the shallop went 'willingly' because they thought that once the mutineers had found the victuals Hudson was supposed to have hidden they would be taken back on board. And Billet claimed that he thought the eviction into the shallop was only temporary (Ewen, pp. 4, 6). Yet these suggestions of a somewhat gentler beginning to the mutiny do not square well with the 'great distress' of Woodhouse when he was 'put away' (Christy, p. 629), or the fact that Lodlo and Bute were put out 'with much ado' (Pricket, p. 162/11). If the mutineers as a whole thought something less violent was going to take place, and if it was Greene who was mainly responsible for the brutality and ruthlessness shown to the victims and for the final abandonment of the shallop, it is apparent that no one was strongly enough opposed to what went on to do anything about it.

It may be helpful at this point to list the crew again to indicate what happened to each person.

Put in the shallop:
  Henry Hudson
  John Hudson

Philip Staffe (voluntarily)
John King
Thomas Woodhouse (sick)
Adam Moore (sick)
Syrack Faner (sick)
Arnold Lodlo (in place of John Thomas)
Michael Bute (in place of Silvanus Bond)

Remained in the Discovery:

Henry Greene ⎤
William Wilson ⎬ Killed at Cape Digges
John Thomas ⎟
Michael Perce ⎦

Robert Juet   Died on the voyage home

Robert Billet ⎤
Abacuck Pricket ⎟
Edward Wilson ⎟
Francis Clements ⎬ The survivors
Adrian Moter ⎟
Bennet Mathews ⎟
Silvanus Bond ⎟
Nicholas Sims ⎦

Died on the voyage out:

John Williams

When the Discovery eventually reached London in September or October 1611, Billet and Pricket reported at once to Sir Thomas Smith. The Trinity House investigation was on 24 October; it had a double purpose—to enquire into the events on board, and to ascertain what, geographically, the voyage had achieved. I have already mentioned their findings on the first; as regards the second, it was concluded that Hudson was nowhere near a route to the South Sea, but that there could be a passage via the Hudson Strait, going west-north-west from Cape Salisbury.

Following the conclusion of the Trinity House investigators that all the survivors were accomplices, the High Court of Admiralty examined the surgeon, Edward Wilson, on 11 January 1611 (Ewen, p. 4). Remarkably, proceedings then ceased, and on April 12 Prince Henry issued instructions to Thomas Button to take the Discovery and the Resolution and search for the north-west passage westwards from Hudson Strait.

Button set sail towards the end of April (Christy, p. 164), and with him were Robert Billet and Abacuck Pricket—and possibly Edward Wilson too. All three men were named in the Royal Charter of 26 July 1612 as members of the new 'Company of the Merchants Discoverers of the North-West Passage', a very large company with Prince Henry as its patron. The Archbishop of Canterbury, Francis Bacon, and Richard Hakluyt were members, as were the promoters of the previous voyage, Smith, Digges, Wolstenholme, and Lady Romney.

Button explored the western side of Hudson Bay and wintered there, but of course he found no exit and he returned in September 1613. In March 1614, the Discovery was sent out again, and this time Robert Billet served under William Gibbons. They returned after very little success. Billet was now given command of the Discovery, and he set out in March 1615 with William Baffin as mate. John Wolstenholme came aboard in St Katharine's Pool and promised triple wages if the passage was found (Dodge, p. 135). They explored and charted the northern reaches of Hudson Bay, returning in September 1615. In March 1616, the Discovery set out on her sixth northern voyage, again with Billet and Baffin, and this time, sailing past Hudson Strait to the north, they found Lancaster Sound without realizing that there if anywhere was the coveted passage. They were back in England on 30 August 1616 (Dodge, p. 142).

The proceedings against Hudson's men were suspended for five years while on successive voyages the Discovery ranged Hudson Bay and Davis Strait trying to follow up Hudson's lead. At some date unknown, the High Court of Admiralty issued a bill of indictment for murder against the survivors (Public Record Office, HCA, 1/6/193; see Ewen, p. 3); the first person to be examined, Pricket, did not make his deposition until 7 February 1617. The examinations were spread over what seems an inordinately long period of six months. Several of those named in the indictment had understandably made themselves scarce; there is no record of Moter, Bond, or Sims being examined.

The questions asked of each are not extant, only the replies. Clearly the judges wanted to know about conspiracy and about violence done to Hudson and his fellow-victims. All the deponents agreed that the bloodstains found in the ship came from those who died after being eviscerated by the Inuits. As Bennet Mathews put it: 'the clothes became bloody by reason the Cannibals cut up their bellies and otherwise wounded them, that they presently died, one in the boat and three in the ship' (PRO, HCA, 1/6/127).

The depositions have the same burden; all the accused said that they did not know what was being planned, that they took no active part in seizing Hudson and the others and forcing them into the shallop, and that Greene and Wilson were the instigators and perpetrators of the mutiny. Pricket said that Staffe and Hudson 'were the best friends he had in the ship'. Billet said that both he and Pricket had tried to stop Greene putting men into the shallop. Bennet Mathews gave the surprising and perhaps untrue information that Hudson and the others were allowed out of the shallop to get warm clothes. Several thought that Greene and Wilson intended to turn pirate.

It is rather strange that one of the judges' questions, apparently, was why the survivors thought the Admiralty proceedings had been interrupted. Billet said it 'was deferred by means of Sir Thomas Smith, Sir Dudley Digges and Master Worseman as he thinketh' (Quinn 1979, iv. 295–6).

The extraordinary upshot of these proceedings was that a year later, possibly after a period of imprisonment, four of the five were brought to trial: Wilson the surgeon, Pricket, Bennet Mathews, and Francis Clements, but not Billet. On 24 July 1618 Pricket and Wilson were charged with 'feloniously pinioning and putting of Henry Hudson, master of the Discovery, out of the same ship with eight more of his company ... without meat, drink, clothes or other provision, whereby they died.' The charge against Mathews and Clements seems to have been dropped. Pricket and Wilson pleaded not guilty and chose to be tried by jury. The verdict was that they were not guilty, 'nor have they fled' (Powys, pp. 190–8).

One final point might be made concerning Abacuck Pricket's narrative. Its worst feature is the rather deadening detail recording changes of course. The information is largely useless, because it often makes obscure what it is intended to make clear, the ship's course and position. These confused and confusing details should be borne with because in their way they are quite eloquent of the bewilderment, anxiety, and frustration of the company as the ship twisted and turned in uncharted waters, trying to free herself from the ice, looking for the opening that would lead to warm seas and the spice islands.

# NARRATIVES

## 1. *Henry Hudson*

*An abstract of the journal of Master* HENRY HUDSON *for the discovery of the North-west Passage, begun the seventeenth of April, 1610, ended with his end, being treacherously exposed by some of the company.*[1]

The seventeenth of April, 1610, we brake ground[2] and went down from Saint Katharine's Pool and fell down to Blackwall; and so plied[3] down with the ships to Lee, which was the two and twentieth day.[4]

The two and twentieth, I caused Master Coleburne[5] to be put into a pink[6] bound for London, with my letter to the adventurers importing the reason wherefore I so put him out of the ship, and so plied forth.

The second of May, the wind southerly, at even we were thwart of Flamborough Head.

The fifth, we were at the Isles of Orkney, and here I set the north end of the needle and the north of the fly[7] all one.

The sixth, we were in the latitude of 59 degrees 22 minutes, and there perceived that the north end of Scotland, Orkney, and Shotland[8] are not so northerly as is commonly set down. The eighth day, we saw Farre[9] Islands, in the latitude of 62 degrees 24 minutes. The eleventh day, we fell with the easter part of Island,[10] and then plying along the souther part of the land we came to Westmony,[11] being the fifteenth day, and still plied about the main island until the last of May, with contrary winds; and we got some fowls of divers sorts.

The first day of June, we put to sea out of an harbour in the westermost part of Island, and so plied to the westward in the latitude of 66 degrees 34 minutes, and the second day plied and found ourselves in 65 degrees 57 minutes, with little wind easterly.

---

[1] This is a mere fragment of the journal. The question of who gutted it and why is discussed in the Introduction, p. 129.    [2] Weighed anchor.

[3] Plying means working one's way to windward by tacking.

[4] St Katharine's Pool is by the Tower of London; Blackwall is 6 miles down river; Leigh-on-Sea is by Southend in the Thames Estuary.

[5] See the Introduction, p. 131.

[6] 'In the 15th and 16th centuries the name was loosely applied to all small ships with narrow sterns' (Kemp).

[7] Compass-card.    [8] Shetland.    [9] Faroe.    [10] Iceland.

[11] Vestmannaeyjar, 63° 27′ N., 20° 15′ W., an island off the south coast of Iceland.

The third day we found ourselves in 65 degrees 30 minutes, with wind at north-east. A little before this we sailed near some ice.

The fourth day we saw Groneland[12] over the ice perfectly, and this night the sun went down due north, and rose north-north-east. So, plying the fifth day, we were in 65 degrees, still encumbered with much ice, which hung upon the coast of Groneland.

The ninth day, we were off Frobisher's Straits with the wind northerly, and plied unto the south-westwards until the fifteenth day.

The fifteenth day, we were in sight of the land, in latitude 59 degrees 27 minutes, which was called by Captain John Davis, Desolation, and found the error of the former laying down of that land. And then, running to the north-westward[13] until the twentieth day, we found the ship in 60 degrees 42 minutes, and saw much ice, and many ripplings or overfalls, and a strong stream setting from east-south-east to west-north-west.

The one and twenty, two and twenty, and three and twenty days, with the wind variable, we plied to the north-westward in sight of much ice, into the height of 62 degrees 29 minutes.

The four and twenty, and five and twenty days, sailing to the westward, about midnight we saw land north,[14] which was suddenly lost again. So we ran still to the westward in 62 degrees 17 minutes.

The fifth of July, we plied up upon the souther side, troubled with much ice in seeking the shore until the fifth day of July, and we observed that day in 59 degrees 16 minutes.[15] Then we plied off the shore again until the eighth day, and then found the height of the pole in 60 degrees no minutes. Here we saw the land from the north-west by west, half northerly, unto the south-west by west, covered with snow, a champaign land, and called it Desire Provoketh.[16]

[12] Greenland, or rather the northern part. Asher (p. 94) explains that the northern part was thought to be separated from the southern part, called Desolation, by 'Frobisher's Strait'.

[13] They have now rounded Cape Farewell, the southernmost point of Greenland.

[14] This might be Queen Elizabeth Foreland, the southern tip of Lok's Land at the entrance to Frobisher Bay on Baffin Island. At 62° 17′ Hudson would still be well north of the entrance to Hudson Strait. All the material about entering the Strait, and going south into Ungava Bay where the unpleasantness recorded by Pricket and Woodhouse occurred, must have been deleted.

[15] They are now following the eastern shore of Ungava Bay, near Cape Kattaktok in Kegla Bay, 65° 40′ W.

[16] Asher (p. 102) calls this Aktapok Island. Hudson cannot be right in saying that the land extended from NW by W. ½ N. to SW by W., an angle of 73°. Only the west coast of Ungava Bay could fill such a huge angle from approximately 60° latitude. 'Champaign land' means level, open country.

We still plied up to the westward, as the land and ice would suffer, until the eleventh day, when, fearing a storm, we anchored by three rocky islands in uncertain depth, between two and nine fathoms, and found it an harbour unsufficient, by reason of sunken rocks, one of which was next morning two fathoms above water. We called them the Isles of God's Mercies.[17] The water floweth here better than four fathoms. The flood cometh from the north, flowing eight the change-day.[18] The latitude in this place is 62 degrees 9 minutes. Then plying to the south-westward the sixteenth day, we were in the latitude of 58 degrees 50 minutes, but found ourselves embayed with land,[19] and had much ice. And we plied to the north-westward until the nineteenth day, and then we found by observation the height of the pole in 61 degrees 24 minutes, and saw the land, which I named Hold With Hope.[20] Hence I plied to the north-westward still, until the one and twentieth day, with the wind variable. Here I found the sea more grown[21] than any we had since we left England.

The three and twentieth day, by observation the height of the pole was 61 degrees 33 minutes. The five and twentieth day, we saw the land and named it Magna Britannia. The six and twentieth day, we observed and found the latitude in 62 degrees 44 minutes. The eight and twentieth day we were in the height of 63 degrees 10 minutes, and plied southerly of the west. The one and thirtieth day, plying to the westward, at noon we found ourselves in 62 degrees 24 minutes.

The first of August we had sight of the northern shore,[22] from the north-by-east to the west-by-south off us; the north part twelve leagues and the wester part twenty leagues from us; and we had no ground there at one hundred and eighty fathoms. And I think I saw land on the sun side, but could not make it perfectly, bearing east-north-east. Here I found the latitude 62 degrees 50 minutes.

The second day, we had sight of a fair headland on the norther shore six leagues off, which I called Salisbury's Foreland.[23] We ran from thence west-south-west fourteen leagues, in the mid-way of which we

[17] They have now gone right across to the northern shore of the Hudson Strait. These are the Middle Savage Islands, 62° 10′ N., 68° 0′ W.

[18] When the moon changes from one phase to another. Properly, the new moon, but here obviously meaning the time of spring tides, which occur twice every lunar month.

[19] Their zigzag course has now brought them back south into Ungava Bay.

[20] Cape Hopes Advance, 61° 06′ N., 69° 35′ W.

[21] With a higher swell.

[22] If he could indeed see the northern shore, Hudson must have been a good deal further north than his observations made him out to be.

[23] Salisbury Island, 63° 50′ N., 77° 00′ W., at the western exit of Hudson Strait.

were suddenly come into a great and whirling sea, whether caused by meeting of two streams or an overfall I know not. Thence sailing west and by south seven leagues farther, we were in the mouth of a strait, and sounded, and had no ground at one hundred fathoms, the strait being there not above two leagues broad in the passage in this wester part; which, from the easter part of Fretum Davis, is distant two hundred and fifty leagues thereabouts.[24]

The third day, we put through the narrow passage, after our men had been on land, which had well observed there *that the flood did come from*
10 *the north*, flowing by the shore five fathoms. The head of this entrance on the south side I named Cape Worsenholme,[25] and the head on the north-wester shore I called Cape Digs.[26] After we had sailed with an easterly wind west and by south ten leagues, the land fell away to the southward, and the other isles and land left us to the westward. Then I observed and found the ship at noon in 61 degrees 20 minutes, and a sea to the westward.

## 2. *Abacuck Pricket*

*A larger discourse of the same voyage, and the success thereof, written by*
ABACUCK PRICKET.

We began our voyage for the North-west passage the seventeenth of April, 1610. Thwart of Sheppey, our master sent Master Colbert back to the owners with his letter. The next day we weighed from hence and stood for Harwich, and came thither the eight and twentieth of April. From Harwich we set sail the first of May along the coast to the north, till we came to the Isles of Orkney; from thence to the Isles of Faro, and from thence to Island,[1] on which we fell in a fog, hearing the rut[2] of the sea ashore but saw not the land, whereupon our master came to an anchor. Here we were embayed in the south-east part of the land. We
10 weighed and stood along the coast on the west side towards the north. But one day, being calm, we fell a-fishing and caught good store of fish, as cod and ling and butt,[3] with some other sorts that we knew not. The

---

[24] i.e. 750 miles; an overestimate. It is about 400 miles. (Asher says, incredibly, 'about one thousand English miles'.)

[25] Cape Wolstenholme, 62° 32′ N., 77° 30′ W., the north-western tip of the mainland, named after John Wolstenholme, one of the main promoters of the voyage.

[26] After Sir Dudley Digges.

[1] Iceland.    [2] Noise of the surf.    [3] Flat-fish (of various kinds).

next day we had a good gale of wind at south-west and raised the Isles of Westmony, where the King of Denmark hath a fortress, by which we passed to raise the Snow Hill[4] foot, a mountain so called on the north-west part of the land. But in our course we saw that famous hill Mount Hecla, which cast out much fire, a sign of foul weather to come in short time. We leave Island astern of us, and met a main of ice which did hang on the north part of Island and stretched down to the west. Which when our master saw, he stood back for Island to find an harbour, which we did on the north-west part, called Derefor,[5] where we killed good store of fowl. From hence we put to sea again, but, neither wind nor weather serving, our master stood back for this harbour again, but could not reach it, but fell with another to the south of that, called by our Englishmen Lousy Bay;[6] where on the shore we found an hot bath, and here all our Englishmen bathed themselves; the water was so hot that it would scald a fowl.

From hence, the first of June, we put to sea for Groneland, but to the west we saw land as we thought, for which we bear the best part of a day, but it proved but a foggy bank. So we gave it over, and made for Groneland, which we raised the fourth of June. Upon the coast thereof hung good store of ice so that our master could not attain to the shore by any means. The land in this part is very mountainous, and full of round hills like to sugar-loaves, covered with snow. We turned the land on the south side, as near as the ice would suffer us. Our course for the most part was between the west and north-west, till we raised the Desolations, which is a great island in the west part of Groneland.[7] On this coast we saw store of whales, and at one time three of them came close by us, so as we could hardly shun them; then, two passing very near and the third going under our ship, we received no harm by them, praised be God.

From the Desolations, our master made his way north-west, the wind being against him, who else would have gone more to the north; but in this course we saw the first great island or mountain of ice, whereof after we saw store. About the latter end of June we raised land to the north of us, which our master took to be that island[8] which Master Davis setteth down in his chart on the west side of his strait. Our master would have

---

[4]  Snæfellsjökull, 4,750 ft.
[5]  Dýrafjörður, 65° 50′ N., 23° 30′ W.
[6]  Breiðafjörður.
[7]  See n. 12 to Hudson's log, p. 141.
[8]  Resolution, the northern entrance to Hudson Strait.

gone to the north of it but the wind would not suffer him, so we fell to the south of it, into a great rippling or overfall of current, the which setteth to the west. Into the current we went, and made our way to the north of the west till we met with ice which hung on this island. Wherefore our master, casting about, cleared himself of this ice and stood to the south, and then to the west, through store of floating ice, and upon the ice store of seals. We gained a clear sea and continued our course till we meet ice, first with great islands, and then with store of the smaller sort. Between them we made our course north-west till we met with ice again. But in this our going between the ice, we saw one of the great islands of ice overturn, which was a good warning to us not to come nigh them nor within their reach. Into the ice we put ahead, as between two lands. The next day we had a storm, and the wind brought the ice so fast upon us that in the end we were driven to put her into the chiefest of the ice and there to let her lie. Some of our men this day fell sick; I will not say it was for fear, although I saw small sign of other grief.

The storm ceasing, we stood out of the ice where we saw any clear sea to go to, which was sometime more and sometime less. Our course was as the ice did lie, sometime to the north, then to the north-west, and then to the west, and to the south-west; but still enclosed with ice. Which when our master saw, he made his course to the south, thinking to clear himself of the ice that way.[9] But the more he strove, the worse he was, and the more enclosed, till we could go no further. Here our master was in despair, and, as he told me after, he thought he should never have got out of this ice, but there have perished. Therefore he brought forth his card,[10] and showed all the company that he was entered above an hundred leagues further than ever any English was;[11] and left it to their choice whether they would proceed any further, yea or nay. Whereupon some were of one mind and some of another, some wishing themselves at home, and some not caring where, so they were out of the ice. But there were some who then spake words which were remembered a great while after.[12]

There was one who told the master that if he had an hundred pounds,

[9] They are now deep in Ungava Bay.

[10] Chart. Pricket underplays the disaffection of the company at this time. See Introduction, p. 132.

[11] An overestimate. They were about 125 nautical miles inside the entrance to the Strait. In any case it is probable that Waymouth had sailed some way into the Strait in 1602.

[12] Two months. The date is approximately 5 July, and the 'trial' of Juet took place on 10 Sept.

he would give fourscore and ten to be at home. But the carpenter[13] made answer that if he had an hundred he would not give ten upon any such condition, but would think it to be as good money as ever he had any, and to bring it as well home, by the leave of God.[14] After many words to no purpose, to work we must on all hands, to get ourselves out, and to clear our ship. After much labour and time spent, we gained room to turn our ship in, and so by little and little to get clear in the sea a league or two off, our course being north and north-west.

In the end we raised land to the south-west, high land[15] and covered with snow. Our master named this land Desire Provokes. Lying here, we heard the noise of a great overfall of a tide, that came out of the land. For now we might see well that we had been embayed before. And time had made us know, being so well acquainted with the ice, that when night, or foggy or foul weather took us, we would seek out the broadest island of ice and there come to anchor, and run and sport, and fill water that stood on the ice in ponds, both sweet and good. But after we had brought this land to bear south of us, we had the tide and the current to open the ice, as being carried first one way and then another; but in bays they lie as in a pond, without moving. In this bay where we were thus troubled with ice, we saw many of those mountains of ice aground, in six or seven score fathom water. In this our course we saw a bear upon a piece of ice by itself, to the which our men gave chase with their boat; but before they came nigh her the tide had carried the ice, and the bear on it, and joined it with the other ice; so they lost their labour and came aboard again.

We continued our course to the north-west, and raised land to the north of our course toward which we made, and coming nigh it, there hung on the eastermost point many islands of floating ice, and a bear on one of them which from one to another came towards us till she was ready to come aboard. But when she saw us look at her, she cast her head between her hinder legs and then dived under the ice; and so from one piece to another till she was out of our reach. We stood along by the land on the south side ahead of us; we met with ice that hung on a point of land that lay to the south, more than[16] this that we came up by; which when our master saw, he stood in for the shore. At the west end of this

---

[13]  Philip Staffe.
[14]  Staffe means that his £100 would be quite safe; he does not need to buy his way home with it; he will get back safely with his money intact.
[15]  The highest point of Aktapok Island is less than 1,000 ft. See note to Hudson's log, p. 141/26.
[16]  i.e. worse than.

island (for so it is) we found an harbour, and came in at a full sea over a rock which had two fathom and a half on it, and was so much bare at a low water. But by the great mercy of God we came to an anchor clear of it and close by it. Our master named them the Isles of God's Mercy. This is an harbour for need,[17] but there must be care had how they come in.

Here our master sent me, and others with me, to discover[18] to the north and north-west. And in going from one place to another we sprung a covey of partridges which were young, at the which Thomas Woodhouse shot, but killed only the old one. This island is a most
10  barren place, having nothing on it but plashes of water and riven rocks, as if it were subject to earthquakes. To the north there is a great bay, or sea (for I know not what it will prove) where I saw a great island of ice aground between the two lands, which with the spring-tide was set afloat and carried into this bay or sea to the north-westward, but came not back again, nor within sight. Here we took in some driftwood that we found ashore.

From hence we stood to the south-west to double the land to the west of us, through much floating ice. In the end we found a clear sea, and continued therein till we raised land to the north-west. Then our master
20  made his course more to the south than before, but it was not long ere we met with ice which lay ahead of us. Our master would have doubled this ice to the north, but could not, and in the end put into it down to the south-west through much ice, and then to the south, where we were embayed again.[19] Our master strove to get the shore, but could not for the great store of ice that was on the coast. From out of this bay we stood to the north, and were soon out of the ice; then down to the south-west and so to the west, where we were enclosed (to our sight) with land and ice. For we had land from the south to the north-west on one side, and from the east to the west on the other; but the land that was to the north
30  of us, and lay by east and west, was but an island. On we went till we could go no further for ice. So we made our ship fast to the ice which the tide brought upon us, but when the ebb came the ice did open and made way; so as in seven or eight hours we were clear from the ice, till we came to weather, but only some of the great islands, that were carried along with us to the north-west.[20]

[17]  In case of necessity.
[18]  Not so much to explore as to get height and survey the terrain.
[19]  In Ungava Bay once more, about 16 July.
[20]  After 7 or 8 hours they had the wind astern and were free of the ice, except for some big floes which were driven north-west with them.

Having a clear sea, our master stood to the west along by the south shore and raised three capes or headlands, lying one above another. The middlemost is an island, and maketh a bay or harbour which (I take) will prove a good one. Our master named them Prince Henry's Cape or Foreland. When we had laid this we raised another, which was the extreme point of the land looking towards the north. Upon it are two hills, but one, above the rest, like an hay-cock; which our master named King James his Cape. To the north of this lie certain islands which our master named Queen Anne's Cape or Foreland.[21] We followed the north shore still. Beyond the King's Cape there is a sound or bay that  10 hath some islands in it; and this is not to be forgotten, if need be. Beyond this lieth some broken land, close to the main; but what it is I know not, because we passed by it in the night.

We stood to the north to double this land, and after to the west again till we fell with land that stretched from the main like a shewer,[22] from the south to the north, and from the north to the west, and then down to the south again. Being short of this land, a storm took us, the wind at west. We stood to the north and raised land. Which when our master saw, he stood to the south again, for he was loath at any time that we should see the north shore. The storm continuing, and coming to the  20 south shore again, our master found himself shot to the west a great way, which made him muse, considering his leeward way.[23] To the south-west of this land, on the main, there is an high hill which our master named Mount Charles. To the north, and beyond this, lieth an island that to the east hath a fair head, and beyond it to the west other broken land which maketh a bay within, and a good road may be found there for ships. Our master named the first Cape Salsbury.

When we had left this to the north-east, we fell into a rippling or overfall of a current, which at the first we took to be a shoal; but, the lead being cast, we had no ground. On we passed, still in sight of the south  30 shore, till we raised land lying from the main some two leagues. Our master took this to be a part of the main of the north land, but it is an island, the north side stretching out to the west more than the south. This island hath a fair head to the east, and very high land,[24] which our

---

[21]  Christy suggests this may be the eastern end of Charles Island.

[22]  Is this 'shore', as Luke Fox reads it (Christy, p. 126), 'skewer', as Asher suggests (p. 105), or 'shoe' (a misreading of 'shewe')?

[23]  i.e. he was puzzled at the distance he had drifted to leeward.

[24]  Powys (p. 139) says that the Cape Digges cliffs rise to over 1,000 ft., and that Cape Wolstenholme is nearly twice that height.

master named Digges Cape; and the land on the south side, now falling away to the south, makes another cape or headland, which our master named Worsenham's Cape.

When we were nigh the north or island cape, our master sent the boat ashore, with myself (who had the charge) and the carpenter and divers others, to discover to the west and north-west, and to the south-west. But we had further to it than we thought, for the land is very high, and we were overtaken with a storm of rain, thunder, and lightning. But to it we came on the north-east side, and up we got from one rock to another till
10 we came to the highest of that part. Here we found some plain ground and saw some deer; at first four or five, and after a dozen or sixteen in an herd, but could not come nigh them with a musket shot.

Thus, going from one place to another, we saw to the west of us an high hill above all the rest, it being nigh us; but it proved further off than we made account, for, when we came to it, the land was so steep on the east and north-east parts that we could not get unto it. To the south-west we saw that we might, and towards that part we went along, by the side of a great pond of water which lieth under the east side of this hill; and there runneth out of it a stream of water, as much as would drive an
20 overshot mill,[25] which falleth down from an high cliff into the sea on the south side. In this place great store of fowl breed, and there is the best grass that I had seen since we came from England. Here we found sorrel, and that which we call scurvy-grass, in great abundance. Passing along, we saw some round hills of stone like to grass-cocks, which at the first I took to be the work of some Christian. We passed by them till we came to the south side of the hill; we went unto them and there found more. And being nigh them, I turned off the uppermost stone and found them hollow within, and full of fowls hanged by their necks.[26] Then Greene[27] and I went to fetch the boat to the south side, while Robert
30 Billet and [the others][28] got down a valley to the sea-side, where we took them in.

Our master (in this time) came in between the two lands and shot off

---

1 Digges] Deepes *Purchas*   11 at first] as first *Purchas*   30 the others]
he *Purchas*

[25] Mill with a wheel turned by water falling from above.

[26] Storage caches like this are mentioned by B. Saladin d'Anglure in 'Inuit of Quebec', in *Handbook of North American Indians*, v, *Arctic*, ed. D. Damas, 1984, p. 491.

[27] In Purchas there is a gap before Greene's name, but presumably Pricket, who everywhere else refers to him as 'Henry Greene', here used the surname only. This is the first mention of the villain of the piece, who enters on p. 152.

[28] 'He' in Purchas cannot be correct.

some pieces to call us aboard, for it was a fog. We came aboard and told him what we had seen, and persuaded[29] him to stay a day or two in this place, telling him what refreshing might there be had; but by no means would he stay, who was not pleased with the motion. So we left the fowl, and took our way down to the south-west. Before, they went in sight of the land, which now bears to the east from us, being the same mainland that we had all this while followed. Now we had lost the sight of it because it falleth away to the east after some five and twenty or thirty leagues. Now we came to the shallow water, wherewith we were not acquainted since we came from Island. Now we came into broken 10 ground and rocks, through which we passed down to the south. In this our course we had a storm, and the water did shoal apace. Our master came to an anchor in fifteen fathoms water.

We weighed and stood to the south-east, because the land in this place did lie so. When we came to the point of the west land (for we now had land on both sides of us)[30] we came to an anchor. Our master sent the boat ashore to see what that land was, and whether there were any way through. They soon returned, and showed that beyond the point of land to the south, there was a large sea. This land on the west side was a very narrow point. We weighed from hence, and stood in for this sea 20 between the two lands, which in this place is not two leagues broad, down to the south, for a great way in sight of the east shore. In the end we lost sight thereof, and saw it not till we came to the bottom of the bay, into six or seven fathoms water. Hence we stood up to the north by the west shore, till we came to an island in 53,[31] where we took in water and ballast.

From hence we passed towards the north. But some two or three days after (reasoning concerning our coming into this bay, and going out)[32] our master took occasion to revive old matters,[33] and to displace Robert Juet from being his mate, and the boatswain[34] from his place, for words 30

5  took] lost *Purchas*

[29]  Urged.

[30]  Asher (p. 108) thinks they were already in James Bay, but Christy is more likely to be right that they were in the passage between the mainland and Smith Island, which Hudson named Romney's Island, 60° 46′ N.

[31]  Presumably Akimiski Island in James Bay.

[32]  Woodhouse's notes make it clear that Pricket's obscure phrase refers to the charge that once again, when the ship had become deeply 'embayed' as it was in Ungava Bay, Juet had begun to demoralize the company. See Introduction, p. 132.

[33]  The date of this 'court martial', fully described by Woodhouse, is 10 Sept.

[34]  Francis Clements.

spoken in the first great bay of ice.[35] Then he made Robert Billet his mate and William Wilson our boatswain.

Up to the north we stood till we raised land, then down to the south, and up to the north, then down again to the south. And on Michaelmas Day[36] came in and went out of certain lands which our master sets down by the name of Michaelmas Bay, because we came in and went out on that day. From hence we stood to the north and came into shoal water; and the weather being thick and foul we came to an anchor in seven or eight fathom water, and there lay eight days, in all which time we could not get one hour to weigh our anchor. But the eighth day, the wind beginning to cease, our master would have the anchor up, against the mind of all who knew what belonged thereunto. Well, to it we went, and when we had brought it to a peak,[37] a sea took her and cast us all off from the capstan, and hurt divers of us.[38] Here we lost our anchor, and if the carpenter had not been,[39] we had lost our cable too; but he (fearing such a matter) was ready with his axe, and so cut it.

From hence we stood to the south and to the south-west through a clear sea of divers sounding, and came to a sea of two colours, one black and the other white, sixteen or seventeen fathom water, between which we went four or five leagues. But the night coming, we took in our topsails and stood afore the wind with our mainsail and foresail, and came into five or six fathoms, and saw no land, for it was dark. Then we stood to the east and had deep water again, then to the south and south-west, and so came to our westermost bay of all,[40] and came to an anchor nearest to the north shore. Out went our boat to the land that was next us. When they came near it, our boat could not float to the shore, it was so shallow; yet ashore they got. Here our men saw the footing of a man and a duck in the snowy rocks, and wood good store, whereof they took some and returned aboard. Being at anchor in this place we saw a ledge of rocks to the south of us, some league of length. It lay north and south, covered at a full sea; for a strong tide setteth in here. At midnight we weighed and stood to go out as we came in; and had not gone long but the carpenter came and told the master that if he kept that course he would be upon the rocks. The master conceived that he was past them,

[35] Ungava Bay.

[36] 29 Sept.

[37] The anchor is a-peak 'when the bows of a ship have been drawn directly above it, ... just before it is broken out of the ground' (Kemp).

[38] Adam Moore never fully recovered; see p. 160.

[39] i.e. if it had not been for the carpenter.

[40] Hannah's Bay?

when presently we ran on them and there stuck fast twelve hours. But (by the mercy of God) we got off unhurt, though not unscarred.

We stood up to the east and raised three hills, lying north and south. We went to the furthermost and left it to the north of us, and so into a bay, where we came to an anchor. Here our master sent out our boat, with myself and the carpenter, to seek a place to winter in;[41] and it was time, for the nights were long and cold, and the earth covered with snow. Having spent three months in a labyrinth without end, being now the last of October, we went down to the east, to the bottom of the bay; but returned without speeding of that we went for. The next day we went to  10 the south and the south-west, and found a place whereunto we brought our ship and haled her aground. And this was the first of November. By the tenth thereof we were frozen in; but now we were in, it behoved us to have care of what we had, for that we were sure of; but what we had not, was uncertain.

We were victualled for six months in good proportion, and of that which was good. If our master would have had more, he might have had it at home and in other places.[42] Here we were now, and therefore it behoved us so to spend that we might have (when time came) to bring us to the capes where the fowl bred, for that was all the hope we had to  20 bring us home. Wherefore our master took order, first for the spending of that we had, and then to increase it by propounding a reward to them that killed either beast, fish or fowl, as in his journal you have seen. About the middle of this month of November, died John Williams our gunner. God pardon the master's uncharitable dealing with this man. Now for that I am come to speak of him out of whose ashes (as it were) that unhappy deed grew which brought a scandal upon all that are returned home, and upon the action itself (the multitude, like the dog, running after the stone but not at the caster),[43] therefore, not to wrong the living nor slander the dead, I will (by the leave of God) deliver the  30 truth as near as I can.

You shall understand that our master kept in his house at London a young man named Henry Greene, born in Kent of worshipful parents,

---

[41] There has been much discussion of the exact point where Hudson wintered. It was most probably Rupert Bay, at the bottom of James Bay.

[42] Pricket means that they were not provisioned for wintering; if Hudson wanted a longer voyage he could easily have made the proper arrangements.

[43] If you throw a stone at a dog, the dog will bite the stone and not the thrower. This proverb had a variety of rather clumsy applications (see *Oxford Dictionary of Proverbs*, 'Dog bites the stone'). Here, the public fastens its attention on the slander and not the slanderer.

but by his lewd life and conversation he had lost the good will of all his friends, and had spent all that he had. This man our master would have to sea with him because he could write well.[44] Our master gave him meat and drink and lodging, and, by means of one Master Venson, with much ado got four pounds of his mother to buy him clothes, wherewith Master Venson would not trust him, but saw it laid out himself. This Henry Greene was not set down in the owners' book, nor any wages made for him. He came first aboard at Gravesend, and at Harwich should have gone into the field with one Wilkinson.[45] At Island, the surgeon and he fell out in Dutch[46] and he beat him ashore in English, which set all the company in a rage, so that we had much ado to get the surgeon aboard. I told the master of it, but he bade me let it alone, for (said he) the surgeon had a tongue that would wrong the best friend he had. But Robert Juet, the master's mate, would needs burn his finger in the embers, and told the carpenter a long tale when he was drunk, that our master had brought in Greene to crack his credit that should displease him. Which words came to the master's ears, who, when he understood it, would have gone back to Island, when he was forty leagues fom thence, to have sent home his mate Robert Juet in a fisherman.[47] But being otherwise persuaded, all was well.

So Henry Greene stood upright, and very inward with the master, and was a serviceable man every way for manhood; but for religion, he would say he was clean paper, whereon he might write what he would. Now, when our gunner was dead, and (as the order is in such cases) if the company stand in need of anything that belonged to the man deceased, then is it brought to the mainmast and there sold to them that will give most for the same—this gunner had a gray cloth gown, which Greene prayed the master to friend him so much as to let him have it, paying for it as another would give. The master said he should; and thereupon he answered some that sought to have it that Greene should have it and none else; and so it rested.

Now, out of season and time, the master calleth the carpenter to go in hand with an house on shore, which at the beginning our master would

[44] A striking indication of the importance attaching to the written record of a voyage; see General Introduction, p. 8.

[45] The *Discovery* was in Harwich for three days; the implication is that Greene quarrelled with Wilkinson ashore, and if the ship had not sailed there would have been a duel.

[46] This almost certainly means when drunk; cf. 'Dutch courage' and 'Dutch bargain'.

[47] This looks like another version of a row between Hudson and Juet, during which Woodhouse said it was *Juet* who threatened to turn the ship around.

not hear, when it might have been done. The carpenter told him that the snow and frost were such as he neither could nor would go in hand with such work. Which when our master heard, he ferreted him out of his cabin to strike him, calling him by many foul names and threatening to hang him. The carpenter told him that he knew what belonged to his place better than himself, and that he was no house carpenter. So this passed, and the house was (after) made with much labour, but to no end. The next day after the master and the carpenter fell out, the carpenter took his piece and Henry Greene with him, for it was an order that none should go out alone, but one with a piece and another with a pike. This 10 did move the master so much the more against Henry Greene that Robert Billet his mate must have the gown, and had it delivered unto him. Which when Henry Greene saw, he challenged the master's promise. But the master did so rail on Greene, with so many words of disgrace, telling him that all his friends would not trust him with twenty shillings, and therefore why should he? As for wages, he had none, nor none should have, if he did not please him well. Yet the master had promised him to make his wages as good as any man's in the ship, and to have him one of the Prince's guard when we came home.[48] But you shall see how the devil out of this so wrought with Greene that he did the 20 master what mischief he could in seeking to discredit him, and to thrust him and many other honest men out of the ship in the end.

To speak of all our trouble in this time of winter, which was so cold as it lamed the most of our company, and myself do yet feel it, would be too tedious.[49] But I must not forget to show how mercifully God dealt with us in this time. For the space of three months we had such store of fowl of one kind, which were partridges as white as milk,[50] that we killed above an hundred dozen, besides others of sundry sorts (for all was fish that came to the net). The spring coming, this fowl left us; yet they were with us all the extreme cold. Then in their places came divers sort of 30 other fowl, as swan, geese, duck, and teal; but hard to come by. Our master hoped they would have bred in those broken grounds, but they do not, but came from the south and flew to the north further than we were this voyage. Yet if they be taken short with the wind at north or north-west or north-east, then they fall and stay till the wind serve them, and then fly to the north. Now in time these fowls are gone, and few or

[48] This would seem to indicate that Hudson had personal assurance of Prince Henry's interest in the voyage.

[49] In the old sense of distressing; *not* boring.

[50] Ptarmigans.

none to be seen. Then we went into the woods, hills, and valleys, for all things that had any show of substance in them, how vile soever. The moss of the ground, than the which I take the powder of a post to be much better, and the frog (in his engendering time as loathsome as a toad) was not spared. But amongst the divers sorts of buds, it pleased God that Thomas Woodhouse brought home a bud of a tree full of a turpentine substance. Of this our surgeon made a decoction to drink, and applied the buds hot to them that were troubled with ache in any part of their bodies. And for my part, I confess I received great and
10 present ease of my pain.

About this time, when the ice began to break out of the bays, there came a savage to our ship, as it were to see and to be seen, being the first that we had seen in all this time. Whom our master entreated well, and made much of him, promising unto himself great matters by his means; and therefore would have all the knives and hatchets which any man had to his private use; but received none but from John King, the carpenter, and myself. To this savage our master gave a knife, a looking glass, and buttons, who received them thankfully, and made signs that after he had slept he would come again, which he did. When he came, he brought
20 with him a sled which he drew after him, and upon it two deer's skins and two beaver skins. He had a scrip[51] under his arm, out of which he drew those things which the master had given him. He took the knife and laid it upon one of the beaver skins, and his glasses and buttons upon the other, and so gave them to the master, who received them; and the savage took those things which the master had given him and put them up into his scrip again. Then the master showed him an hatchet, for which he would have given the master one of his deer skins, but our master would have them both; and so he had, although not willingly. After many signs, of people to the north and to the south, and that after
30 so many sleeps he would come again, he went his way; but never came more.

Now, the ice being out of the sounds, so that our boat might go from one place unto another, a company of men were appointed by the master to go a-fishing with our net. Their names were as followeth: William Wilson, Henry Greene, Michael Perce, John Thomas, Andrew Moter, Bennet Mathews, and Arnold Lodlo. These men, the first day they went, caught five hundred fish, as big as good herrings, and some trouts; which put us all in some hope to have our wants supplied and our

---

[51] Bag.

commons amended. But these were the most that ever they got in one day; for many days they got not a quarter so many. In this time of their fishing, Henry Greene and William Wilson, with some others, plotted to take the net and the shallop,[52] which the carpenter had now set up, and so to shift for themselves. But, the shallop being ready, our master would go in it himself to the south and south-west, to see if he could meet with the people; for to that end was it set up, and (that way)[53] we might see the woods set on fire by them. So the master took the sayne[54] and the shallop, and so much victual as would serve for eight or nine days, and to the south he went. They that remained aboard were to take in water, wood, and ballast, and to have all things in a readiness against he came back. But he set no time of his return; for he was persuaded, if he could meet with the people he should have flesh of them, and that good store. But he returned worse than he went forth, for he could by no means meet with the people, although they were near them; yet[55] they would set the woods on fire in his sight.

Being returned, he fitted all things for his return, and first delivered all the bread out of the bread-room, which came to a pound a piece for every man's share, and delivered also a bill of return,[56] willing them to have that to show, if it pleased God that they came home. And he wept when he gave it unto them. But to help us in this poor estate with some relief, the boat and sayne went to work on Friday morning and stayed till Sunday noon; at which time they came aboard and brought four-score small fish, a poor relief for so many hungry bellies. Then we weighed, and stood out of our wintering place, and came to an anchor without, in the mouth of the bay; from whence we weighed and came to an anchor without, in the sea; where, our bread being gone, that store of cheese we had was to stop a gap, whereof there were five;[57] whereat the company grudged, because they made account of nine. But those that were left were equally divided by the master, although he had counsel to the

10

20

30

8 sayne] sayue *Purchas*

[52] A ship's boat, but not the only one the Discovery had, because a second boat plays an important part in the story after the shallop had been cut adrift.
[53] In that direction.
[54] The seine net, which hangs vertically in the water.
[55] Implies continuation, 'and still'.
[56] Probably a certificate that he was not returning under duress. See Introduction, p. 126. The inference is that having failed to meet the Inuits who might have revictualled the ship, Hudson was under strong pressure to return—and to attest that he was returning voluntarily.
[57] i.e. whole cheeses.

contrary; for there were some who having it would make haste to be rid thereof, because they could not govern it. I knew when Henry Greene gave half his bread (which he had[58] for fourteen days) to one to keep, and prayed him not to let him have any until the next Monday; but before Wednesday at night he never left till he had it again, having eaten up his first week's bread before. So Wilson the boatswain hath eaten in one day his fortnight's bread, and hath been two or three days sick for his labour. The cause that moved the master to deliver all the cheese was because they were not all of one goodness, and therefore they should see that they had no wrong done them, but every man should have alike the best and the worst together, which was three pounds and a half for seven days.

The wind serving, we weighed and stood to the north-west, and on Monday at night (the eighteenth day of June) we fell into the ice, and the next day the wind being at west, we lay there till Sunday, in sight of land. Now being here, the master told Nicholas Sims that there would be a breaking up of chests and a search for bread; and willed him, if he had any, to bring it to him, which he did, and delivered to the master thirty cakes in a bag. This deed of the master (if it be true) hath made me marvel what should be the reason that he did not stop the breach in the beginning, but let it grow to that height as that it overthrew himself and many other honest men.[59] But *there are many devices in the heart of man, yet the counsel of the Lord shall stand.*[60]

Being thus in the ice, on Saturday the one and twentieth of June, at night Wilson the boatswain and Henry Greene came to me, lying in my cabin lame, and told me that they and the rest of their associates would shift[61] the company, and turn the master and all the sick men into the shallop and let them shift for themselves. For there was not fourteen days victual left for all the company, at[62] that poor allowance they were at, and that there they lay, the master not caring to go one way or other, and that they had not eaten anything these three days, and therefore were resolute either to mend or end, and what they had begun, they would go through with it or die. When I heard this, I told them I marvelled to hear so much from them, considering that they were

---

[58] i.e. was to last him.

[59] Why does Pricket think this action of Hudson's so significant? Is it because it shows Hudson's unawareness of the crew's suspicions that it was Hudson who was concealing food?

[60] Prov. 19, 21.

[61] Divide in two; see *OED*, 2.

[62] Even at.

married men, and had wives and children,[63] and that for their sakes they should not commit so foul a thing in the sight of God and man as that would be. For why should they banish themselves from their native country? Henry Greene bade me hold my peace, for he knew the worst, which was to be hanged when he came home, and therefore of the two he would rather be hanged at home than starved abroad. And for the good will they bare me, they would have me stay in the ship.[64] I gave them thanks, and told them that I came into her, not to forsake her, yet not[65] to hurt myself and others by any such deed. Henry Greene told me then that I must take my fortune in the shallop. If there be no remedy, said I, the will of God be done.[66]

Away went Henry Greene in a rage, swearing to cut his throat that went about to disturb them, and left Wilson by me, with whom I had some talk, but to no good; for he was so persuaded that there was no remedy now but to go on while it was hot, lest their party should fail them, and the mischief they had intended to others should light on themselves. Henry Greene came again, and demanded of him what I said. Wilson answered, 'He is in his old song, still patient.'[67] Then I spake to Henry Greene to stay three days, in which time I would so deal with the master that all should be well. So I dealt with him to forbear but two days, nay, twelve hours. 'There is no way,' then say they, 'but out of hand.' Then I told them that if they would stay till Monday, I would join with them to share[68] all the victuals in the ship, and would justify it when I came home; but this would not serve their turns. Wherefore I told them it was some worse matter they had in hand than they made show of, and that it was blood and revenge he sought, or else he would not at such a time of night undertake such a deed. Henry Greene with that taketh my Bible which lay before me and sware that he would do no man harm, and what he did was for the good of the voyage, and for nothing else; and that all the rest should do the like. The like did Wilson swear.

Henry Greene went his way, and presently came Juet, who, because

10

20

30

---

[63] It does not seem possible, from what Pricket has earlier said, that Greene was a family man.

[64] Very likely Purchas is correct in saying that the conspirators badly wanted Pricket because of the influence he might have with the promoters, whose agent he was. See p. 174.

[65] Nor yet.

[66] This highly ambiguous remark may refer to the prospect of being put into the shallop, but it can also signify a reluctant acquiescence in the fact of the mutiny. Three lines later, 'no remedy' certainly means that the mutiny cannot be stopped.

[67] Willing to suffer (Hudson's command).          [68] Share out.

he was an ancient man, I hoped to have found some reason in him. But he was worse than Henry Greene, for he sware plainly that he would justify this deed when he came home. After him came John Thomas[69] and Michael Perce, as birds of one feather; but because they are not living I will let them go, as then I did. Then came Moter and Bennet, of whom I demanded if they were well advised what they had taken in hand. They answered they were, and therefore came to take their oath.[70]

Now, because I am much condemned for this oath, as one of them
10 that plotted with them, and that by an oath I should bind them together to perform what they had begun, I thought good here to set down to the view of all how well their oath and deeds agreed. And thus it was. *You shall swear truth to God, your prince and country. You shall do nothing but to the glory of God, and the good of the action in hand, and harm to no man.* This was the oath, without adding or diminishing.

I looked for more of these companions (although these were too many) but there came no more. It was dark, and they in readiness to put this deed of darkness in execution. I called to Henry Greene and Wilson and prayed them not to go in hand with it in the dark, but to stay till the
20 morning. Now every man, I hope, would go to his rest, but wickedness sleepeth not; for Henry Greene keepeth the master company all night (and gave me bread, which his cabin-mate gave him)[71] and others are as watchful as he. Then I asked Henry Greene whom he would put out with the master. He said the carpenter, John King, and the sick men. I said they should not do well to part with the carpenter, what need soever they should have. Why the carpenter was in no more regard amongst them was, first, for that he and John King were condemned for wrong done in the victual. But the chiefest cause was for that the master loved him, and made him his mate upon his return out of our wintering place,
30 thereby displacing Robert Billet;[72] whereat they did grudge, because he

[69] Although Thomas seems to have been of Greene's party, he was at first put in the shallop, then brought back into the ship at the intercession of Clements.
[70] The account given of this important oath is confused. Above, it is Greene who proposes the oath; here, Pricket seems to be administering it. Then he goes on to imply that it was he who instigated it, as though he were perhaps attempting to defuse the plot by binding the conspirators in an oath which vows non-violence. See Introduction, p. 136.
[71] Pricket cannot mean that Greene was in Hudson's cabin; probably Greene kept watch on Hudson's cabin all night. The curiously irrelevant recollection that Greene brought the helpless Pricket some bread (apparently secreted by the resourceful boy Sims) suggests the use of the most valued commodity in the ship as a bribe.
[72] This is the only mention of this extraordinary act. See Introduction, p. 134.

could neither write nor read. And therefore, said they, the master and his ignorant mate would carry the ship whither the master pleased, the master forbidding any man to keep account or reckoning, having taken from all men whatsoever served for that purpose.[73] Well, I obtained of Henry Greene and Wilson that the carpenter should stay, by whose means I hoped, after they had satisfied themselves, that the master and the poor men might be taken into the ship again. Or I hoped[74] that some one or other would give some notice either to the carpenter, John King, or the master; for so it might have come to pass by some of them that were the most forward.[75]                                                                    10

Now, it shall not be amiss to show how we were lodged. And to begin in the cook-room, there lay Bennet[76] and the cooper,[77] lame. Without the cook-room, on the steerboard side, lay Thomas Wydhouse,[78] sick. Next to him lay Sydrack Faner,[79] lame; then the surgeon,[80] and John Hudson[81] with him. Next to them lay Wilson the boatswain, and then Arnold Lodlo next to him. In the gunroom lay Robert Juet and John Thomas. On the larboard side lay Michael Bute and Adam Moore, who had never been well since we lost our anchor. Next to them lay Michael Perce and Andrew Moter. Next to them, without the gunroom, lay John King, and with him Robert Billet. Next to them myself, and next to me      20 Francis Clements. In the midship, between the capstan and the pumps, lay Henry Greene and Nicholas Sims.

This night John King was late up, and they thought he had been with the master, but he was with the carpenter, who lay on the poop; and coming down from him was met by his cabin-mate,[82] as it were by chance, and so they came to their cabin together. It was not long ere it was day; then came Bennet for water for the kettle.[83] He rose[84] and went

---

7 men] man *Purchas*          17 Adam] Adria *Purchas*

[73] A remarkable indication of Hudson's distrust of his company. Staffe was convinced by Hudson's claim that no one knew enough about the ship's position to 'carry her home' (p. 161/34).

[74] Not an alternative but an additional hope.

[75] Presumably meaning that those whose quarters were forward could have got up on deck and gone aft to the poop without being noticed.

[76] Bennet Mathews, cook and trumpeter.          [77] Silvanus Bond.

[78] Woodhouse, the 'student in the mathematics'.

[79] Shadrach? The surname appears elsewhere as Fanner, Funer, Farmer.

[80] Edward Wilson.          [81] Hudson's son.

[82] Robert Billet, whose complicity is thus established.

[83] Bennet Mathews, the cook, is not allowed to get water from the casks himself; he must get it from the quartermaster.

[84] i.e. John King.

into the hold; when he was in they shut the hatch on him (but who kept it down I know not). Up upon the deck went Bennet.

In the meantime, Henry Greene and another went to the carpenter and held him with a talk till the master came out of his cabin, which he soon did. Then came John Thomas and Bennet before him, while Wilson bound his arms behind him. He asked them what they meant. They told him he should know when he was in the shallop. Now Juet, while this was-a-doing, came to John King into the hold, who was provided for him, for he had got a sword of his own and kept him at a bay, and might have killed him, but others came to help him; and so he came up to the master. The master called to the carpenter and told him that he was bound, but I heard no answer he made. Now Arnold Lodlo and Michael Bute railed at them[85] and told them their knavery would show itself.

Then was the shallop haled up to the ship side; and the poor, sick, and lame men were called upon to get them out of their cabins into the shallop. The master called to me, who came out of my cabin, as well as I could, to the hatchway to speak with him.[86] Where, on my knees, I besought them for the love of God to remember themselves, and to do as they would be done unto. They bade me keep myself well and get me into my cabin, not suffering the master to speak with me. But when I came into my cabin again, he called to me at the horn which gave light into my cabin,[87] and told me that Juet would overthrow us all. 'Nay,' said I, 'it is that villain Henry Greene.' And I spake it not softly.

Now was the carpenter at liberty, who asked them if they would be hanged when they came home. And as for himself, he said, he would not stay in the ship unless they would force him. They bade him go then, for they would not stay him. 'I will,' said he, 'so I may have my chest with me, and all that is in it.' They said he should, and presently they put it into the shallop. Then he came down to me to take his leave of me, who persuaded him to stay, which if he did, he might so work that all should be well. He said he did not think but they would be glad to take them in again. For he was so persuaded by the master, that there was not one in all the ship that could tell how to carry her home. But (saith he) if we must part, which we will not willingly do (for they would follow the ship),

[85] i.e. at the mutineers; these two were later put in the shallop.
[86] Presumably his lameness prevented him from managing the ladder to the upper deck.
[87] Without a plan of the ship one cannot say where this scuttle was. Luke Fox in his paraphrase reads 'horn window' for 'horn' (Christy, p. 143).

he prayed me, if we came to the capes[88] before them, that I would leave some token that we had been there, near to the place where the fowls bred, and he would do the like for us. And so, with tears, we parted.

Now were the sick men driven out of their cabins into the shallop. But John Thomas was Francis Clements' friend, and Bennet was the cooper's; so as there were words between them and Henry Greene, one saying that they should go, and the other swearing that they should not go, but such as were in the shallop should return. When Henry Greene heard that, he was compelled to give place, and to put out Arnold Lodlo 10 and Michael Bute, which with much ado they did.[89]

In the mean time, there were some of them that plied their work as if the ship had been entered by force, and they had free leave to pillage, breaking up chests and rifling all places. One of them came by me, who asked me what they should do. I answered, he should make an end of what he had begun, for I saw him do nothing but shark[90] up and down. Now were all the poor men in the shallop, whose names are as followeth: Henry Hudson, John Hudson, Arnold Lodlo, Sidrack Faner, Philip Staffe, Thomas Woodhouse, or Wydhouse,[91] Adam Moore, John King, Michael Bute. The carpenter got of them a piece, and powder and shot, 20 and some pikes, an iron pot, with some meal, and other things.

They stood out of the ice, the shallop being fast to the stern of the ship; and so, when they were nigh out (for I cannot say they were clean out) they cut her head-fast[92] from the stern of our ship. Then out with their topsails, and towards the east they stood in a clear sea. In the end they took in their topsails, righted their helm, and lay under their foresail till they had ransacked and searched all places in the ship. In the hold they found one of the vessels of meal whole, and the other half spent, for we had but two. We found also two firkins of butter, some twenty-seven piece of pork, half a bushel of pease. But in the master's cabin we found 30 two hundred of biscuit cakes, a peck of meal, of beer to the quantity of a butt, one with another. Now it was said that the shallop was come within

---

19 John King] Henrie King *Purchas*

[88] Digges and Wolstenholme.

[89] It looks as though John Thomas and Silvanus Bond, the sick cooper, had been put into the shallop and that Clements and Bennet Mathews objected. Greene and Wilson must have insisted on two other victims to replace them, and the unhappy Lodlo and Bute were forced in.

[90] Pilfer.

[91] Purchas probably inserted this alternative spelling.

[92] Bow rope.

sight; they let fall the mainsail and out with their topsails, and fly as from an enemy.

Then I prayed them yet to remember themselves; but William Wilson, more than the rest, would hear of no such matter. Coming nigh the east shore, they cast about and stood to the west, and came to an island, and anchored in sixteen or seventeen fathom water. So they sent the boat and the net ashore to see if they could have a draught, but could not for rocks and great stones. Michael Perce killed two fowl, and here they found good store of that weed which we called cockle-grass[93] in our wintering place, whereof they gathered store and came aboard again. Here we lay that night, and the best part of the next day, in all which time we saw not the shallop, or ever after.

Now Henry Greene came to me and told me that it was the company's will that I should come up into the master's cabin and take charge thereof. I told him it was more fit for Robert Juet. He said he should not come in it, nor meddle with the master's card or journals. So up I came, and Henry Greene gave me the key of the master's chest, and told me then, that he had laid the master's best things together, which he would use himself when time did serve. The bread was also delivered me by tale.[94]

The wind serving, we stood to the north-east; and this was Robert Billet's course, contrary to Robert Juet, who would have gone to the north-west. We had the eastern shore still in sight, and in the night had a stout gale of wind, and stood afore it till we met with ice, into the which we ran from thin to thick till we could go no further for ice, which lay so thick ahead of us (and the wind brought it after us astern) that we could not stir, backward nor forward; but so lay embayed fourteen days in worse ice than ever we met to deal withal, for we had been where there was greater store, but it was not so broad upon the water as this; for this floating ice contained miles and half-miles in compass, where we had a deep sea, and a tide of flood and ebb which set north-west and south-east.

Here Robert Juet would have gone to the north-west, but Robert Billet was confident to go through to the north-east, which he did. At last, being clear of this ice, he continued his course in sight of the eastern shore till he raised four islands which lay north and south;[95] but we passed them six or seven leagues, the wind took us so short. Then we

93 Scurvy-grass.  94 By number as distinguished from weight (*OED*, tale, *sb.*, 6*b*).
95 Not easily identifiable.

stood back to them again and came to an anchor between two of the most northermost. We sent the boat ashore to see if there were anything there to be had, but found nothing but cockle-grass, whereof they gathered store, and so returned aboard.

Before we came to this place, I might well see that I was kept in the ship against Henry Greene's mind, because I did not favour their proceedings better than I did.[96] Then he began, very subtly, to draw me to take upon me to search for those things which himself had stolen, and accused me of a matter no less than treason amongst us, that I had deceived the company of thirty cakes of bread. Now they began to talk  10 amongst themselves that England was no safe place for them, and Henry Greene swore the ship should not come into any place, but keep the sea still till he had the king's majesty's hand and seal to show for his safety. They had many devices in their heads, but Henry Greene in the end was their captain, and so called of them.

From these islands we stood to the north-east, and the easter land still in sight. We raised those islands that our master called Romney's Islands.[97] Between these islands and the shallow ground to the east of them, our master went down into the first great bay. We kept the east shore still in our sight, and coming thwart of the low land we ran on a  20 rock that lay under water, and struck but once, for if she had,[98] we might have been made inhabitants of that place; but God sent us soon off without any harm that we saw. We continued our course and raised land ahead of us which stretched out to the north, which when they saw they said plainly that Robert Billet by his northerly course had left the capes to the south, and that they were best to seek down to the south in time for relief before all was gone, for we had small store left. But Robert Billet would follow the land to the north, saying that he hoped in God to find somewhat to relieve us that way as soon as to the south. I told them that this land was the main of Worsenhome Cape, and that the shallow rocky  30 ground was the same that the master went down by when he went into the great bay. Robert Juet and all said it was not possible, unless the master had brought the ship over land; and [I] willed them[99] to look

33  and I willed] and willed *Purchas*

[96]  i.e. at the time of the mutiny.

[97]  (Now Smith Island.) Named after Rebecca, Lady Romney, one of the backers of the voyage, and later a member of the North-Western Company. She was the wife of Sir William Romney, a City associate of Sir Thomas Smith.

[98]  Something is missing; the meaning is 'and if she had struck more heavily'.

[99]  Pricket is presumably speaking of his effort to convince the sceptics that they had not overshot the capes.

into the master's card, and their course, how well they did agree.

We stood to the east, and left the mainland to the north, by many small islands, into a narrow gut[100] between two lands, and there came to an anchor. The boat went ashore on the north side, where we found the great horn,[101] but nothing else. The next day we went to the south side, but found nothing there save cockle-grass, of which we gathered. This grass was a great relief unto us, for without it we should hardly have got to the capes for want of victual. The wind serving, we stood out, but before we could get clean out the wind came to the west, so that we were
10 constrained to anchor on the north side.

The next day we weighed and doubled the point of the north land, which is high land, and so continueth to the capes, lying north and south, some five and twenty or thirty leagues. To the north we stood to see store of those fowls that breed in the capes, and to kill some with our shot, and to fetch them with our boat. We raised the capes with joy, and bare for them, and came to the islands that lie in the mouth of the strait; but bearing in between the rocky isles we ran on a rock that lay under water, and there stuck fast eight or nine hours. It was ebbing water when we thus came on, so the flood set us afloat, God guiding both wind and sea
20 that it was calm and fair weather. The ebb came from the east and the flood from the west.[102] When we were afloat, we stood more near to the east shore, and there anchored.

The next day, being the seven and twentieth of July, we sent the boat to fetch some fowl, and the ship should weigh and stand as near as they could, for the wind was against us. They had a great way to row, and by that means they could not reach to the place where the fowl bred; but found good store of gulls, yet hard to come by, on the rocks and cliffs; but with their pieces they killed some thirty, and towards night returned. Now, we had brought our ship more near to the mouth of the straits, and
30 there came to an anchor in eighteen or twenty fathom water, upon a reef or shelf of ground, which after they had weighed their anchor and stood more near to the place where the fowl bred, they could not find it again, nor no place like it, but were fain to turn to and fro in the mouth of the

---

30 reef] Riffe *Purchas*

[100] Passage or channel.

[101] Presumably a large tusk or horn which they had brought home. Luke Fox was probably right in assuming that it came from the 'sea-unicorn' (narwhal) (Christy, p. 150).

[102] Christy's long note (p. 150) describes the extraordinary attention paid by Trinity House, by Purchas, and by Dudley Digges to this 'flood from the west', arguing that 'it came from the Southern sea'. This grounding is confirmed in Billet's log (Christy, p. 633).

strait, and to be in danger of rocks, because they could not find ground to let fall an anchor in, the water was so deep.

The eight and twentieth day, the boat went to Digges his Cape for fowl, and made directly for the place where the fowl bred, and being near, they saw seven boats come about the eastern point towards them. When the savages saw our boat, they drew themselves together, and drew their lesser boats into their bigger. And when they had done, they came rowing to our boat and made signs to the west; but they made ready for all assays. The savages came to them, and by signs grew familiar one with another, so as our men took one of theirs into our boat, and they took one of ours into their boat. Then they carried our man to a cove where their tents stood, toward the west of the place where the fowl bred. So they carried him into their tents, where he remained till our men returned with theirs. Our boat went to the place where the fowl bred, and were desirous to know how the savages killed their fowl. He showed them the manner how, which was thus. They take a long pole with a snare at the end which they put about the fowl's neck, and so pluck them down. When our men knew that they had a better way of their own, they showed him the use of our pieces, which at one shot would kill seven or eight. To be short, our boat returned to their cove for our man, and to deliver theirs. When they came, they made great joy, with dancing and leaping and stroking of their breasts. They offered divers things to our men, but they only took some morse's teeth,[103] which they gave them for a knife and two glass buttons. And so, receiving our man, they came aboard, much rejoicing at this chance, as if they had met with the most simple and kind people of the world.

And Henry Greene, more than the rest, was so confident, that, by no means, we should take care to stand upon our guard; God blinding him so, that where he made reckoning to receive great matters from these people, he received more than he looked for, and that suddenly, by being made a good example for all men that make no conscience of doing evil; and that we take heed of the savage people, how simple soever they seem to be.[104]

The next day, the nine and twentieth of July, they made haste to be ashore, and because the ship rid too far off, they weighed and stood as near to the place where the fowl bred as they could. And because I was lame, I was to go in the boat to carry such things as I had in the cabin, of everything somewhat. And so, with more haste than good speed, and not

---

[103] Walrus tusks.
[104] This moralizing strongly suggests the hand of Samuel Purchas.

without swearing, away we went; Henry Greene, William Wilson, John Thomas, Michael Perce, Andrew Moter, and myself. When we came near the shore, the people were on the hills, dancing and leaping. To the cove we came, where they had drawn up their boats. We brought our boat to the east side of the cove, close to the rocks. Ashore they went, and made fast the boat to a great stone on the shore. The people came, and everyone had somewhat in his hand to barter. But Henry Greene swore they should have nothing till he had venison, for that they had so promised him by signs.

10    Now when we came, they made signs to their dogs (whereof there were many, like mongrels, as big as hounds) and pointed to their mountain, and to the sun, clapping their hands. Then Henry Greene, John Thomas, and William Wilson stood hard by the boat head; Michael Perce and Andrew Moter were got up upon the rock, a-gathering of sorrel. Not one of them had any weapon about him, not so much as a stick, save Henry Greene only, who had a piece of a pike in his hand. Nor saw I anything that they had wherewith to hurt us. Henry Greene and William Wilson had looking-glasses and jew's trumps,[105] and bells, which they were showing the people. The savages standing round about them, one of them came into the boat's head to me to show me a bottle. I made signs to him to get him ashore, but he made as though he had not understood me, whereupon I stood up, and pointed him ashore. In the meantime, another stole behind me to the stern of the boat, and when I saw him ashore that was in the head of the boat, I sat down again, but suddenly I saw the leg and foot of a man by me. Wherefore I cast up my head and saw the savage with his knife in his hand, who struck at my breast over my head. I cast up my right arm to save my breast; he wounded my arm and struck me into the body under my right pap. He struck a second blow, which I met with my left hand,

30    and then he struck me into the right thigh, and had like to have cut off my little finger of the left hand. Now I had got hold of the string of the knife, and had wound it about my left hand, he striving with both his hands to make an end of that he had begun. I found him but weak in the grip (God enabling me), and getting hold of the sleeve of his left arm, so bare him from me. His left side lay bare to me, which when I saw, I put his sleeve off his left arm into my left hand, holding the string of the knife fast in the same hand, and having got my right hand at liberty, I sought for somewhat wherewith to strike him, not remembering my dagger at my

---

[105] The same as jew's harps.

side; but looking down I saw it, and therewith struck him into the body and the throat.

Whiles I was thus assaulted in the boat, our men were set upon on the shore. John Thomas and William Wilson had their bowels cut, and Michael Perce and Henry Greene being mortally wounded came tumbling into the boat together. When Andrew Moter saw this medley, the boat, hanging on the stern thereof till Michael Perce took him in, who manfully made good the head of the boat against the savages, that manfully made good the head of the boat against the savages, that pressed sore upon us. Now Michael Perce had got an hatchet, wherewith I saw him strike one of them, that he lay sprawling in the sea. Henry Greene crieth 'Coragio!' and layeth about him with his truncheon. I cried to them to clear the boat, and Andrew Moter cried to be taken in. The savages betook them to their bows and arrows, which they sent amongst us, wherewith Henry Greene was slain outright, and Michael Perce received many wounds, and so did the rest. Michael Perce cleareth the boat, and puts it from the shore, and helpeth Andrew Moter in. But in turning of the boat, I received a cruel wound in my back with an arrow. Michael Perce and Andrew Moter rowed the boat away, which when the savages saw, they ran to their boats, and I feared they would have launched them, to have followed us, but they did not; and our ship was in the middle of the channel, and could not see us.

Now, when they had rowed a good way from the shore, Michael Perce fainted and could row no more. Then was Andrew Moter driven to stand in the boat head, and waft[106] to the ship, which at the first saw us not, and when they did, they could not tell what to make of us, but in the end they stood for us, and so took us up. Henry Greene was thrown out of the boat into the sea, and the rest were had aboard, the savage being yet alive yet without sense. But they died all there that day, William Wilson swearing and cursing in most fearful manner.[107] Michael Perce lived two days after, and then died. Thus you have heard the tragical end of Henry Greene and his mates, whom they called captain; these four being the only lusty men[108] in all the ship.

The poor number that was left[109] were to ply our ship to and fro in the

---

[106] Wave.

[107] At the Admiralty examination in 1617, Francis Clements spoke of those 'who were slain by the savages, having their bellies ripped up, then their gut hung out when they came on board, and died aboard' (Quinn 1979, iv, p. 296).

[108] Healthy men.

[109] Of the nine left in the ship, Abacuck Pricket, Edward Wilson, Bennet Mathews, and Silvanus Bond were not seamen.

mouth of the strait, for there was no place to anchor in near hand. Besides, they were to go in the boat to kill fowl to bring us home, which they did, although with danger to us all. For if the wind blew, there was an high sea, and the eddies of the tides would carry the ship so near the rocks as it feared[110] our master, for so I will now call him.[111] After they had killed some two hundred fowl, with great labour, on the south cape, we stood to the east; but when we were six or seven leagues from the capes, the wind came up at east. Then we stood back to the capes again, and killed an hundred fowl more. After this the wind came to the west, so we were driven to go away, and then our master stood (for the most) along by the north shore, till he fell into broken ground about the Queen's Foreland, and there anchored. From thence we went to God's Mercies, and from thence to those islands which lie in the mouth of our strait, not seeing the land till we were ready to run our bowsprit against the rocks in a fog. But it cleared a litle, and then we might see ourselves enclosed with rocky islands, and could find no ground to anchor in. There our master lay a-try[112] all night, and the next day, the fog continuing, they sought for ground to anchor in, and found some in an hundred and odd fathomes of water. The next day we weighed and stood to the east, but before we came here we had put ourselves to hard allowance, as half a fowl a day with the pottage. For yet we had some meal left, and nothing else. Then they began to make trial of all whatsoever. We had flayed our fowl, for they will not pull; and Robert Juet was the first that made use of the skins by burning of the feathers; so they became a great dish of meat, and as for the garbage, it was not thrown away.

After we were clear of these islands, which lie out with two points, one to the south-east and the other to the north, making a bay to the sight as if there were no way through, we continued our course east-south-east and south and by east to raise the Desolations, from thence to shape our course for Ireland. Thus we continued divers days, but the wind coming against us made us to alter our course, and by the means of Robert Juet, who persuaded the company that they should find great relief in Newfoundland if our countrymen were there, and if they were gone before we came, yet should we find great store of bread and fish left ashore by them. But how true, I give God thanks we did not try. Yet we stood to the south-west and to the west almost to 57 degrees, when, by

---

110 Frightened.
111 Billet.
112 Lay to, under bare poles or with trysail only.

the will of God, the wind came up at south-west. Then the master asked me if he should take the benefit of this wind, and shape his course for Ireland. I said it was best to go where we knew corn grew, and not to seek it where it was cast away and not to be found.

Towards Ireland now we stood, with prosperous winds for many days together. Then was all meal spent, and our fowl resty[113] and dry. But, being no remedy, we were content with the salt broth for dinner and the half fowl for supper. Now went our candles to wrack, and Bennet our cook made a mess of meat of the bones of the fowl, frying them with candle-grease till they were crisp, and with vinegar put to them made a   10 good dish of meat. Our vinegar was shared, and to every man a pound of candles delivered for a week, as a great dainty. Now Robert Juet, by his reckoning, saith we were within sixty or seventy leagues of Ireland, when we had two hundred thither. And sure, our course was so much the longer through our evil steerage, for our men became so weak that they could not stand at the helm, but were fain to sit.

Then Robert Juet died, for mere want, and all our men were in despair, and said we were past Ireland, and our last fowl were in the steep-tub.[114] So our men cared not which end forward, insomuch as our master was driven to look to their labour as well as his own. For some of   20 them would sit and see the foresail or mainsail fly up to the tops, the sheets[115] being either flown or broken, and would not help it them- selves, nor call to others for help, which much grieved the master. Now in this extremity it pleased God to give us sight of land, not far from the place our master said he would fall withal, which was the Bay of Galloway,[116] and we fell to the west of the Derses,[117] and so stood along by the coast to the south-west. In the end, there was a joyful cry, 'A sail! a sail!', towards which they stood, then they saw more; but to the nearest we stood, and called to him. His bark was of Fowy,[118] and was at anchor a-fishing. He came to us, and brought us into Berehaven.[119]   30

Here we stayed a few days and dealt with the Irish to supply our wants, but found no relief, for in this place there was neither bread, drink, nor money to be had amongst them. Wherefore they advised us to deal with

---

[113] Stale.
[114] i.e. had been put to soak.
[115] Lines attached to sails.
[116] Galway.
[117] Dursey Island, Co. Cork.
[118] Fowey, Cornwall.
[119] In Bantry Bay. The date of reaching Ireland is given by Purchas as 6 Sept. 1611 (Asher, p. 144).

our countrymen who were there a-fishing; which we did, but found them so cold in kindness that they would do nothing without present money, whereof we had none in the ship. In the end, we procured one John Waymouth, master of the bark that brought us into this harbour, to furnish us with money, which he did, and received our best cable and anchor in pawn for the same. With this money, our master, with the help of John Waymouth, bought bread, beer, and beef.

Now, as we were beholding to Waymouth for his money, so were we to one Captain Taylor[120] for making of our contracts with Waymouth,
10 by whose means he took a bill for our cable and anchor, and for the men's wages, who would not go with us unless Waymouth would pass his word for the same; for they made show that they were not willing to go with us for any wages.[121] Whereupon Captain Taylor swore he would press them, and then if they would not go, he would hang them.[122]

In conclusion, we agreed for three pound ten shillings a man to bring our ship to Plymouth or Dartmouth, and to give the pilot five pound. But if the wind did not serve, but that they were driven to put into Bristow, they were to have four pound ten shillings a man, and the pilot six pound. Omitting therefore further circumstances, from Berehaven we
20 came to Plymouth, and so to an anchor before the castle; and from Plymouth, with fair wind and weather, without stop or stay we came to the Downs,[123] from thence to Gravesend, where most of our men went ashore, and from thence came on this side Erith, and there stopped; where our master Robert Billet came aboard,[124] and so had me up to London with him, and so we came to Sir Thomas Smith's together.

---

[120] It becomes clear that he must have been in command of a man-of-war. Pirates infested the south-west coast of Ireland, very well organized under English 'admirals'. In the autumn of 1611 a squadron of nineteen pirate ships had been sighted. 'Sometimes there was a King's ship at hand and sometimes there was not' (R. Bagwell, *Ireland Under the Stuarts*, i. 1909, pp. 101–7). It looks as though Captain Taylor was on fishery protection duty.

[121] This refers to the sailors who had been recruited to take the ship back to England.

[122] Initially, when they tried to muster a crew to take the Discovery back to England, they met with a refusal, whatever wages were to be paid. Then the men in question agreed to go only if Waymouth guaranteed their wages. At this Taylor threatened to use his authority to press them as if for naval service.

[123] The roadstead off the east Kent coast between north and south Foreland.

[124] He must have gone ashore at Gravesend. He is described as being 'of St. Katharine's' in the Admiralty examinations.

## 3. *Thomas Woodhouse*
### (introduced by Samuel Purchas)

*Forasmuch as this report of Pricket may haply be suspected by some as not so friendly to Hudson, who returned with that company which had so cruelly exposed Hudson and his, and therefore may seem to lay heavier imputation, and rip up occasions[1] further than they will believe, I have also added the report of Thomas Widhouse, one of the exposed company, who ascribeth those occasions of discord to Juet. I take not on me to sentence; no, not to examine. I have presented the evidence just as I had it; let the bench censure, hearing with both ears that which with both eyes they may see in those and these notes. To which I have first prefixed his letter to Master Samuel Macham.[2]*

Master Macham,                                                                          10
    I heartily commend me unto you, &c. I can write unto you no news, though I have seen much, but such as every English fisherman haunting these coasts can report better than myself.
    We kept our Whitsunday in the north-east end of Island, and I think I never fared better in England than we feasted there. They of the country are very poor, and live miserably; yet we found therein store of fresh fish and dainty fowl. I myself in an afternoon killed so much fowl as feasted all our company, being three and twenty persons, at one time only, with partridges, besides curlew, plover, mallard, teal, and goose. I have seen two hot baths in Island, and have been in one of them. We are resolved to   20
try the uttermost, and lie only expecting a fair wind, and to refresh our selves, to avoid the ice, which now is come off the west coasts, of which we have seen whole islands, but God be thanked have not been in danger of any. Thus I desire all your prayers for us.
    From Island, this thirtieth of May, 1610.

A note found in the desk of Thomas Wydowse, student in the mathematics, he being one of them who was put into the shallop.

The tenth day of September, 1610, after dinner, our master called all the company together, to hear and bear witness of the abuse of some of the company, it having been the request of Robert Juet that the master

---

[1] Present circumstances (in a discrediting way).
[2] A London publisher and bookseller, originally from Ashby-de-la-Zouch. This same year (1611) he published John Donne's *Anatomy of the World*. I assume that Woodhouse sent his letter back by an English fishing-boat, and that Purchas got the letter from Macham.

should redress some abuses and slanders, as he called them, against this Juet. Which thing after the master had examined and heard with equity what he could say for himself, there were proved so many and great abuses and mutinous matters against the master and action, by Juet, that there was danger to have suffered them longer; and it was fit time to punish and cut off farther occasions of the like mutinies.

It was proved to his face, first with Bennet Mathew our trumpet, upon our first sight of Island, and he confessed, that he supposed that in the action would be manslaughter, and prove bloody to some.

10 Secondly, at our coming from Island, in hearing of the company, he did threaten to turn the head of the ship home from the action; which at that time was by our master wisely pacified, hoping of amendment.

Thirdly, it was deposed by Philip Staffe, our carpenter, and Ladlie Arnold, to his face upon the holy Bible, that he persuaded them to keep muskets charged and swords ready in their cabins, for they should be charged with shot ere the voyage were over.

Fourthly, we being pestered in the ice, he had used words tending to mutiny, discouragement, and slander of the action, which easily took effect in those that were timorous; and had not the master in time 20 prevented, it might easily have overthrown the voyage. And now lately being embayed in a deep bay, which the master had desire to see for some reasons to himself known, his word tended altogether to put the company into a fray of extremity, by wintering in cold;[3] jesting at our master's hope to see Bantam by Candlemas.[4]

For these and divers other base slanders against the master, he was deposed, and Robert Bylot, who had showed himself honestly respecting the good of the action, was placed in his stead the master's mate.

Also Francis Clement, the boatswain, at this time was put from his office, and William Wilson, a man thought more fit, preferred to his 30 place. This man had basely carried himself to our master and to the action.

Also Adrian Mooter was appointed boatswain's mate; and a promise by the master that from this day Juet's wages should remain to Bylot, and the boatswain's overplus of wages should be equally divided between Wilson and one John King, to the owners' good liking, one of the quartermasters, who had very well carried themselves to the furtherance of the business.

[3] i.e. put them into extreme terror by talk of having to winter in the ice.
[4] i.e. be in Java by the beginning of Feb. Juet's scepticism may have been dispiriting but it was fully justified.

Also the master promised, if the offenders yet behaved themselves henceforth honestly, he would be a means for their good, and that he would forget injuries, with other admonitions.

*These things thus premised touching Hudson's exposing, and God's just judgements on the exposers, as Pricket hath related (whom they reserved, as is thought, in hope by Sir Dudley Digges his master to procure their pardon at their return), I thought good to add that which I have further received from good intelligence, that the ship coming aground at Digges' Island, in 62 degrees 44 minutes, a great flood came from the west and set them on float; an argument of an open passage from the South Sea to that, and consequently to these seas.*[5]  10 *The weapons and arts which they saw, beyond those of other savages, are arguments hereof. He which assaulted Pricket in the boat had a weapon broad and sharp indented of bright steel, such as they use in Java, riveted into a handle of morse tooth.*

[5]  See note to Pricket, p. 165/21.

# III

*The Last Voyage of*
*Sir Walter Ralegh*
*1617–1618*

FIG. 5. Sir Walter Ralegh. Engraving by Simon Passe, published by Compton Holland. This first appeared in the third edition of Ralegh's *History of the World*, which, though dated 1617, was actually the first of two issues of 1621. Possibly commissioned for Henry Holland's *Herwologia* of 1620, but left out as too risky to publish. See Lionel Cust, 'The Portraits of Sir Walter Ralegh' (Walpole Society, vol. viii, 1919–20), pp. 1–15. (Reproduced by permission from the copy of the 1628 edition of *The History of the World* in the City of Birmingham Public Library)

# INTRODUCTION

## 1. *The Voyage*

THE story of Ralegh's last voyage is more than a story of ships and men. It is a complex story of considerable political importance, spanning many years and involving the relationship of several governments. At its most critical points the story, always confused, becomes shrouded in complete mystery, in spite of a host of contemporary witnesses and a library of later commentary and argument.

The documents which follow tell the story only from Ralegh's point of view; in his journal, where he recorded events as they happened until the moment when he heard of the failure of the Orinoco task force; in his letters to Winwood and to his wife reporting that failure and the death of his son; in his 'Apology', written back in England during a few days' respite on his final journey under escort to London; and in two letters, to Lord Carew and to the King, written in the weeks before his execution. This part of the introduction offers a brief overview of the whole enterprise in order to put the documents in their context.

Ralegh fell from favour with Queen Elizabeth in 1592 because she had discovered his secret marriage to Elizabeth Throckmorton, one of her maids-in-waiting, who bore their first child, Damerei, in March of that year. In August husband and wife were imprisoned for a time in the Tower. Ralegh claimed, with reason, that his first expedition to Guiana in 1595 was in part undertaken in order to regain royal favour, or 'the least taste of the greatest plenty formerly possessed', as he wrote in the Epistle Dedicatory of *The Discovery of Guiana*. In 1603 Ralegh was in the Tower again, this time on a suspended sentence of death, having been put on trial by Elizabeth's successor, James, and found guilty, on negligible evidence, of high treason. His second voyage to Guiana, after twelve years' imprisonment, was also undertaken to reinstate himself with his monarch.

Guiana mesmerized Ralegh. He was as determined to establish the English in Guiana as he had been to establish them in Virginia in the 1580s. It is 'a country that hath yet her maidenhead,' he wrote in *The Discovery*; 'a better Indies for her majesty than the king of Spain hath any, which if it shall please her highness to undertake, I shall most willingly end the rest of my days in following the same' (Schomburgk, pp. 115, x). It did not so please Queen Elizabeth, but Ralegh did not give up. The special attraction of Guiana was El Dorado, golden man or golden city, centre of the legendary civilization of Manoa, situated on a vast lake somewhere in the interior. The prospect of gold was the central point in Ralegh's advocacy of imperial development.

In his 1595 expedition, with a royal commission to discover and subdue heathen lands, he had attacked and overcome the soldiers of Antonio de Berrio, the Spanish governor in Trinidad, and penetrated the Orinoco as far as the Caroní River, 150 miles from the seaboard. He was particularly concerned to make contact with the Indian chieftains, the caciques, whom he treated with great courtesy, and on whom he impressed the role of the English as their deliverer from the cruelty and oppression of the Spaniards. These contacts and these promises were the groundwork of his later relations with the country and the foundation of almost all his hopes of an English future in Guiana. The remainder of his hopes centred on gold. Obviously he made no progress towards Manoa and El Dorado. But at the mouth of the Caroní near the settlement of the influential Topiawari (with whom Ralegh had very full negotiations) he found what he regarded as very promising ore. More important, as has come to light from some recently discovered Spanish documents, it seems that Topiawari secretly took Ralegh and Lawrence Keymis and one other to a place five or six miles east of his town and, after digging in the sand, exposed deposits of alluvial gold. Ralegh brough some of the earth away (Lorimer 1982). Some miles further to the east, a cacique called Putijma took Keymis to see a mine near Mount Iconuri. He was not shown the actual mine, which was supposed to be very secret and very special (Hakluyt, x. 468–9).

Ralegh sent Keymis back the following year to make a further exploration of the Guianan coast and possible routes to Manoa, and to keep in touch with the Indian leaders. Keymis's account, promptly published on his return (1596), supported Ralegh's own vivid and impressive *Discovery of the Large, Rich, and Beautiful Empire of Guiana*, also published in 1596, as a vigorous advertisement for colonial investment in the land. Keymis's account was prefaced by Chapman's imperialist poem, 'De Guiana carmen epicum', and Keymis's own Latin poem to his fellow-scholar Thomas Harriot (Keymis had been a fellow of Balliol). His purpose in writing his account, he said, was 'to remove all fig-leaves from our unbelief'; an odd image, but with some relevance to the Edenic description of the country. A theme not found in *The Discovery* is that of conversion to Protestantism. Might it not be the case, he asked, that the Almighty 'hath a work in this place, instead of papistry, to make the sincere light of His gospel to shine on this people?'

If the Castilians, pretending a religious care of planting Christianity in those parts, have in their doings preached nought else but avarice, rapine, blood, death, and destruction to those naked and sheeplike creatures of God, erecting statues and trophies of victory unto themselves in the slaughters of millions of innocents, doth not the cry of the poor succourless ascend unto the heavens? (Hakluyt, x. 488)

Keymis did not revisit the sites of any of the possible gold-mines. When he reached Topiawari's Port, near the mouth of the Caroní, he found that the Spaniards had established a settlement of 'some twenty or thirty houses'. Nervous of this new threat, his resolution to seek Putijma's mine weakened with the failure of the Indians to rally to him. But, he declared, 'myself and the remain of my few years I have bequeathed wholly to Raleana, and all my thoughts live only in that action'.

In later years, Ralegh attributed his own failure to return to Guiana to the Cadiz and Islands voyages of 1596 and 1597, and the Queen's refusal to allow a fleet to leave English waters during Tyrone's rebellion in Ireland (see p. 249). Nevertheless, he kept in touch with Guiana and the Indians by regularly sending out a ship or helping to finance other men's ventures even while in the Tower. Others followed his lead. The Dutch had faith enough in *The Discovery* to send an expedition up the Orinoco to look for gold, but found none. In 1602 Charles Leigh reconnoitred Guiana for a suitable site for a colony. He chose the River Wiapaco (now Oiapoque) and returned there in 1604 with forty-six people. The little colony endured until 1606. Leigh's main interest was in solving his personal financial problems by means of Guiana gold. His successor, Robert Harcourt, had wider views and hoped to exploit a whole range of commodities as well as find gold. He had the support of Prince Henry, who got James's consent for the founding of a Guiana colony in 1609. Again the Wiapaco was chosen. Harcourt made use of Ralegh's name to establish good relations with the Indians. His brother Michael stayed with the colony while Harcourt went back to England seeking further funds. He had little success, although in 1613 the Privy Council drew up a grant of colonial rights to Harcourt. It is not clear when his brother abandoned the colony (Williamson, pp. 41–51).

Meanwhile, San Thomé (Santo Tomé), the Spanish settlement on the Orinoco near the River Caroní, was doing well. It had become a boom town at the turn of the century when the search for Manoa was brisk, and its subsequent decline was halted when the new governor of 'Trinidad y Guayana', Fernando, son of old Berrio, decided he could make money out of tobacco. A flourishing illegal international trade developed. It was reckoned that Fernando sold 60,000 pounds of tobacco a year at Port of Spain in Trinidad and at San Thomé. As many as thirty foreign vessels might be found at Port of Spain, many of them English. In the season of October to December 1610, eight or nine ships visited San Thomé for the contraband traffic, and one English merchant left his factor there, John Brewer. Ralegh had a ship at Port of Spain in 1608 (Lorimer 1978, p. 132).

The Spanish authorities closed in on this traffic in 1611, and Berrio managed to sell off the last of his season's crop while manfully firing his guns at the buyers' ships (ibid. 142). To put himself in a good light with the authorities he massacred the crew of an English merchant, Captain Hall, in Trinidad—an atrocity which Ralegh indignantly, justifiably, and repeatedly cited as an example of the 'peace' which he was held to have broken (Apology, p. 247; letters to Carew and James, pp. 249 and 251).

All this activity in Guiana was fully known to the Government in London. Robert Cecil, Earl of Salisbury, Lord High Treasurer and Secretary of State, was much interested in Guianan ventures. He was receiving detailed information about the situation in the Orinoco from Sir Thomas Roe, who went out in 1609 with two ships (financed in part by Ralegh) to explore the Amazon, the Wiapoco, and the Orinoco in the hope of finding the way to Manoa. In 1611 Roe sent a letter to Salisbury (Harlow, pp. 104–6). 'I am now past the Wild Coast [the Guiana seaboard] and arrived at Port d'Espagne in the island of Trinidad, where are fifteen sail of ships freighting smoke [tobacco], English, French, Dutch.' The Spaniards were doing their best to make 'a new city' of San Thomé, but Roe thought Berrio was too lazy to carry the plans forward. He thought the settlement could easily be captured and held, particularly since (in his opinion) there was disaffection within and a possibility of enlisting Spaniards themselves against the town.

A prisoner in the Tower, Ralegh longed to join in this activity on 'the Wild Coast'. All the time that he was writing *The History of the World*, with its solemn warnings against the vanity of worldly aspiration, Guiana was beckoning to him as a means of obtaining his release. Its gold became the more real and tangible as the frustration of his inhibited life increased. In 1607 he had written to Salisbury a passionate pleading letter, telling him that samples he had brought back from Guiana in 1595 had been reassayed and were certainly gold-bearing. If he were freed to work the mine, it could be pretended that he was going to Virginia, and he would not go near the Spaniards. The mountain where the mine lay was near the riverside (Harlow, pp. 100–2). In a letter to Haddington, he swore to bring his party 'to a mountain, near a navigable river, covered with gold and silver ore' (ibid. 103).

It is clear that by 1611 the expedition was a possibility. But when Salisbury suggested sending Keymis ahead on his own, Ralegh at once became more cautious about the ease with which the mine could be found. It was sixteen years since they had visited the place, he wrote to Salisbury, and it would be a hard task for the pair of them to find the exact location (ibid. 110). But it seems that, with reluctance, he agreed to Keymis being sent ahead. A letter of 1611, written apparently to the Lords of the Council (ibid. 112–13), expresses his faith both in Keymis and the mine, but gives ample indication of the problems which he so often made light of.

And though it be a difficult matter—of exceeding difficulty—for any man to find the same acre of ground in a country desolate and overgrown which he hath seen but once, and that sixteen years since (which were hard enough to do upon Salisbury Plain), yet that your lordships may be satisfied of the truth I am contented to venture all I have, but my reputation, upon Keymis's memory.   (ibid. 113)

Ralegh stated that the gold he sought 'is found but at the root of the grass, in a broad and flat slate' (ibid. 110). This is what he said to Carew in 1611, and he repeated it in a document to the king which has only come to light in recent years; it dates perhaps from 1613.

And although I did not work this mine to any depth, because I valued it at nothing, yet seeing it lay within nine inches of the superficies and did rise up in a broad slate, and not in small veins, there was never a mine of gold in the world promising so great abundance.   (Strathmann, p. 263)

These words cannot apply to the deep ore of the Caroní mine, nor to Putijma's mine which Ralegh had never seen; they must refer to the gold which Topiawari uncovered for him by digging in the ground on that secret expedition a few miles from his town.

The 1611 negotiations had fizzled out, and Salisbury, like Ralegh's champion Prince Henry, died in 1612. But Ralegh refused to give up his scheme, as is quite clear from the Folger document just quoted. In it he proposed an expedition of four ships and two barks. He asked James to lend him two of the king's ships, being of smaller draught than the usual merchant ships and better armed. He argued that the enterprise would not 'breed unkindness' between James and the Spanish king because the undertaking was 'upon a place of mine own discovery, and of which the natural lords have submitted themselves to our late sovereign lady, Queen Elizabeth' (Strathmann, p. 266). The document provided a detailed costing of the expedition, from the charge of victualling 425 men for ten months, at £3,966. 13s. 4d., to the cost of four copper furnaces for distilling sea-water at £40.

By 1615 the political atmosphere had altered very much in Ralegh's favour with the appointment of the anti-Spanish Sir Ralph Winwood as Secretary of State. Ralegh sent him copies of his earlier correspondence with Salisbury and the King. With James moving towards the deeply unpopular project of marrying Prince Charles to the Infanta of Spain, the anti-Spain party was more than ready to let loose the renowned enemy of Spain on an expedition which must inevitably anger the Spaniards and make a decisive breach in the relations between the two countries (Gardiner, ii. 369). On 19 March 1616, a royal warrant instructed the Lieutenant of the Tower to 'permit Sir Walter Ralegh to go abroad to make preparations for his voyage'. He had to be attended by his keeper until January, when he was officially freed; but he was never pardoned.

James's motives in allowing Ralegh his freedom can only be guessed. Perhaps the most important was cupidity. He was extremely short of money; the dowry expected with the Infanta would be of very great benefit to the treasury, and so would Guiana gold. The possession of one would preclude the possession of the other. James could not have both, but, unwilling to forgo either, he continued to play for both. There was also the pressure of public opinion, and the desirability of being the champion of Protestantism (in conflict with a larger view of himself as European peacemaker). There must also have been the thought that by permitting Ralegh to go on this expedition he might have the opportunity of destroying a man he hated, whom he had crippled, but who still had the temerity, in prison, to write a *History of the World* whose contempt for princes had so angered James that he made a vain attempt to suppress it. Ralegh's failure, or his aggressiveness, might provide the grounds for putting him down for good.

What exactly Ralegh was going to do with his freedom now he had obtained it was a question in everyone's mind, including Ralegh's. He at once commissioned Phineas Pett, the king's shipwright, to build him a ship of 450 tons, to be named the Destiny, and he set about raising money by every possible means, selling land, borrowing, enlisting adventurers. His readiness to use the fleet he was gathering for purposes over and above Guiana is clearly indicated by the proposal that he should try to seize Genoa on behalf of Savoy, then at war with Spain. In his Protestant-champion mood, James agreed; but then changed his mind and told the Savoy ambassador he would not divert Ralegh from Guiana (Gardiner, iii. p. 52).

Ralegh was also negotiating with Huguenot interests in France. He seems to have suggested in particular that some French ships should join him in the Orinoco, and that in the event of failure he should have the haven of a French port. Sadly, the emissaries Ralegh used betrayed him (Harlow, p. 31).

The commission which James granted to Ralegh he later printed in his *Declaration*, put out to justify his action in executing Ralegh. It is well known that when the King saw the draft of the commission, he ordered that the phrase 'trusty and well-beloved' before Ralegh's name should be struck out. The commission nowhere specifically forbade Ralegh to enter land claimed by Spain or to attack Spaniards; nor, on the other hand, did it license Ralegh to take over and subdue lands held by the heathen. All it did was to permit him to visit places 'possessed and inhabited by heathen and savage people' to obtain commodities, including gold. The inhibiting restrictions which shackled the liberated Ralegh did not appear in the commission.

The role of the Spanish ambassador Sarmiento (soon to become Count Gondomar) in providing the shackles is very well known. He was understandably furious that one who was promising to meet all the Spanish king's stipulations for the marriage of Prince Charles to the Infanta should at the same time be countenancing the release into the open sea of a large armed fleet whose objctives could not fail to harm Spanish interests. Gondomar did not believe that Ralegh was going to Guiana; he thought he would be making spoil wherever he could. In so far as the Orinoco was indeed his objective, he was proposing an invasion of Spanish territory.

James did not respond to Gondomar's indignation by halting the expedition. But he tells us in the *Declaration* that he extracted from Ralegh a 'close letter'—a confidential or private letter, that is—'containing a solemn profession' that he had no other objective than the gold-mines of Guiana, and that 'he never meant or would commit any outrages or spoils upon the king of Spain's subjects' (Harlow, p. 336). Ralegh himself acknowledged in his journal, when he was not writing directly for publication, that he had received 'express commandment' from James not 'to invade any of the Spanish king's territories' (p. 200/ 4). Winwood was instructed to give Ralegh's letter of assurance to Gondomar, and also to hand him a complete list and description of Ralegh's vessels and their proposed route. A letter from the Spanish authorities conveying this information was found by Keymis in the settlement of San Thomé.

Neither Ralegh nor James could have believed for one minute that it would be possible to perform this expedition without trespassing on what the Spaniards claimed as their territory, or, if the mine were to be fully exploited, without some physical confrontation with the Spanish forces whose presence on the banks of the Orinoco had been a fact of life for years. Ralegh must have assumed that if he struck it rich James would openly accept Ralegh's position that Guiana was English territory by right, and would varnish over any clash with the Spaniards. The main burden of Ralegh's Apology is that by letting him go to Guiana James had acceded to Ralegh's claim that Guiana did not belong to Spain. Even after his eventual and total failure, it looks as though on returning to England Ralegh was astounded that James was proposing to treat so very seriously a minor clash at a small Spanish settlement.

Ralegh had everything to lose on this expedition, James nothing. If Ralegh succeeded, James had his gold; if Ralegh failed, James had his head.

The fleet which Ralegh got together by the spring of 1617 numbered in all fourteen ships and a thousand men. Lawrence Keymis was with him, of course, his own son Walter Ralegh, and his nephew George Ralegh. Gondomar said with justice that this was a very large force just to exploit a gold-mine. There can be no doubt that, although gold was the key to get Ralegh out of the Tower and was the bait to attract ships, men, and finance, Ralegh was out for very much more than gold. He was out to establish a major English colony with the enthusiastic support of the native peoples of the region, disaffected by Spanish oppression. He was banking on an Indian rising, and this is the only explanation of the deep penetration of the Orinoco by Keymis's task force, 250 miles west of the Caroní, after the capture of San Thomé. This journey is never mentioned by Ralegh; but the Spaniards knew what was afoot (Harlow, p. 179). The expedition as a whole was basically opportunistic; it was meant to exploit whatever opening for gold or territorial advantage offered itself. What eventually happened was the worst possible case, allowing no response whatever.

At Plymouth on 3 May 1617 Ralegh issued his 'Orders to be observed by the commanders of the fleet'. They were based on earlier orders of the kind, including probably instructions worked out for the Islands voyage of 1597 (Sandison). They enjoin daily divine service, forbid smoking between decks, encourage the training of the landsmen in simple nautical tasks, instruct in keeping station at night, and give rules for naval engagements. Particular warnings are given about conduct ashore, forbidding absolutely the forcing of 'any woman, be she Christian or heathen, upon pain of death', and also forbidding the eating of strange fruit, or bathing except where Indians swim 'because most of the rivers are full of alligators'.

The expedition made a very bad start by running into a storm which drove the ships into Irish harbours for shelter. From Cork Ralegh wrote to Lord Boyle: 'There is no middle course but perish or prosper' (Grosart, p. 85). It was not until 19 August 1617 that the fleet sailed again. Here Ralegh's journal begins; it gives a vivid account of the adventures in the Canaries and the Cape Verde Islands, and the agonizingly slow crossing of the Atlantic with the flagship in particular in the grip of an appalling infection which killed forty-two men, including some on whom Ralegh was relying most, and 'my honest friend Mr John Talbot, one that had lived with me eleven years in the Tower, an excellent general scholar and a faithful true man as lived' (p. 208/26). Ralegh himself caught the fever and was still very ill when they made their landfall by the Wiapoco, 750 miles south-east of the Orinoco, on 11 November.

Ralegh sent a letter to his wife by Captain Peter Alley, who returned because of ill health. He was worried about reinforcements which the Spaniards might have brought in. (They had not in fact arrived.) He was pleased with his reception by the Indians: 'To tell you I might be here king of the Indians were a vanity; but my name hath still lived among them' (Harlow, p. 159). One 'R.M.'—perhaps Robert Mearing, who was a witness at Ralegh's examination—sent back the report which was printed as *Newes of S* Walter Rauleigh*. He wrote with enormous enthusiasm about the land they had reached—

a landskip of that excellent perfection which no art could better, hardly imitate. For truly hitherto to mine eye this country hath appeared a very earthy paradise, and therefore doubtless is full of strong promises that our attemptings cannot return without much honour and reward. (Harlow, pp. 151–2)

Lawrence Keymis also wrote home, not as jubilant as R.M., but

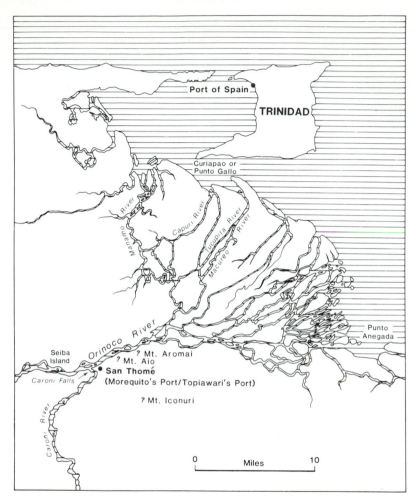

Port of Spain

TRINIDAD

Curiapao or
Punto Gallo

*River*

*Capuri River*

*Tucupita River*

*River*

*Macureo River*

*Manamo*

*Orinoco River*

Punto
Anegada

Seiba
Island

? Mt. Aromai

? Mt. Aio

● San Thomé

(Morequito's Port/Topiawari's Port)

*Caroni Falls*

*Caroni River*

? Mt. Iconuri

0      Miles      10

Map 4. Ralegh's Guiana

certainly not indicating that, as Harlow put it, 'he was already losing heart' (p. 56). Ralegh's own feelings may be imagined. However good his reception by the Indians, he had lost many weeks, some of his best men were dead, including the lieutenant-general Pigott, and neither he nor Sir Warham St Leger was well enough to make the journey into the interior.

Keymis was put in charge of the expedition up-river, with George Ralegh as military commander. Five ships with 300 men were sent on the expedition, while Ralegh with the rest of the fleet waited at Trinidad, ready to intercept Spanish reinforcements. Ralegh instructed Keymis (according to the Apology) to land a force between Mount Aio and San Thomé to protect the finding and working of the mine, which was supposed to be about three miles from Mount Aio. In the event, an Indian spotted the task force when it was over thirty miles from San Thomé and informed the governor, Diego Palomeque, who put the town in readiness. Keymis proceeded westwards without two of his ships, under Wollaston and Whitney, which had gone aground. He claimed in his second letter to Ralegh (Latham, pp. 109–10) that San Thomé had been resited since he discovered the settlement in 1596, and that he came upon it unawares. The settlement might have been rebuilt but its location in 1617 was substantially the same as in 1596. It may well be the case that Keymis came upon the settlement 'before . . . we thought ourselves to be near it', but that is most likely because in this enormously wide and heavily forested river he did not know exactly where he was.

The English force landed on the south bank of the Orinoco on 2 January. There was a clash with the Spanish defenders, and who began it is impossible to determine. Captain Parker wrote later of the 'unadvised daringness' of Ralegh's son Walter, who rushed forward and was killed (Harlow, p. 231). The Spanish governor was killed. But though there were deaths on both sides, the casualties were very light. After some opposition from within the houses the garrison fled, and the English took the town. They eventually burned it.

That Keymis did not at once prosecute the search for the mine with any confidence or vigour was probably owing to a number of reasons. He was demoralized by this disastrous commencement: a battle with the Spaniards and the death of Ralegh's son. He found it hard to cope with his unco-operative officers and men, who were expecting instant results. He was appalled at the extreme difficulty of the terrain, of finding his way through it without native guides to a mine whose precise location he was probably hazy about, of maintaining supplies, and a safe line of communication once it was found. He was harassed and harried by fire from the Spaniards and Indians in the woods and on Seiba island.

He wrote informing Ralegh of the death of his son on 7 or 8 January, and sent the letter by Ralegh's servant Peter Andrews and an Indian pilot. But Andrews must have been held up; it was not until 13 February—the day the journal breaks off—that Ralegh got Keymis's news of the disaster, as the chaplain Samuel Jones reported (Harlow, p. 236).

George Ralegh with three boats ascended the Orinoco for a further 250 miles, and it was three weeks before they got back to San Thomé. The very detailed narrative of Father Pedro Simón, which Harlow translates, speaks of their efforts to persuade the tribes to rise against the Spaniards; they were certainly not looking for any mine which Ralegh knew of. When the force returned Keymis, having failed to discover gold, abandoned the whole venture. On their slow journey back, one of the caciques, Caranapa, tried to persuade them to stay, offering to find them gold; some wanted to accept his offer but they were outvoted. On leaving the main river in order to reach Trinidad via the Macureo, in early February, Keymis must have learned that Ralegh had not got his earlier letter; presumably he was met by one of the search parties that Ralegh had sent out. So he wrote a second long and rambling letter, beginning 'I am very sorry that my letters from St. Thome to Trinidado bearing date 7 January 1617 came not to your lordship's hands; however, I wish (were God so pleased) you might never hear nor read the contents thereof' (Latham, p. 106). This letter is dated 9 February and Keymis sent it ahead. He and his ships reached the rest of the fleet at Trinidad on 2 March.

Ralegh gave his own account several times of how he received Keymis and laid the blame for failure on him, and how, after several days of discussing what had been done and not done, Keymis committed suicide. Although extreme depression at his failure and Ralegh's unforgiving attitude are enough to explain what Keymis did, the thought crosses one's mind that he may have freely sought death in order to enable Ralegh to use him as a scapegoat, and to return an unanswering silence to questions about his instructions, his intentions, his thoughts, his actions.

The fleet now broke up. Wollaston and Whitney went off looking for ships to rob. Captain Charles Parker, a close friend of Ralegh, was undecided what course to take, but 'about the latter end of August I hope we shall have feathered our nest' (Harlow, p. 232). At St Christopher's in the Leeward Islands, on 21 March 1618, three weeks after Keymis's empty-handed return, Ralegh wrote a long report to Secretary of State Winwood, not knowing that he had died, and on the following day a letter to his wife; both of these are printed in the pages following.

Ralegh had considered going back for the gold and had rejected the idea. The plan to intercept the Mexican plate fleet, which had been hovering ever since Ralegh left the Tower, again offered itself. He was heard to speak of a French commission that he had. Whatever else he would face in going back to England, he would certainly encounter financial ruin. He finally put the Destiny and the remnant of his fleet on course for Newfoundland, there to victual, trim, and consider. However, Ralegh found out that there was a conspiracy on board, which included 'some of the best men I had, some of them being gentlemen', to desert at Newfoundland, take another ship, and turn pirate. On deciding to alter course for England he faced open mutiny. He quelled it by promising to make for Ireland and to let the company disperse. He brought the Destiny back to England with a skeleton crew of loyal men on 21 June 1618.

Before Ralegh reached Plymouth, James issued a proclamation expressing his indignation at Ralegh's breach of his promise not to commit any act of hostility against the territories and subjects of his 'dear brother the king of Spain', and at the nature of the act, the killing, sacking, and burning, which had maliciously broken the peace and amity which had 'so long inviolably continued' between the two nations. He asked anyone with information to bring it forward, so that 'exemplary punishment' could be visited on the authors of these 'scandalous and enormous outrages'. Gondomar insisted that Ralegh should be handed over to the King of Spain to be hanged, and James, supported by Buckingham, at first agreed (Gardiner, iii. 133–5).

When he realized the full import of what James had in store for him, Ralegh decided to flee the country, with the help of the one captain who remained loyal to him, Samuel King. While being rowed out to a French vessel, he changed his mind and returned, and set off for London in the custody of Sir Lewis Stukeley. He faked illness at Salisbury in order to write his Apology, which appears in the documents which follow. Confined to his own house in London, he made secret plans to escape again, but he was betrayed, arrested in the act, and imprisoned yet again in the Tower. This was August.

Philip of Spain had now yielded to James the office of executing Ralegh, but James found himself in a legal quandary. Since the show trial of 1603, Ralegh had been under sentence of death for treason; he could not be tried again, for he was 'civilly dead' (Harlow, p. 295). In view of public feeling, it was necessary that some judicial procedure should take place, even if he were to be executed in fulfilment of the old suspended sentence. Commissioners were appointed to get a case ready—Bacon, Coke, Abbot, Worcester, Caesar, Naunton; and on 22 October Ralegh was brought before these. He was charged with the crimes he had committed by reason of his late voyage but his defence was interrupted by Lord Chief Justice Montague, who said it was 'not to the purpose', and advised him: 'Fear not death too much, nor fear death too little'; he ended 'Execution is granted' (Harlow, pp. 303–4). The sentence of death of 1603, for supposed treasonable complicity with the Spaniards, was eventually to be put into effect because of acts hostile to the Spaniards.

Ralegh's request for a delay was not granted by James, and he was told to prepare for death the following morning. The king did, however, remit the original stipulation regarding the manner of death, namely that he should be drawn, hanged, and quartered. 'Instead thereof, our pleasure is to have the head only of the said Sir Walter Ralegh cut off.'

'He was very cheerful that morning he died,' wrote the Dean of Westminster, 'ate his breakfast heartily, and took tobacco; and made no more of his death than if [it] had been to take a journey; and left a great impression in the minds of those that beheld him' (E. Edwards, ii. 491). On the scaffold, at 9 a.m. on Thursday, 29 October 1618, Ralegh said, 'I thank my God heartily that he hath brought me into the light to die, and not suffered me to die in the dark prison of the Tower, where I have suffered a great deal of adversity and a long sickness.' He made a speech to clear himself of 'two main points of suspicion'. The first concerned his relations with France. The second was the question of disloyalty to James. 'In this I speak now, what have I to do with kings? I have nothing to do with them, neither do I fear them; I have now to do with God.' But he denied he had spoken dishonourably of James. After rebutting various accusations, 'he looked over his note of remembrance. "Well, (saith he) thus far I have gone; now a little more, and I will have done by and by."' He spoke of the mutiny off Newfoundland, and of the charge that the Guiana venture was a pretext to get his liberty. He finally denied that he had rejoiced at the death of Essex and taken tobacco at his execution.

He asked his auditors to join him in a prayer for his forgiveness, 'being a man full of all vanity, and have lived a sinful life in all sinful callings, having been a soldier, a captain, a sea-captain, and a courtier, which are all places of wickedness and vice'.

Then putting off his gown and doublet, he called to the headsman to show him the axe, which being not presently showed him, he said, *I pray thee let me see it; dost thou think that I am afraid of it?* And having it in his hands, he felt along upon the edge of it, and smiling, spake to the sheriff, saying, *This is a sharp medicine, but it is a physician for all diseases.* Then going to and fro upon the scaffold, on every side he prayed the company to pray to God to assist him and strengthen him.

And so being asked which way he would lay himself, on which side the block, as he stretched himself along and laid his head on the block, he said, *So the heart be right, it is no matter which way the head lieth.* And then praying, after he had forgiven the headsman, having given him a sign when he should do his office, at two blows he lost both head and life, his body never shrinking nor moving. His head was showed on each side of the scaffold, and then put into a red leather bag, and his wrought velvet gown thrown over it, which was afterwards conveyed away in a mourning coach of his lady's.   (*The History of the World*, 1687, p. 40)

## 2. *The Documents*

Of the voluminous documentation of Ralegh's last voyage, which was a matter of national and international interest and concern, I am giving, as I have indicated, only Ralegh's own writings, and only the most important of these. Much of the additional material is in V. T. Harlow's eccentric but indispensable work of 1932, *Ralegh's Last Voyage*. The two major writings I give are Ralegh's journal, which is not in Harlow, and the Apology, which has been wholly re-edited. There are also the two letters from St Christopher's relating the failure of the expedition to Sir Ralph Winwood and to his wife, and two letters written to Sir George Carew and to the King not long before his execution.

There is a good deal of repetition in these six documents. The record of events in the journal was used for the Apology, and the five later documents tend to repeat the same incidents (such as the suicide of Keymis and the massacre of Hall's men) and rehearse the same arguments vindicating or justifying Ralegh's procedures. These arguments are as follows:

1. Guiana does not belong to Spain; it is English, ceded to me by the native chiefs in 1595.
2. James must have recognized this claim or he would not have allowed me to go.

3. I have not broken peace with Spain because the Spaniards have been warring against us.
4. I did not use the mine as a pretext to get my freedom.
5. The mine is a reality; both Keymis and I had seen it.
6. The failure to find the gold was Keymis's fault, not mine.

Reiteration is inescapable; it is the essence of these documents, for they show Ralegh writing for his life, fighting for his life by writing, and for a period of six months, on board the Destiny, on his way in custody to London, and finally in the Tower, he returned to the same incidents, the same arguments, modifying and rearranging them as in a new context he justified his conduct to a new hearer. For all the repetition, each document reshapes the voyage.

## (i)  *The Journal*

The journal which Ralegh kept from the time the fleet left Ireland in August 1617 until the day in February 1618 when he received the news of the failure to find the gold-mine and the death of his son exists as an untitled manuscript in Ralegh's hand in the British Library (MS Cotton Titus B. VIII, fos. 162–75, now separately bound). My text is based on the transcript by R. H. Schomburgk in the Hakluyt Society edition of Ralegh's *Discovery of Guiana*, which I have corrected in a number of places by collation with the original MS. The spelling is modernized and Ralegh's contractions are expanded (e.g. L. becomes leagues, S.W. becomes south-west, D. becomes degrees). Numbers under 100 are regularized as figures for dates, times, distances, positions; otherwise they are written as words. Gaps which Ralegh left in his manuscript (for dates he was not sure of, etc.) are indicated by square brackets.

The journal is long, and I have made three cuts where the material becomes a rather humdrum record of navigational or other detail. But it would not have done to have given only the highlights; I thought it essential to let the reader have the flow of a day-by-day narrative which inevitably includes periods of monotony. At sea, Ralegh generally entered up the record of each day's run after the noon observation or reckoning. In harbour at the Canaries, however, he created a narrative, describing the scene, explaining and justifying his actions, which must have been intended as material for the history of the voyage which he foresaw himself writing. Then, as the fleet left the Canaries, the journal became a grim roll-call of the dead as the contagion spread through the ship, culminating in the 'lamentable twenty-four hours' when under

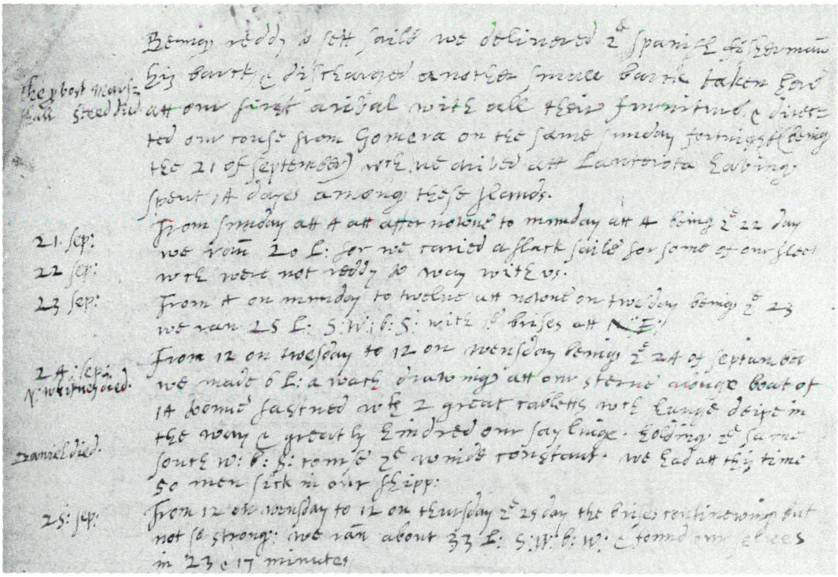

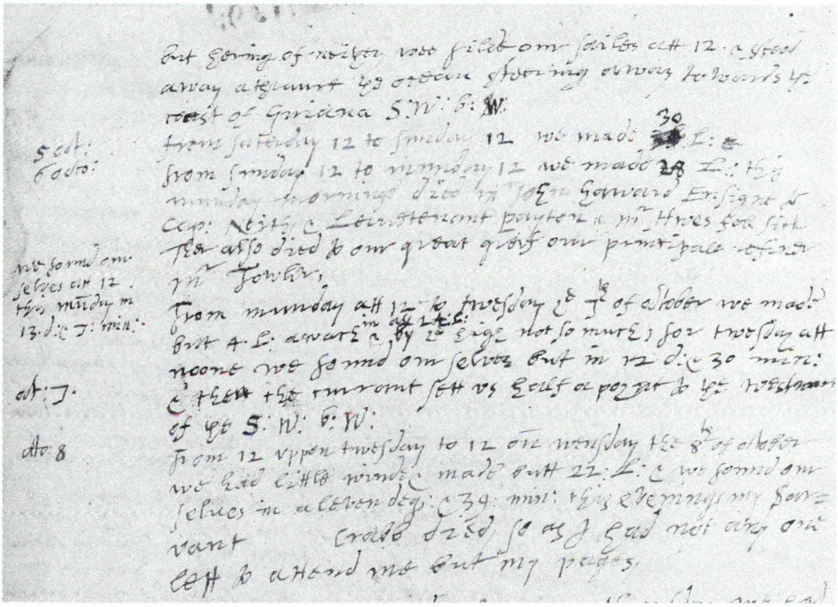

FIG. 6. Ralegh's journal. Two passages from the original manuscript, for the periods 21–25 September and 4–8 October, 1617, showing the marginal insertions. Transcription on pp. 204–5, 207. British Library, Cotton MS, Titus B VIII, folios 167v, 168v. (Reproduced by permission of the British Library)

dark and heavy skies came the deaths of John Pigott, who was to have led the land forces, and John Talbot, Ralegh's companion in the Tower.

The journal was of course not kept up during the worst part of Ralegh's illness, and the entries are fitful and irregular during the increasingly nerve-racking wait off Trinidad. The strain on Ralegh as trickles of news begin to come in from Indian sources is very clear. The journal breaks off abruptly on 13 February.

### (ii) *The Letters to Winwood and Lady Ralegh*

The text of Ralegh's letter to Winwood is taken from the official transcript now in the Public Record Office: State Papers, Domestic, James I (SP 14), vol. xcvi, no. 70. The transcript is mutilated, and the missing portions are supplied from another transcript in the Cecil papers at Hatfield as given by E. Edwards (ii. 350–8) and Hadow (pp. 185–92). Hadow's text of the letter as a whole (which according to his preface was prepared for him by Frederick Page) is much more accurate than Edward Edwards's, and it meticulously indicates the words and letters supplied from the Cecil MS.

The letter to Winwood is an attempt at a cool, measured, sorrowful report of an expedition that went wrong, commending those who have done good service in an unfortunate defeat by the Spanish forces. But brooding self-pity and helpless anger are not to be suppressed, and they break out above all in the postscript, written when Ralegh had just learned from the others that Keymis had said he could have reached the mine but chose not to.

There is no authoritative manuscript of Ralegh's famous letter to his wife. Edward Edwards chose MS Harley 4761, fos. 23–5; Hadow chose MS Sloane 3520, fos. 2–4; Harlow chose MS Add. 34631, fo. 47. All these are in the British Library. The MS used by Harlow (from the Macvey–Napier papers, vol. xvi) is the least satisfactory, but neither the Harley nor the Sloane manuscript can be taken as a copy-text since each contains what seems to be authentic material lacking from the other. There is nothing for it but to prepare an eclectic text from the two of them, and guess whether Ralegh wrote 'dear Bess' or 'dearest Bess'. The more important variants are noted.

Rather strangely, Ralegh's letter to his wife has the same 'format' as the letter to Winwood. Ralegh comes to the end of a reasonably controlled letter and then bursts out in a tempestuous postscript. The letter is in another sense curiously divided; having failed to limit himself to a brief consolation, Ralegh sees the value of the longer letter as a means of giving the bitter news to his friends, and what he writes is both a private letter and a public communication.

(iii) *The Apology*

Ralegh's Apology, of which there is no autograph or authoritative manuscript, though there are many manuscript copies (Lefranc, p. 54), was first printed in 1650, in *Judicious and Select Essays and Observations*, with separate title-page and pagination (Brushfield, pp. 135 and 218). It was execrably printed, with careless and extensive omissions, unthinking misreadings, and confused punctuation. But this text was several times reprinted. The next major edition, in Ralegh's *Works* of 1751 (vol. ii) must have been set up from a marked-up copy of 1650 or one of its reprints, because it reproduces not only its omissions but some of its ludicrous misreadings, such as 'cheins' for 'thieves'. When 1650 says that 'we tarried' Captain Hastings instead of 'we buried' him, 1751 improves this to 'we tarried for' Captain Hastings. All the same, there are in 1751 many additions and corrections which can hardly have been supplied without reference to a manuscript, as for example the phrase 'being now over with your son' from Keymis's letter, omitted from 1650.

Arthur Cayley, reprinting the Apology in his life of Ralegh in 1806 (ii. 82–117), immeasurably improved the text of 1751, filling in lacunae and correcting errors by reference to manuscripts in the Sloane collection and St John's College, Cambridge. For the eight-volume Oxford edition of Ralegh's *Works* of 1829, Philip Bliss made further corrections from manuscripts in the Bodleian and the British Museum. But at the same time he tidied up and modernized the text; 'dislike his majesty' became 'offend his majesty', 'weakly' became 'sickly', 'departed London' became 'departed from London'. It is also clear that the manuscripts which Bliss consulted (like that which Harlow used) derive from an early copy of the Apology which had been extensively polished to get rid of the roughness arising from the hectic speed of Ralegh's composition. Time and again one feels that in spite of their omissions and mistakes, 1650 and 1751 are nearer to what Ralegh wrote than the fuller and more elegant version of 1829. Cayley's is probably the best text as a whole, but it is often necessary to follow the corrections of 1829. The more important variants are recorded in the notes.

In his Apology, a work of pedantic detail suffused with paranoia and obsessive self-justification, Ralegh attempted (vainly) to place the ill success of his expedition within a philosophic view of the limits of human achievement. The grand opening invokes the fellowship of failure; it is a mighty procession of 'if'-clauses marshalling his predecessors in defeat from Charles V to Francis Drake. The simple and sombre thesis is that success is a matter of luck. The early ventures of both Cavendish and Drake succeeded because fortune favoured them. When fortune 'left them to the trial of their own virtues' they inevitably came to grief (p. 234). Every successful endeavour is riddled with culpability and error; we succeed in spite of ourselves. When we succeed, no questions are asked about our misjudgements and offences; but when, with no worse a record of transgression, we fail, no one shows mercy. 'But as good success admits no examination, so the contrary allows of no excuse' (p. 233/4).

In a successful enterprise fortune overrules our self-destructive efforts; when fortune deserts us we reap what we have sown and the outcome is our responsibility. 'As many things succeed both against reason and our best endeavour, so it is most commonly true that men are the cause of their own misery.' But not Ralegh; even though he adds, 'as I was of mine' (p. 229). Ralegh admits one error and one only—setting out without a royal pardon, for his status ('*non ens* in law') fatally weakened his authority. There is no further admission of error; the expedition failed partly because of unnatural ill luck (like the unprecedented adverse winds) but above all because of the malevolence and weakness of others. Ralegh makes himself the great exception to his theory of failure. He is a man surrounded by ill will, whether in Gondomar or Captain Bailey. His men, with a few exceptions, were 'the very scum of the earth'.

Ralegh's rejection of his responsibility shows itself most painfully in his brutal treatment of Keymis—not on board the Destiny but in the pages of the Apology. The affray at San Thomé was the Spaniards' fault. But for everything else Keymis was to blame; his whole conduct receives not one word of pity or understanding or forgiveness. It cannot be but that Keymis's words and actions have been misrepresented. It is obvious that the two vital documents which Ralegh quotes—his instructions to Keymis and Keymis's letter to him—have been doctored. The tortuousness of Ralegh's case against Keymis puts an intolerable strain on his sentences. He tries at the same time to repudiate Keymis's reasons for not working the mine and to accentuate the problems of getting there. Any claim by Keymis to his companions that he did not know where the mine was has to be circumvented by a bewildering deviousness of language (see especially pp. 239–41).

But everywhere the language shows the stress of his situation; the Apology is hardly a sane document. There is too much to say; emotion forces pieces of evidence into the sentences in defiance of coherence and grammar. A long list of the wonderful commodities of Guiana thrusts itself into the middle of his rejection of Keymis's excuses (p. 240/11).

In spite of all this, a work that began with an appeal to recognize the hazards of all human enterprise also ends on a level above that of personal complaint, with a challenge to James on the status of England on the international scene. If we admit to Spain that the expedition to Guiana was an attack on the legal rulers of that part of the world, 'we must for ever abandon the Indies, and lose all our knowledge, and all our pilotage of that part of the world'.

### (iv) *The Letter to Carew*

The manuscript of this letter is in the British Library, MS Cotton Vitellius C. xvii, fos. 439–40. There is also a copy in the Folger Library, Washington. The Cotton MS was badly damaged by fire, but the letter had been printed in *Judicious and Select Essays and Observations* and by Cayley (ii. 117–22) and the portions missing from the Cotton MS have been supplied from there.

This is the only writing in which Ralegh remains dispassionate and cool. The letter summarizes and condenses the major political arguments of the Apology, rising to the most important paragraph (p. 250) which argues that for James to acknowledge that his subjects have offended Spain in this enterprise is to devalue and diminish Britain's rights in the world and, worse still, to deny to Englishmen the protection they have a right to look for from their King. It shows a cowardice towards Spain, Ralegh ends, which is not shared by France and Holland.

### (v) *The Letter to James I*

The text is from the official transcript in the Public Record Office, State Papers, Domestic, James I (SP 14), vol. xcix, no. 69.1, though a second transcript which follows (no. 70) sometimes provides a better reading. Harlow used a Bodleian manuscript, Eng. Hist. d. 138. There is also a copy in MS Jones B 60 in Dr Williams's Library, London.

# NARRATIVES

## 1. Ralegh's Journal

[1617]

19 day    The 19th of August at 6 o'clock in the morning, having the wind at north-east, we set sail in the river of Cork where we had attended a fair wind seven weeks.[1]

20 day    From 6 in the morning[2] till 10 at night we ran 14 leagues south by west. From 10 at night till 10 in the morning we had no wind, so as between 10 in the morning and 4 at afternoon we made not above 2 leagues.

At 4 the 20th day the wind began to fresh, and we stirred away south-south-west, keeping a westerly course fearing the westerly winds, and from 4 to 2 o'clock after midnight, being the morning of the 21 day, we ran 13 leagues.

[*For the next ten days the entries record only courses, positions, winds, and distances sailed. On 30th August they were off southern Portugal, and had 'brought Lisborne east-northerly'.*]

At 12 the same 30 day we discovered four sails and giving them chase ran west-south-west till 7 at night. Then leaving the chase we stood

31 day    south-south-east till 12 at night, and then south, so as by 8 o'clock Sunday morning we had gone 18 leagues and were 20 leagues short of the Cape Saint Vincent.[3]

These four ships were French, and came from Cape Blank[4] laden with fish and train oil, and were bound as they pretended[5] for Civile in Spain;[6] but because they should not give knowledge that I was then passed by, carried them with me 100 leagues to the southward; and then, buying of them a pinnace of seven ton and three pipes[7] of train oil, for which I gave them in ready money sixty-one crowns, I dismissed them. It

---

[1] The fleet had set sail from Plymouth on 12 June 1617 and had been driven by bad weather to Ireland.

[2] i.e. 19 Aug.

[3] The south-western tip of Portugal.

[4] Cape Blanco, or Cap Blanc, Mauritania, on the west coast of Africa, between the Canaries and the Cape Verde islands, 20° N. 17° W.; an important rendezvous and point of departure.

[5] Claimed.          [6] Seville.          [7] Large casks.

is true that I had arguments enough to persuade me that they had not fished but robbed the Portugals and Spaniards at Cape Blank, for they were not only provided and furnished like men of war but had in them store of Spanish apparel and other things taken there. But because it is lawful for the French to make prize of the Spanish king's subjects to the south of the Canaries and to the west of the Azores, and that it did not belong to me to examine the subjects of the French king, I did not suffer my company to take from them any pennyworth of their goods, greatly to the discontentment of my company,[8] who cried out that they were men
10 of war and thieves; and so indeed they were, for I met with a Spaniard afterward of the Grand Canaries[9] whom they had robbed.

From 8 Sunday morning to 12 Monday being the 1 of September we ran 40 leagues, and were in 35 degrees lacking 8 minutes, and made our way south by east.

From 12 on Monday to 12 on Tuesday the 2 day we ran 30 leagues, having lien by the lee[10] four hours, and were in 33 degrees and half.

From 12 on Tuesday to 12 on Wednesday the 3 day we ran 30 leagues.

From 12 on Wednesday to 12 on Thursday the 4 of September we ran
20 but 14 leagues south by east. Friday the 5 and Saturday the 6 day we ran with a good gale and made Lancerota[11] on Saturday before noon; but on Saturday night we stood off till midnight and then stood in, and on Sunday the 7 day came to anchor near the shore of Lancerota, where we landed our men to stretch their legs. The people, fearing that we had been the same fleet of Turks which had spoiled Porta Sancta,[12] put themselves in arms and came to the seaside with a flag of truce, the Governor being desirous to speak with me; to which I yielded, taking with me [Lieutenant] Bradshaw,[13] with each of us a sword. And the Governor with one of his so armed came into the plain[14] to meet me, our
30 troops staying at equal distance from us.

After he had saluted me, his first desire was to know whether we were

*(right margin:)*
1 September

2 September

3 September

4 September
5 and 6 September

---

28 Lieutenant] *not in MS*

[8] Chiefly Captain John Bailey of the Southampton, who deserted at the Canaries; see Apology, p. 230.

[9] Grand Canary, or Gran Canaria, the major island of the group.

[10] They had been driven to leeward.

[11] Lanzarote, Canary Islands.

[12] Porto Santo, Madeira islands.

[13] There is a gap in the MS; 'Lieutenant' is taken from the Apology; Bradshaw was Captain Pennington's lieutenant (Apology, p. 234).

[14] The open space where two parties in conflict meet.

Christians or Turks, whereof being satisfied he demanded what I sought for from that miserable and barren island, peopled in effect all with Moriscoes.[15] I answered him that although I landed many men to refresh them, I had no purpose to invade any of the Spanish king's territories, having received from the king my master express commandment to the contrary. Only I desired for my money such fresh meat as that island yielded. And because he should not doubt of what nation we were, I willed him to be informed by the English merchant whose ship lay by us,[16] and whom we found in his port at our arrival trading with him and others of the island, and had lately brought them wine from 10 Tenerife, and stayed for his lading of corn. Whereupon he prayed me to set down in writing what I desired and it should be furnished the next day, promising to send me that night some few muttons and goats for myself and the captains.

8 September        In the morning, being Monday the 8 day, the English merchant's man came to me, by whom I sent him[17] a note for a quantity of wheat, goats, sheep, hens, and wine, for which the merchant should make the price, and to whom I would deliver so much ready money or other truck[18] as it amounted to, promising him that my companies should not go from the seaside above a mile or two, nor offend any of the inhabitants. I stayed 20 the next day, but nothing came; which day we spent in training and mustering our companies on the seashore. The next, he wrate[19] me a letter in Spanish wherein he protested on the faith of a caballero that he would send the provisions the 3 day being the 11 of September, and sent me the English merchant, which lay above at his town, with two French factors to assure me, whom he abused by protesting as much to them. For mine own part, I never gave faith to his words, for [I] knew he sought to gain time to carry the goods of the town, being seven miles from us, into the mountains.

My company pressed me that they might march towards the town, but 30 besides that I knew that it would offend his majesty, I am sure that the poor English merchant should have been ruined, whose goods he had in his hands; and the way being mountainous and most extreme stony, I

27 I knew] knew *MS*
[15] Moors, arabs.
[16] The name of the ship's master was Reekes, who reported on the events when he returned to England in Dec. (Harlow, pp. 144–5).
[17] The governor.
[18] Material for barter.
[19] Ralegh's normal spelling; cf. his 'Ocean to Cynthia', 124, 'So wrate I once...'.

knew that I must have lost twenty good men in taking a town not worth two groats, for they were three hundred men, whereof ninety musketeers, upon a ground of infinite advantage.

When the 3 day was past, I sent the merchant's man with a letter charging him[20] with his promise and faith given, and that did I not know that it would offend the king my sovereign I would pull his Moriscoes out of their town by the ears; and by the merchant's man I sent some twenty shillings to buy some hens and other trifles. By whom he returned answer that we were the same Turks which had taken and
10 destroyed Porta Sancta, and therefore he was resolved to stand upon his guard, and were we English, yet if he gave us any relief he was sure to be hanged; taking the money from the merchant's man and beat him for offering to buy anything for us without his leave.

I sent back the merchant's man and wrate unto him that because he was a poor fellow and needed apparel, if he would send back the merchant's [man] I would send him forty rial more to buy him a doublet to his hose. And for the rest it was enough for me to know his master's disposition, who notwithstanding the peace with our king, yet he had given order that no relief should be given to any of his subjects; and that
20 evening departed, and came the next day at night to the Grand Canaries, and from the south part sent a Spaniard which was a fisherman of that island with a letter to the governor, to whom the other islands were subject as to the supreme audience,[21] with the copy of the governor of Lancerota his letter to me and mine to him, and how I had no intent to invade any of those islands nor to offend any of the Spanish king's subjects, but only sought for water, and for fresh meat for my money, praying the governor to take knowledge that I had it in commandment from the king my master not to offer any violence nor to take any places belonging to the Spanish king. Only I desired from him to know if any
30 such commandment were given to the governor of Lancerota not to trade with us but to offend us in all he could, or whether himself, being the king's lieutenant of all the islands, had any such order.

In the meanwhile, landing to get a little water, which I did with great difficulty, the quantity being not half a ton, I thought it perilous to stay in those extreme hot calms, my company in all the ships falling extremely sick, whereof many died for want of water.[22] I did therefore determine

16 man] *not in MS*

[20] The governor.    [21] (Sp. *audiencia*) colonial court of justice.
[22] This is the first mention of the dangerous fever which ran through Ralegh's ship, at last attacking himself, causing 42 deaths.

to stay but one day more for the governor's answer. Where being on the land with a few men I set two or three sentinels, doubting the people might come down on the sudden. The islanders finding a sentinel of two of our company somewhat far off from the rest, they crept near them by the favour of the trees and on the sudden ran upon them. Our musketeer shooting off gave us the alarm. Our pike,[23] being charged with three of them received three wounds, being one Smith, a master mate[24] of Sir J. Ferne's ship, but behaved himself so well as he slew one of them and recovered his pike. Captain Thornhurst,[25] being a valiant and active man, hasted to their rescue and with a horseman's piece[26] shot another 10 of them. Mr Hawton with his pike wounded the third, so as all three died in the place, the rest taking their heels. We were now out of their debts, for at Lancerota, by the vanity and madness of a sergeant who standing sentinel would needs force the governor's sentinel from his ground,[27] they being twenty and ours but three, whereof we lost two.

From the calms of the Great Canaries, where at this time of the year the springs being dried up there was no water to be had, we set sail the [   ] of September and stood for Gomera,[28] where some of our company assured us there was water enough; but we fell to leeward of it that night. The next day being Thursday the [   ] we turned it up and recovered the 20 port, being the best of all the Canaries, the town and castle standing on the very breach of the sea; but the billows do so tumble and overfall as it is impossible to land upon any part of the strand but by swimming, saving in a cove under steep rocks, where there can pass towards the town but one after another, and could they pass ten men in front,[29] yet from the steep mountain of rock over the way they were all sure to be beaten in pieces with massy stones.

Before we were at anchor they shot at us from those rocks, and we, to let them know that we had good ordnance, gave them some twenty demi-culverin[30] through their houses and then forbare. I then sent a 30

---

5   sudden] sunday *MS*          6   pike] pick *MS*

[23]   Pikeman.          [24]   Master's mate?

[25]   Thomas Thornhurst; he wrote his own narrative (Harlow, pp. 145–8). He was badly wounded after the taking of San Thomé.

[26]   Presumably a pistol.

[27]   Ralegh has left out something, such as 'there was a brief skirmish'. This set-to on Lanzarote, which Ralegh does not mention in its proper place, is briefly referred to in the *Apology* (p. 231/7).

[28]   An island SW of Tenerife.

[29]   i.e. abreast.

[30]   i.e. shots from his demi-culverin, or nine-pounder cannon.

Spaniard on shore to the Count, lord and governor of the island, and wrate unto him that I came not hither as the Hollanders did, to sack their town and burn their churches as the Hollanders did in the year [ ]³¹ but being in necessity of water, for it only. And therefore, as he had begun the war in shooting first, so it should be his fault to continue it by denying us to relieve ourselves, whereunto we were mainly constrained.

To this he made answer in writing and in fair terms that he was advertised from the other islands that we were the same Turks which had taken Porta Sancta, otherwise he would be ready to do me service. I
10 answered that he received that advertisement from the Morisco of Forteventura,³² but to put him altogether out of doubt I would send him six other Spaniards of the Gran Canaries, taken on Africa side in a small bark, who should resolve him that we were Christians and the vassals of the king of Great Britain in perfect league and amity with the king of Spain.

This being done, we made an agreement that his soldiers and others to the number of 300 should quit their trenches upon the landing places, where they were so well assured by divers redoubts one above another as the Hollanders were forced to land their army six mile from this port
20 when they took it as aforesaid, and where in passing the mountains they lost eighty soldiers. And I for my part should promise on the faith of a Christian not to land above thirty mariners without weapons to fill water, [which] was within a pistol shot of the wash of the sea; myself farther promising that none of those should enter their houses nor their gardens.

Upon this agreement I sent my boat ashore with my barricoes,³³ adventuring but two poor sailors ashore and four to keep the boat, which had in her head two good murderers;³⁴ and for the more safety brought six ships with their broadsides towards the town, which I would have
30 beaten down in ten hours if they had broken the agreement.

By the Spaniard which carried my letter to the Count, I sent his lady³⁵ six exceeding fine handkerchers and six pair of gloves, and wrate unto her that if there were anything worthy of her in my fleet she should

---

23 which was] we was *MS*; we were *Schomburgk*    28 brought] and brought *MS*

³¹ Gap left in MS; Schomburgk notes the ill-success of a big Dutch fleet which attacked in 1599.
³² Fuerteventura, the island south of Lanzarote.
³³ Casks (Spanish).
³⁴ Small cannons.
³⁵ She was of an English family; Ralegh gives more details in the Apology (p. 232).

command it and me. She sent me answer that she was sorry that her barren island had nothing worthy of me, and with her letter sent me four very great loaves of sugar, a basket of lemons which I much desired to comfort and refresh our many sick men, a basket of oranges, a basket of most delicate grapes, another of pomegranates and of figs, which trifles were better welcome unto me than a thousand crowns could have been. I gave her servants two crowns to each, and answering her letter in the fairest terms I could, because I would not rest in her debt I sent her two ounces of ambergris, an ounce of the delicate extract of amber, a great glass of rose water in high estimation here, and a very excellent picture  10 of Mary Magdalen, and a cutwork ruff. These presents were received with so great thanks and so much acknowledgement of debt as could be expressed, and upon Saturday there was sent me a basket of delicate white manchet,[36] and two dozen of fat hens with divers fruits.

In the meanwhile, Friday, Saturday, and part of Sunday we filled 240 pipes of water, and on the Sunday evening we departed without any offence given or received to the value of a farthing. For testimony whereof, the earl sent his friar aboard my ship with a letter to Don Diego Sarmiento, ambassador in England, witnessing how noble we had behaved ourselves, and how justly we had dealt with the inhabitants of  20 the island.

Being ready to set sail, we delivered the Spanish fisherman his bark and discharged another small bark, taken here at our first arrival, with all their furniture, and directed our course from Gomera on the same Sunday fortnight (being the 21 of September) which we arrived at Lancerota, having spent fourteen days among these islands.

From Sunday at 4 at afternoon to Monday at 4, being the 22 day, we ran 20 leagues, for we carried a slack sail for some of our fleet which were not ready to weigh with us.

From 4 on Monday to 12 at noon on Tuesday, being the 23, we ran 25  30 leagues south-west by south, with the breezes at north-east.

From 12 on Tuesday to 12 on Wednesday, being the 24 of September, we made 6 leagues a watch, drawing at our stern a longboat of 14 ton fastened with two great cablets which hung deep in the way and greatly hindered our sailing, holding the same south-west by south course, the wind constant. We had at this time fifty men sick in our ship.

The provost-marshall Steed died[37]

21 September

22 September

24 September
N. Whitney died[38]

Daniel died[39]

---

[36]  A small loaf made of fine flour.
[37]  The provost-marshal carried a special responsibility for discipline.
[38]  Presumably a relative of Captain Whitney.
[39]  Unidentified.

From 12 on Wednesday to 12 on Thursday the 25 day, the breezes continuing but not so strong, we ran about 33 leagues south-west by west and found ourselves in 23 [degrees] and 17 minutes. *25 September*

From Thursday 12 to Friday 12, being the 26 day, we brought ourselves into 22 [degrees] northerly, the wind continuing and the course south-south-west, for whereas we resolved to fall with the westermost island of Cap de Vert, called St Antoine,[40] being informed that the same was desolate and could yield us no refreshing, and that we had sixty men sick aboard us, we determined to touch at Bravo,[41] where I was told that there were people and fresh meat. *September 26*

From 12 the 26 to 12 the 27 we ran 38 leagues and were in 19 degrees 20 minutes; the course south by west. *27 September*

From 12 the 27 to 12 the 28 being Sunday we had a few hours calm and ran but 27 leagues, and were at 12 o'clock in 18 degrees. *28 September*

Monday at noon we found ourselves in 16 degrees and 20 minutes, and Monday night by the star we found ourselves in 15 degrees and half, and then we lay at hull from 8 at night to 6 in the morning, whenas we saw the island of St Iago[42] fair by us. Monday, being Michaelmas Day, there died our master surgeon Mr Nubal, to our great loss. The same day also died Barber, one of our quartermasters and our sailmaker; and we had sixty men sick, and all mine own servants amongst them, that I had none of mine own but my pages to serve me. *Nubal the master-surgeon died. Barber died. The sailmaker died.* *29 September*

Tuesday night we stood off because we meant to water at Bravo, four leagues to the westward of Fuego,[43] being 12 leagues to the west of St Iago. Holcroff, the sergeant of my son's company, died. *Last September*

That night, the pinnace[44] that was Captain Barker's having all her men asleep and not anyone at the watch, drave under our bowsprit and sunk, but the men were saved, though better worthy to have been hanged than saved.

Wednesday we stood back with Bravo but found very inconvenient anchoring and rough ground. And that night, having the Vice-admiral[45] with me at supper, myself being newly come from the shore to seek out a *October 1*

7 westermost] *MS*; wethermost *Schomburgk*
24 Fuego] Fuego Fuego *MS*; fridgo fuego *Schomburgk*
   *Schomburgk*
18 St Iago] Stiago *MS*
32 seek] *MS*; feel

[40] Santo Antão.
[41] Brava, a small island at the SW corner of the Cape Verde islands.
[42] São Tiago.
[43] Fogo. Ralegh accidentally wrote the name twice.
[44] The Page.
[45] Pennington.

better road, a hurlecano[46] fell upon us with most violent rain, and brake both our cables at the instant, greatly to the damage of the ship and all our lives, but it pleased God that her head cast from the shore and drave off. I was myself so wet as the water ran in at my neck and out at my knees as if it had been poured on me with pails. All the rest of our fleet lost their cables and anchors. Three of our small men that rid in a cove close under the land had like all to have perished. Captain Snedall grated on the rocks; Wollaston and King scaped them not their ships' length.[47]

2 October    Thursday we stood up upon a tack to recover the island, for I had sent off my skiff to fish not half a quarter of an hour before the hurlecan, and I gave her lost, and six of my men in her, to my great discomfort, having had so great mortality. But I thank my God I found them in the morning under the shore and recovered them. But I lost another of my pinnaces called the Fifty Crowns (because I paid fifty crowns to the Frenchmen for her) in this storm.

Friday one of my trumpeters and one other of the cookroom died.

Finding that the rains and storms were not yet past in this place, and finding no fair ground to ride in, I resolved rather to leave the island and the refreshing we hoped for here than to endanger our ships, the most of them having lost a cable and anchor, and myself two. This island of Bravo standeth in [    ],[48] a little island but fruitful, having store of goats, cattle, maize, figs, and water; it hath on the north side little islands and broken grounds, which doth as it were impale it; on the west side it hath an excellent watering place in a cove in which there may ride a dozen ships, if they come either before or after the rains and storms which begin in the middle of July and end in the middle of August; and in this cove and all alongst the west side abundance of fish. There is a current which sets very strong from the south to the north and runs in effect all ways so. This night Captain Pigott's lieutenant, called Allen, died.[49]

3 October    Thursday night I stood off a league and then lay by the lee the most

10

20

30

---

7  Snedall] Snedul *MS*

[46] One of the many versions of the Carib word which eventually established itself in English as 'hurricane'.

[47] Snedall died before reaching the American shore. Captain Richard Wollaston commanded the Confidence in the Orinoco but, with Whitney, was delayed and reached San Thomé after it was taken. Like Whitney, he in the end deserted Ralegh. Keymis said hard things about him before they went up the river (Harlow, p. 160). Samuel King also commanded one of the ships in the task force. He remained faithful to Ralegh, and tried to engineer his escape to France.

[48] Gap left in MS. Brava is 14° 50′ N.

[49] He is mentioned by Thornhurst (Harlow, p. 146).

part of the night to stay for some of our ships that were in the cove to take water; so as by 12 on Friday we were about 10 leagues off the island. On Friday morning being the 3 of October our cape-merchant [    ] Kemishe died.[50] Friday at noon, we lay again by lee to stay for King who was in my flyboat, and lay so till Saturday, having sent back Captain Barker[51] in the carvel to seek him; but hearing of neither we filled our sails at 12 and stood away athwart the ocean, steering away towards the coast of Guiana, south-west by west.

From Saturday 12 to Sunday 12 we made 30 leagues.

From Sunday 12 to Monday 12 we made 28 leagues. This Monday morning died Mr John Hayward, ensign to Captain North, and Lieutenant Payton and Mr Hews[52] fell sick. There also died to our great grief our principal refiner Mr Fowler.

From Monday at 12 to Tuesday the 7th of October we made but 4 leagues a watch and in all 24 leagues, by the high[53] not so much, for Tuesday at noon we found ourselves but in 12 degrees and 30 minutes, and then the current set us half a point to the westward of the south-west by south.

From 12 upon Tuesday to 12 on Wednesday the 8th October we had little wind and made but 22 leagues, and we found ourselves in 11 degrees and 39 minutes. This evening my servant [    ] Crabb died, so as I had not any one left to attend me but my pages.

From 12 on Wednesday to 12 on Thursday we had a fresher gale and made 30 leagues, but all the day we bare little sail, the weather being rainy with gusts and much wind, as it is commonly in these parts at the small of the moon.

From 12 on Thursday to 12 on Friday we had nothing but rain and not much wind, so as we made but 4 leagues a watch, to wit 24 leagues, and the nearest that we could observe, the sun shining but little and by starts, was 10 degrees and 8 minutes. But in the afternoon it cleared up, which we hoped that God would have continued,[54] for we were all

Marginal notes: 4 October / 5 October / 6 October / We found ourselves at 12 this Monday in 13 degrees and 7 minutes / October 7 / October 8 / October 9 / October 10

---

12 Hews] Hwes *MS*          24 the day] *MS*; this day *Schomburgk*

[50] Ralegh left a blank for his first name. The cape-merchant was the ship's purser. Ralegh's 'Orders' for the fleet indicate that he would also be responsible for all trading with the Indians (Harlow, p. 126). Presumably this man was a relative of Lawrence Keymis (whose name Ralegh always spells 'Kemishe').

[51] James Barker, who had been captain of the Page.

[52] He died at sea. Ralegh calls him 'my cousin' (Harlow, p. 159).

[53] The altitude; i.e. their observation of the sun.

[54] Ralegh originally wrote 'it cleared up, which God continue'. That was presumably the end of the original entry.

drowned in our cabins, but about 4 o'clock there rose a most fearful blackness over the one half of the sky, and it drave against the wind, which threatened a turnado, and yet it pleased God that it brake but into rain, and the evening again hopeful, but there blew no wind at all, so as we lay becalmed all the night; and the next day, at 12 on Saturday, we

October 11 observed and found ourselves in 10 degrees and 10 minutes, and had not made from noon to noon above 5 leagues.

October 12 From Saturday the 11 day at 12 to Sunday at 12 we had all calms as before, and the little breath which we sometime had was for the most part south and to the westward, which hath seldom been seen in this 10 passages and climate, so as we made not above 6 leagues west by south. In the afternoon the wind took us a-stays[55] and blew a little gale from the north-north-west.

This Sunday morning died Mr Hews, a very honest and civil gentleman, having lien sick but six days. In this sort it pleased God to visit us with great sickness and loss of our ablest men, both landmen and seamen. And having by reason of the turnado at Bravo failed of our watering, we were at this time in miserable estate, not having in our ship above seven days water, sixty sick men, and near 400 leagues off the shore, and becalmed.                                                                           20

We found ourselves this day at noon in 10 degrees, so we had raised since Saturday noon but 10 minutes.

October 13 From Sunday noon to Monday noon we made not above 12 leagues. Observe we could not for the dark weather. A lamentable twenty-four hours it was, in which we lost Captain John Pigott, my lieutenant-general by land, my honest friend Mr John Talbot,[56] one that had lived with me eleven years in the Tower, an excellent general scholar and a faithful true man as lived. We lost also Mr Gardner and Mr Mordent, two very fair-conditioned gentlemen, and mine own cook Francis.

October 14 From Monday at 12 to Tuesday at 12, having in the night a fresh gale 30 with much rain, we ran some 26 leagues. I observed this day, and so I did before, that the morning rainbow doth not give a fair day as in England, but there followed much rain and wind, and that we found the winds here for six or seven days together to the southward of the east, as at

9  sometime] *MS*; sometimes *Schomburgk*          19  near] *MS*; nearly *Schomburgk*
26  Talbot] Tabote *MS*

[55]  They were suddenly head to wind.
[56]  Ralegh's protégé and his secretary in the Tower. Just before his execution, in Oct. 1618, he wrote a memorandum asking his wife to look after Talbot's mother 'who, I fear me, her son being dead, will otherwise perish' (Harlow, p. 284).

south-east and south-south-east, and always rain and gusts more or less.

Wednesday morning we saw another rainbow, and about 10 o'clock it began to gather as black as pitch in the south, and from thence there fell as much rain as I have seen, but with little wind. October 15

From Tuesday 12 to 12 this Wednesday we ran not above 14 leagues. Observe we could not, neither Monday, Tuesday, nor Wednesday, for the darkness of the sky, which is very strange in these parts. For most of the afternoon we steered our ship by candlelight.

From Wednesday 12 to Thursday 12 we had all calms saving some few hours in the night, and from 7 in the morning till 10, and the wind we had was so weak as we made not above 6 leagues. About 10 in the morning it began to rain, and it continued strong till 2 after dinner, the effect of the morning rainbow. About 3, the wind, the little that it was, blew at west-south-west, which hath not often been seen. Captain Jennings died and many fell sick. October 16

Thursday morning a windfall in the north

From Thursday 12 to Friday 12 we could make no reckoning, for the wind changed so often between the south and the west, as after the changing of the tack divers times, we found it best to take in all our sails and lie at hull, for the wind that blew was horrible with violent rain, and at south-west and south-south-west. And so it continued all night, and so it doth continue this Saturday morning. And [I] think that since the Indies were discovered never was the like wind found in this high,[57] which we guess to be about nine degrees, for we could not observe since Monday last. 17

Saturday morning it cleared up, and at noon we found ourselves in 9 degrees and 45 minutes as we supposed, but the wind directly contrary as well in the storms as in the sun shining, and lying at hull we drave to the north-west and fell altogether to leeward. We set sail after dinner and stood by a wind to the eastward, but could lie but south-east and by east. October 18

The night proved altogether calm, so as we moved no way, but we hoped that upon the change of the moon, which changed Sunday about 11 o'clock, that God would send us the long-looked-for breeze. This night died my cousin Payton, lieutenant of my son's company.

[*For ten days, until 29 October, the journal has only a continuation of the adverse winds and bad weather to record. A waterspout just missed them. One night when it was fair they saw in the sky 'Magellan's cloud, round and white'.*]

---

[57] Latitude.

*On 23 October Ralegh began to 'fear that we shall not be able to fetch our port'.*
*Water was getting very short.*]

October 29    From Tuesday to Wednesday 12 we had the wind large,[58] but so
gentle a wind as we made not above 10 leagues, and found ourselves by
an obscure observation in 6 degrees. Two rainbows we had in the
morning but fair weather hath hitherto followed, and so we hoped that
the rains had been past, but the circle about the moon the Tuesday night
and the double rainbow on Wednesday morning paid us towards the
evening with rain and wind, in which gust we made shift to save some
three hogheads of water, besides that the company, having been many    10
days scanted and pressed with drought,[59] drank up whole quarter cans
of the bitter rainwater. The Wednesday night was also calm, with
thunder and lightning.

October 30    Thursday morning we had again a double rainbow, which put us in
fear that the rains would never end. From Wednesday 12 to Thursday
12 we made not above 6 leagues, having always uncomfortable rains and
dead calms.

The last of October at night, rising out of bed, being in a great sweat
by reason of a sudden gust and much clamour in the ship before they
could get down the sails, I took a violent cold, which cast me into a    20
burning fever, than which never man endured any more violent, nor
never man suffered a more furious heat and an unquenchable drought.
For the first twenty days I never received any sustenance but now and
then a stewed prune, but drank every hour day and night, and sweat so
strongly as I changed my shirts thrice every day and thrice every night.

11 of    The 11 of November we made the north cape of Wiapoco,[60] the cape
November  then bearing south-west and by west as they told me, for I was not yet
able to move out of my bed. We rode in 6 fathom, 5 leagues off the shore.
I sent in my skiff to enquire for my old servant Leonard the Indian, who
been with me in England three or four years;[61] the same man that took    30
Mr Harcourt's brother and fifty of his men when they came upon that
coast and were in extreme distress, having neither meat to carry them
home nor means to live there, but by the help of this Indian, whom they
made believe that they were my men. But I could not hear of him by my

[58] Abaft the beam; i.e. the wind was at last from the right direction.
[59] Here and elsewhere spelt 'drough' in MS.
[60] Cape Orange, at the mouth of the Oiapoque, 4° 20' N., 51° 30' W., about 750 miles
SE of the mouth of the Orinoco. It was here that Leigh and Harcourt attempted to set up
their colonies in 1604 and 1609; see Introduction, p. 179.
[61] Leonard had returned to his homeland. Harcourt told the settlers he left behind to
look out for him and as indicated he gave them signal help.

boat that I sent in, for he was removed 30 mile into the country, and because I had an ill road and 5 leagues off, I durst not stay his sending for, but stood away for Caliana,[62] where the cacique was also my servant and had lived with me in the Tower two years.[63]

Yet the 12 day we weighed and stood somewhat nearer the land some 3 leagues off. My boat going and returning brought us some of the country fruits, and left in the port two Hollanders,[64] trading for arnotto, gums, and speckled wood.[65]     12 November

The 13 I set sail alongst the coast and anchored that night in 11 fathom near an island where there were so many birds as they killed them with staves. There grows upon it those trees which bear the great cods of hereculla silk.[66] This island is but little and is from the mainland some 4 leagues. The same afternoon we weighed and stood alongst the coast towards Caliana west-south-west and south-west and by west, and anchored again in the evening some 5 leagues south-west from the island of birds, in 5 fathom within a kind of bay.     13 November

The 14th day we stood out of the bay, and passed by three or four islands where there grew many trees of those that bear the cods of silk also. By the islands we had 10 fathom, from whence we stood alongst into 6 fathom and came to an anchor. Thence I sent my barge ashore to enquire for my servant Harry the Indian, who [sent] his brother unto me with two other caciques, promising to come to me with provisions if I came not into the river within a day or two. These Indians stayed with me that night, offering their service and all they had. Mine own weakness, which still continued, and the desire I had to be carried ashore to change the air, and out of an unsavoury ship pestered with many sick men which being unable to move poisoned us with a most filthy stench, persuaded me to adventure my ship over a bar where never any vessel of burden had passed.     14 November

In the road my barge found one Janson of Flushing who had traded

---

7 trading] *MS; omitted Schomburgk*     7 arnotto] Onotto *MS*     21 sent] not in *MS*

[62] Cayenne, 80 miles NW.

[63] This is Harry; see below, p. 212/8.

[64] The interest of the Dutch in Guiana had been aroused by Ralegh's treatise of 1596; an expedition went up the Orinoco in 1597–8.

[65] Arnotto is an orange dye from the shrub *bixa orellana*. Speckled wood is 'the beautiful Letter- or Snake-wood ... from the tree *Piratinera Guianensis* ... now very scarce' (Schomburgk, writing in 1848).

[66] The fibres from the silk-cotton tree cannot be woven, and were used like kapok for stuffing pillows etc.

that place about a dozen years, who came to me where I rid without, offering me his service for the bringing in of my ship, and assuring me that on the top of a full sea there was 3 fathom, whereupon the rest of my fleet went into the river and anchored within in 4 and 5 fathom. It flows there north-east and south-west. Here I stayed at anchor from the 14th
17 November  day to the 17 day, when by the help of Janson I got over the bar in 3 fathom a quarter less,[67] when I drew 17 foot water.

After I had stayed in Caliana a day or two, my servant Harry came to me, who had almost forgotten his English, and brought me great store of very good cassavi bread, with which I fed my company some seven or 10 eight days and put up a hogshead full for store. He brought great plenty of roasted mullets, which were very good meat, great store of plantains and piones[68] with divers other sorts of fruits and pistaches;[69] but as yet I durst not adventure to eat of the pione, which tempted me exceedingly. But after a day or two, being carried ashore and sitting under a tent, I began to eat of the pione, which greatly refreshed me. And after that I fed on the pork of the country[70] and of the armadillios, and began to gather a little strength.

Here I also set all my sick men ashore and made clean my ship, and where they all recovered. And here we buried Captain Hastings,[71] who 20
Captain Pigott  died ten days or more before, and with him my sergeant-majors Hart and Captain Henry Snedall, giving the charge of Snedall's ship to my servant Captain Robert Smith of Cornwall. We also in this river set up our barges, and made clean our ships, trimmed up our cask, and filled store of water, set up our smith's forge and made such iron-work as the fleet needed. In this river we refreshed ourselves from the 17 day of
December 4  November till the 4th of December.

Captain Janson, whom we found a very honest man, departed from Caliana towards Flushing the [    ] and Captain Peter Alley, being still troubled with the vertigo, and desirous therefore to return because 30 unable to endure the rolling of the ship, I got passage for him with Janson, and for [    ], who could not yet recover his health in this hot country.

---

12  plantains] plantens *MS*          30  and] *MS; omitted Schomburgk*
[67]  Ralegh originally wrote '3 fathom & a half'.
[68]  Probably pineapples.
[69]  Pistachio nuts.
[70]  The peccary (Schomburgk).
[71]  It is strange that Hastings and Pigott (he had died a month earlier) were not buried at sea.

The 4th of December I weighed and fell down to the haven's mouth, not daring to lose the spring tide. The rest of my ships had yet somewhat to do about their boats which they newly set up, to wit the Flying Hart, wherein was Sir John Ferne, and the Chudley; all promised to follow within a day or two, and I told them that I would stay them at the Triangle islands called Epinessarie.[72] Only the Vice-admiral followed me, to wit Captain Pennington in the Jason. And notwithstanding that I had sounded the bar twice or thrice before I durst put over, yet I came aground in 16 foot, it being a quarter ebb ere I could get over by reason of the little wind which I found a-seaboard. We used all the help we had by warping[73] and otherwise, being greatly assisted by the Vice-admiral boats and warps, but we stuck two whole tides and two nights, and afterward had foul water in 3 fathom. But God favoured us with very fair weather, and the ground was all ooze and very soft; for had it been hard ground and any weather at all, we had left our bones there.

In this melancholy toil we spent the 5th and 6th day and then came to anchor at the Triangle islands before spoken of in 6 fathom, where I stayed for the rest of the fleet till the 10 day, who, neglecting the spring tide, though they drew by far less water than I did, were like to have perished upon the flats where I struck.

The 10 day the rest of the fleet came to me all but the Chudley. And then I embarked my men in five ships for Orenoke, to wit 400 soldiers and sailors. The ships I sent off were the Encounter, commanded by Captain Whitney, the supply[74] of Captain King, the pink[75] of Robert Smith, Captain Wollaston,[76] and Captain Hall.

Sir Warham St Leger, to whom as to my lieutenant I gave the charge of those companies, fell extreme sick at Caliana, and in his place as sergeant-major I appointed my nephew George Ralegh. The land companies were commanded by Captain Parker, Captain North, my son W. Ralegh, Captain Thornhurst, Captain Hall,[77] and Captain Chudleigh's Lieutenant;[78] Captain Kemys having the chief charge for their landing within the river.

---

26 Warham St Leger] Warran Sentleger *MS*        31 Chudleigh's] Chudles *MS*
31 Kemys] Kemish *MS*

[72] 'At present known as the "îles du Salut"' (Schomburgk).
[73] The levering effect of ropes attached to objects ashore or in another ship.
[74] Supply-boat. Ralegh calls it a flyboat in the Apology.
[75] In the Apology this is called a carvel.        [76] In the Confidence.
[77] This seems to be a mistake; Hall was one of the ships' captains, and in the Apology the fourth company is given to Lieutenant Bradshaw.
[78] His name was Pridieux (Apology).

The 10 day they parted from us with a month victuals or somewhat more. I gave them order to stay a day or two in Shurinamo[79] to get pilots and to bring some of our great barges aground who were weak and leaky by towing them from Caliana. I also gave them order to send into Dessekebe,[80] for I assured them that they could not want pilots there for Orenoke, being the next great river adjoining unto it, and to which the Spaniards of Orenoke had daily recourse.

December 15    The 15 of December we made the land near Puncto Anegada[81] at the mouth of Orenoke, and that night we saw the north-east part of Trinidado, and came to anchor in 30 fathom, 6 leagues off the shore. From thence we coasted the island near the south side in 15 fathom, and near the shore in 10 and 11 fathom, and coming close aboard the point of the road at the west end of the island, which point they naturally call Curiapan,[82] and the Spaniards Puncto de Gallo, we had 5 fathom.

[*Ralegh now briefly records the activities of the next five weeks. They stayed at Punta Gallo till the end of December, then moved up the west coast of Trinidad to 'Terra de Bri', near Port of Spain.*]

[1618]

January the    The 19 of January we sent up Sir John Ferne's ship to the Spanish port
19    to try if they would trade for tobacco and other things, but when her boat was near the shore, while they on the land were in parle with Captain Giles, who had charge of the boat, the Spaniards gave them a volley of some twenty muskets at 40 paces distant, and yet hurt never a man. As our boat put off, they called our men thieves and traitors with all manner of opprobrious speeches.

The [   ] of January we sent back the Vice-admiral, Captain Pennington, to Puncto Gallo to attend the return of our companies in Orenoke.

January 29    The 29 of January we lost one of Sir John Ferne's men, who being ashore boiling of the country pitch was shot by a Spaniard, who lay in the woods all night with five other Spaniards. Our ships taking the alarm, we manned out our boats. I took my barge with six shot, Captain Chudleigh

33  manned] mand *MS*; waied *Schomburgk*          33  Chudleigh] Chudley *MS*
[79]  The River Surinam.
[80]  Essequibo (near modern Georgetown, Guyana).
[81]  'Anegado' in the Apology. Schomburgk believed this to be 'the present point Bariana' (see Map 4, p. 186), although in the Apology it is described as being on 'the north side' of the river.
[82]  i.e. it is so called by the natives.

took his skiff and Sir W. St Leger his. We pursued them with all haste possible and forced them to forsake their canoas and run into the thick woods, leaving behind them their cloaks and all other their implements but their arms. There were of Sir John Ferne's men three and one boy; one of them was slain, one swam aboard, and [the] third hid himself in the woods till my barge came ashore; the boy we suppose was carried with them alive.

The last of January we returned from the pitch land to Puncto Gallo, January the hoping to meet our men which we sent into Orenoke. last

The 1st of February the sentinel which we had laid to the eastward of February the Puncto Gallo to discover if any ships or boats came from the east alongst 1 the coast (for we could not discover anything where we rode till they were within a mile of us, by that the point lay out so far), these of the sentinel discovered seven Indians and brought them unto us.[83] They had a village some 16 mile from us to the eastward, and as it proved afterward came but as spies to discover our forces. They were two days aboard and would be acknown that they could speak any word of Spanish,[84] but by signs they made us know that they dwelt but one day's journey towards the east. I kept three of them aboard and sent twelve of my men with the other four to see their town and to trade with them. But in their way thitherward, one of the Vice-admiral's men espied an Indian, one of the four who two year before he had seen in Orenoke,[85] and taking him by the arm told him that he knew him, and that he could speak Spanish. In the end, after many threats he spake, and confessed that one of the three aboard my ship could also speak Spanish; whereupon the Vice-admiral's man returning aboard me, and I threatening the chief of those which I had kept, one of them spake Spanish, and told me that certain Indians of the drowned lands inhabited by a nation called Tibitivas, arriving in a canoa at his port, told him that the English in Orenoke had taken St Thomé, slain Diego de

---

1 St Leger] Sentleger *MS*     5 the third] third *MS*     27 threatening] *MS*; threating *Schomburgk*

[83] This must have been the party despatched by the Spaniards in a 'pirogue' or dugout to inform the authorities in Trinidad of the fall of San Thomé. Pedro Simon's narrative (Harlow, p. 177) explains that when the pirogue was intercepted the Spaniards got away but some Indians were captured. It was some time before they admitted they were from San Thomé.

[84] Ralegh seems to have left out a negative. They would not be acknown (i.e. they would not acknowledge) that they knew Spanish.

[85] He would have been either on one of the tobacco-smuggling voyages or in a ship that Ralegh is reputed to have sent on reconnaissance in 1615. See Lorimer 1978, p. 148.

Palmita[86] the governor, slain Captain Erenetta[87] and Captain John
Rues,[88] and that the rest of the Spaniards (their captains slain) fled into
the mountains; and that two English captains were also slain. This tale
was also confirmed by another Indian which my men brought from the
Indian town, with divers other particularities, which I forbear to set
down till I know the truth, for the 6 of this month[89] I sent the Vice-
admiral skiff from Puncto Gallo towards Orenoke, manned with ten
musketeers, to understand what my men had done there, and the cause
of their long stay, having received no news from them since they entered
Orenoke, but by these Indians, since the 10 of December, other than    10
that they were at the river's mouth, which news Captain Chudleigh (who
accompanied them so far) brought me.

January the       The 3 of February my men returned from the Indian town and
3[90]          brought with them some cassavi bread with other fruits, and very fair
oranges.

January the 4      The 4 of February a boat that I had sent over to the south side where I
saw a great fire, returned not finding any people there.

January 6         The 6 day I sent a skiff over toward Orenoke manned with ten
musketeers to hear what was become of my men there. The same day
came into this port Captain Giner of the Isle of Wight and his    20
pinnace.

January 8         The 8 day I sent sixteen musketeers by land to the Indian town to
bring away some of the Indians which spake Spanish, and to separate
them from those two which I kept aboard me, because I found them so
divers in their reports as touching Orenoke, and because one of them
had confessed the day before that himself, with the pilot which I sent
into Orenoke in the skiff and one of them in the Indian town, were in St
Thomé when it was taken by the English. I was desirous by taking two or
three of the rest to know the truth, but so careless were the mariners I
sent as they suffered all to go loose and escape. But I had yet two Indians    30
aboard me, and a third went pilot for Orenoke; one of these I sent away
with knives to trade with a nation inhabiting the east part of Trinidado
called the Nepoyios, with this charge, that if he came not again after four
days (which was the time by him required) that I would then hang his

---

[86]  Diego Palomeque de Acuña, the unpopular governor of Trinidad and Guiana.
[87]  Arias Nieto.
[88]  Juan Ruiz Monje.
[89]  i.e. 6 Feb. Ralegh is filling in the journal after the date in question, and is here
anticipating the entry for this date.
[90]  Four times Ralegh enters the wrong month in the margin of the log.

brother which was the pilot as aforesaid, and this other Indian aboard; to which the Indian aboard condescented.[91]

But the 12 of February I went ashore and took the Indian with me, February 12 fastened and well bound to one of my men, so carried him with me to show me the trees which yield balsamum, of which I had recovered a nutful of that kind which smells like angolica and is very rare and precious. And after it was 10 o'clock and very hot, the wood also being full of mosquitoes, I returned and left my Indian in charge with one of my master's mates and three others. But I was no sooner gone but they

10 untied him, and he at the instant took the wood and escaped, notwithstanding that I had told them that if the Indian gat but a tree between him and them and were loose, that all the English in the fleet could not fetch him again. I had now none left but the pilot sent to Orenoke, and I fear me that he also will slip away by the negligence of the mariners, who (I mean the common sort) are diligent in nothing but pillaging and stealing.

The 13 day Captain Giner and I made an agreement that he should 13 February follow me with his small ship and pinnace for six months after this 13 day.

20 The same evening I sent Sir W. St Leger, Captain Chudleigh, and Captain Giles with sixty men to the Indian town to try if I could recover any of them.[92]

## 2. *Letter to Sir Ralph Winwood*
### (21 March 1618)[1]

Sir,

As I have not hitherto given you any account of our proceedings and passage towards the Indies, so have I no other subject to write of since our arrival than of the greatest and sharpest misfortunes that have ever befallen any man.

For whereas, for the first, all those that navigate between Capo Verde and America do pass it in fifteen or twenty days at most, we found the

---

[91] Condescended, agreed.

[92] The journal ends at this point. According to the testimony of the chaplain Samuel Jones to the Privy Council, it was on 13 Feb. that Ralegh received the first news from the task force (Harlow, pp. 234, 236; see Introduction, p. 188). Pedro Simon's narrative, using the evidence of the Indians captured by Ralegh, said that two launches arrived (Harlow, p. 177). These would presumably be Pennington's skiff, despatched on 6 Feb., and Peter Andrews's long-delayed boat. Keymis and the ships did not arrive until 2 Mar.

[1] Unknown to Ralegh, Sir Ralph Winwood had died on 27 Oct. 1617.

winds so contrary (which is also contrary to nature), and so many violent
storms and rains, as we spent six weeks in that passage. By reason
whereof, and that in so great heat we wanted water (for at the Isle Bravo
of Cap de Verd we lost our cables and anchors and our water cask, being
driven from the island with a hurlican, and were all like to have perished)
great sickness fell amongst us and carried away great numbers of our
ablest men both for sea and land.

The 17 of November we had sight of the coast of Guiana, and soon
after came to anchor in five degrees at the river Caliana. Here we stayed
till the 4th of December, landed our sick men, set up the barges and    10
shallops which we brought out of England in quarters, washed our ships,
and took in fresh water; being fed and assisted by the Indians of my old
acquaintance, with a great deal of love and respect.

Myself having been in the hands of death, without hope, some six
weeks (and not yet able otherwise to move than as I was carried in a
chair) gave order to five small ships to sail into Orenoke, having Captain
Keymis for their conductor towards the mine; and in those five ships five
companies of fifty,[2] under the command of Captain Parker[3] and Captain
North[4] (brothers to the Lord Mounteagle[5] and the Lord North[6]),
valiant gentlemen and of infinite patience for the labour, hunger, and    20
heat which they have endured. My son had the third company, Captain
Thornhurst of Kent the fourth, Captain Chudleigh (by his lieutenant[7])
the fifth. But as my sergeant-major, Captain Pigott of the Low
Countries, died in the former miserable passage, so my lieutenant, Sir
Warham St Leger, lay sick without hope of life, and the charge
conferred on my nephew George Ralegh, who had also served long with

---

17 Keymis] Kemish *MS*          22 Thornhurst] Thornix *MS*

[2] It is six companies in the Apology. Again Ralegh seems forgetful about the company
commanded by Lieutenant Bradshaw (compare the journal, p. 213).

[3] Charles Parker.

[4] Roger North. Although his testimony to the Lords was not favourable to Ralegh, he
was a firm believer in the cause of colonizing Guiana and the Amazon, and prepared an
expedition after Ralegh's death. James played with him as he had played with Ralegh, first
countenancing him, then at the instigation of Gondomar trying to stop him. In the 1620s
he made a second venture with Harcourt. A colony was formed on the Amazon, but did not
last.

[5] William Parker, Lord Mounteagle, renowned for revealing the impending Gun-
powder Plot in 1605.

[6] Dudley North, third baron, 1581–1666, discoverer of the springs at Tunbridge
Wells. He was sympathetic to the Parliamentary cause in the Civil War. An essayist and
poet.

[7] Prideux.

singular commendations in the Low Countries, but by reason of my absence and of Sir Warham's was not so well obeyed as the enterprise required.

As they passed up the river, the Spaniards began the war and shot at us both with their ordnance and muskets; whereupon the companies were forced to charge them, and soon after beat them out of their town. In the assault whereof my son (having more desire of honour than of safety) was slain; and with whom (to say the truth) all respect of the world hath taken end in me. And although these five captains had as weak companies as ever followed valiant leaders, yet there were amongst them some twenty or thirty very adventurous gentlemen, and of singular courage, as, of my son's company, Mr Knevet, Mr Hammond, Mr Langworth, Mr John Plessington, his officers; Sir John Hampden, Mr Simon Leak (corporal of the field), Mr Hammond's elder brother, Mr Nicholas of Buckingham, Mr Roberts of Kent, Mr Perin, Mr Tresham, Mr Molineux, Mr Winter, and his brother, Mr Way, Mr Miles Herbert, Mr William Herbert, Mr Bradshaw, Captain Hall, and others.

Sir, I set down the names of these gentlemen to the end that if his majesty shall have cause to use their service, it may please you to take knowledge of them for very sufficient men.

The other five ships stayed at Trinidado, having no other port capable of them near Guiana. The second ship was commanded by my vice-admiral Captain John Pennington, of whom (to do him right) I must confess that he is one of the sufficientest gentlemen for the sea that England hath. The third by Sir Warham St Leger, an exceeding valiant and worthy gentleman. The fourth by Sir John Ferne, and the fifth by Captain Chudleigh of Devon. With these five ships I daily attended the armada of Spain,[8] which had they set upon us, our force divided (the one half in Orenoque, a hundred and fifty miles from us) we had not only been torn in pieces, but all those in the river had also perished, being of no defence at all for a sea fight. For we had resolved to have burnt by their sides[9] and to have died there, had the armada arrived. But belike they stay for us at Marguerita,[10] by which they know we must pass towards the Indies.

For it pleased his majesty to value us at so little as to command me upon my allegiance to set down under my hand the country and the very

---

16 Molineux] Mullinax *MS*

[8] i.e. waited for the fleet which I expected Spain to be sending out.
[9] i.e. fight to the last, and go down in burning ships rather than surrender.
[10] The island of Margarita, 200 miles W. of Trinidad.

river by which I was to enter it; to set down the number of my men, and
burden of my ships, with what ordnance every ship carried. Which being
made known to the Spanish ambassador, and by him in post to the king
of Spain, a despatch was made by him and his letters sent from Madril[11]
before my departure out of the Thames. For his first letter, sent by a
bark of advice, was dated the 19th of March, 1617, at Madril; which
letter I have here-enclosed sent your honour. The rest I reserve, not
knowing whether these may be intercepted or not: the second, of the
king's, dated the 17th of May, sent also by a caravel to Diego de
Palomeque, governor of Guiana, El Dorado, and Trinidado; the third,    10
by the bishop of Puerto Ricco, and delivered to Palomeque the 15th of
July at Trinidado; and the fourth was sent from the farmer and secretary
of his customs in the Indies at the same time. By that of the king's hand,
brought by the bishop, there was also a commission for the speedy
levying of 300 soldiers and ten pieces of ordnance to be sent from Puerto
Ricco for the defence of Guiana; 150 from Nuevo Reino de Granado
under the command of Captain Antonio Musica, and the other 150
from Puerto Rico to be conducted by Captain Francisco Zanchio.

   Now sir, if all that have traded the Indies since his majesty's time
know it that the Spaniards have flayed alive these poor men which they    20
have taken, being but merchant men, what death and torment shall we
expect if they conquer us? Certainly they have hitherto failed grossly,
being set out unto them as we were, both for our numbers, time, and
place.

   Lastly, to make an apology for not working the mine—although I
know not (his majesty excepted) whom I am to satisfy so much as myself,
having lost my son and my estate in the enterprise. Yet it is true that the
Spaniards took more care to defend the passages leading unto it than
they did their town, which (say the king's instructions) they might easily
do, the country being *aspera et fragosa*.[12] But it is true that when Keymis    30
found the rivers low, and that he could not approach the banks in most
places near the mine by a mile, and where he found a descent, a volley of
muskets came from the woods upon the banks and slew two of the
rowers, hurt six others, and shot a valiant gentleman, Captain Thornhurst, in the head, of which wound he hath languished to this day—he
(to wit, Keymis) following his own advice that it was in vain to discover
the mine (for he gave me this for excuse at his return, that the companies

---

[11] Madrid.                    [12] Rough and uneven.

of English in their town of St Thomé were hardly able to defend it against the daily and nightly alarms and assaults of the Spaniards; that the passage to the mine was of thick and impassable woods; that, being discovered, they had no men to work it), did not discover it at all. For it is true that the Spaniards, having two gold mines near the town, the one possessed by Petro Rodrigo de Parama, the second mine by Hernian Fruntino,[13] the third, of silver, by Francisco Fashardo,[14] [left them] for the want of negroes to work them. For as the Indians cannot be constrained, by a law of Charles the Fifth, so the Spaniards will not,
10 neither can they endure the labour of these mines. Whatsoever that braggadochio the Spanish ambassador say, I shall prove it under the proprietaries' hand, by the custom books, and by the king's quinto,[15] of which I recovered an ingot or two. And I shall make it appear, to any prince or state that will undertake it, how easily those mines and five or six more may be possessed, and the most of them in those places which never yet have been attempted by any enemy, nor any passage to them ever discovered by the English, Dutch, or French.

But at Keymis's return from Orenoque, when I rejected his counsel and his course, and told him that he had undone me and wounded my
20 credit with the king past recovery, he slew himself. For I told him that seeing my son was lost, I cared not if he had lost a hundred more in opening the mine, so my credit[16] had been saved. For I protest before God, had not Captain Whitney (whom I gave more countenance unto than to all the captains of my fleet) run from me at the Granados, and carried another ship with him of Captain Wollaston's, I would have left my body at St Thomé by my son's, or have brought with me out of that or other mines so much gold ore as should have satisfied the king that I had propounded no vain thing.

What shall become of me now I know not. I am unpardoned in
30 England and my poor estate consumed; and whether any other prince or state will give me bread I know not. I desire your honour to hold me in your good opinion, and to remember[17] my service to my lords of Arundel and Pembroke; to take some pity on my poor wife, to whom I

7 left them] *E. Edwards*; *not in MS (PRO and Hatfield)*

[13] Cebrian Frontino, reputed to be one of those plotting against the governor of San Thomé (Harlow, p. 221).

[14] Francisco Fajardo, also named in the Spanish narratives as an opponent of the San Thomé governor (Harlow, p. 221).

[15] The fifth part of all bullion reserved for the king.

[16] Credibility, trustworthiness (as regards the existence of the mine).

[17] Give assurance of.

dare not write for renewing the sorrow for her son;[18] and beseech you to give a copy of these to my Lord Carew. For to a broken mind, to a weak body, and weak eyes, it is a torment to write many letters. I have found many things of importance for discovering the estate and weakness of the Indies, which if I live I shall hereafter impart unto your honour, to whom I shall ever remain a faithful servant.[19]

W. Ralegh.

Sir, since the death of Keymis, it is confessed by the sergeant-major and other of his inward friends that he told them, when they were at the river's mouth coming thence, that he could have brought them to the mine within two hours' march from the river's side. But because my son was slain, myself unpardoned and not like to live, he had no reason to open the mine either for the Spaniards or for the king. They answered that the king (though I were not pardoned) had granted me my patent under the great seal. He replied that the grant to me was to a man who was *non ens* in law, and therefore of no force. This discourse he had, which I knew not of till after his death. When I was resolved to write to your honour, he prayed me to join with him in excusing his not going to the mine. I answered him that I would not do it; that if himself could satisfy the king and the state that he had reason not to open it, I should be glad of it, but for my part I must avow it that he knew it, and that he might with little loss have done it; other excuse I would not frame. He then told me that he would wait on me presently and give me better satisfaction. But I was no sooner come from him into my cabin but I heard a pistol go off over my head; and sending up to know who shot it, word was brought that Keymis had shot it out of his cabin window to cleanse it. His boy, going into the cabin, found him lying on his bed with much blood by him, and looking on his face saw he was dead. The pistol being but little, the bullet did but crack his rib; but he, turning him over, found a long knife in his body, all but the handle.

Sir, I have sent into England, in a flyboat,[20] with my cousin Herbert (a very valiant and honest gentleman), divers other unworthy persons, good for nothing either by land or sea; and, though it was at their own suit, yet I know that they will wrong me in all that they can. I beseech

---

[18] How was Lady Ralegh first to receive the news of her son's death?

[19] Ralegh does not realize what awaits him in England. He is expecting Winwood to listen enthusiastically to his information about the vulnerability of Spain's empire.

[20] Two-masted vessel with high square stern, broad beam, and shallow draft. Dutch *vlieboot* (from the Vlie region in northern Holland).

your honour that this scum of men may not be believed of me, who have taken more pain and suffered more than the meanest rascal in the ship. These being gone, I shall be able if I live to keep the sea till the end of August, with four reasonable good ships.

Sir, whensoever God shall permit me to arrive in any part of Europe, I will not fail to let your honour know what we have done. Till then, and ever,

Your honour's servant,<br>W. Ralegh.

10 From St Christophers, one of the islands of the Antillias, the 21th of March, 1617.

## 3. *Letter to Lady Ralegh*
### (22 March 1618)

I was loth to write because I knew not how to comfort you. And God knows, I never knew what sorrow meant till now. All that I can say to you is that you must obey the will and providence of God, and remember that the queen's majesty bare the loss of Prince Henry with a magnanimous heart, and the Lady Harrington of her son.[1] Comfort your heart (dearest Bess), I shall sorrow for us both; and I shall sorrow the less because I have not long to sorrow, because not long to live. I refer you to Mr Secretary Winwood's letter, who will give you a copy of it if you send for it. Therein you shall know what hath past, which I have 10 written by that letter, for my brains are broken, and 'tis a torment for me to write, and especially of misery. I have desired Mr Secretary to give my Lord Carew a copy of his letter. I have cleansed my ship of sick men and sent them home, and hope God will send us somewhat ere we return. Commend me to all at Lothbury.[2] You shall hear from me, if I live, from Newfoundland, where I mean to make clean my ships and to revictual; for I have tobacco enough to pay for it. The Lord bless you, and comfort you, that you may bear patiently the death of your valiant son.

March the 22th, from the fleet, St Christophers.

Your<br>W. Ralegh

1 knew] *Harley*; know *Sloane*     5 son] *Harley*; only son *Sloane*     6 dearest] *Harley*; dear *Sloane*     14 Commend ... Lothbury] *Sloane*; *not in Harley*

[1] Anne, Lady Harington, widow of John, first Baron Harington of Exton (d. 1613). Her eldest son died in infancy; her second son, John, a scholarly young man and a close friend of Prince Henry, died in 1614, aged 22.

[2] A street in the City of London.

I protest before the majesty of God, that as Sir Francis Drake and Sir John Hawkins died heart-broken when they failed of their enterprise,[3] I could willingly do the like, did I not contend against sorrow for your sake in hope to provide somewhat for you, and to comfort and relieve you. If I live to return, resolve yourself that it is the care for you that hath strengthened my heart. It is true that Kemys might have gone directly to the mine, and meant it. But after my son's death, he made them to believe he knew not the way, and excused himself upon the want of water in the river, and, counterfeiting many impediments, left it unfound. When he came back, I told him that he had undone me and that my credit was lost for ever. He answered that when my son was lost and that he left me so weak that he resolved not to find me alive, he had no reason to enrich a company of rascals, who after my son's death made no account of him. He further told me that the English sent up into Guiana could hardly defend the Spanish town of St Thomé which they had taken, and therefore for them to pass through thick woods it was impossible; and more impossible to have victuals brought them into the mountains. And it is true that the governor Diego Palomeque and four other captains being slain, whereof Wat slew one—Plessington, Wat's sergeant, and John of Moroccoes, one of his men, slew other two—I say five of them slain in the entrance of the town, the rest went off in a whole body, and took more care to defend the passages to their mines (of which they had three within a league of the town, besides a mine that was about five miles off) than they did of the town itself.

Yet Keymis at the first was resolved to go to the mine. But when he came to the bank-side to land, he had two of his men slain outright from the bank and six other hurt, and Captain Thornhurst shot in the head, of which wound and the accidents thereof he hath pined away these twelve weeks.

Now when Keymis came back, and gave me the former reasons which moved him not to open the mine—the one, the death of my son; the second, the weakness of the English, and their impossibilities to work it and to be victualled; a third that it were a folly to discover it for the Spaniards; and the last, both my weakness and my being

3 contend ... relieve you] *Harley*; contend with sorrow, to comfort, and relieve you *Sloane*        13 of rascals] *Harley*; *not in Sloane*        19 Wat] *Harley*; my son Wat *Sloane*        24 town] *Harley*; city *Sloane*        34 the last ... my being] *Sloane*; lastly, my weakness being *Harley*

[3] Both Drake and Hawkins died at sea during the unsuccessful West Indian expedition of 1595–6.

unpardoned[4]—and that I rejected all these his arguments, and told him that I must leave him to himself to resolve it to the king and the state, he shut up himself into his cabin and shot himself with a pocket pistol, which broke one of his ribs, and finding that it had not prevailed, he thrust a long knife under his short ribs up to the handle, and died.

Thus much I have written to Mr Secretary, to whose letters I refer you. But because I think my friends will rather hearken after you than any other to know the truth, I did after the sealing break open your letter again to let you know in brief the state of that business, which I pray you impart to my Lord of Northumberland[5] and Sil Skory[6] and to Sir John Leigh.[7]

For the rest, there was never poor man so exposed to the slaughter as I was. For, being commanded upon my allegiance to set down not only the country but the very river by which I was to enter it, to name my ships, number my men and my artillery, this now was sent by the Spanish ambassador to his master, the king of Spain. The king wrote his letters to all parts of the Indies, especially to the governor Palomeque of Guiana, El Dorado, and Trinidado, of which the first letter bare date the 19th of March, 1617, at Madril, when I had not yet left the Thames, which letter I have sent to Mr Secretary. I have also two other letters of the king's, which I reserve, and one of the council. The king also sent a commission to levy 300 soldiers out of his garrison of Nuevo Regno de Granadoes e Porto Rico, with ten pieces of brass ordnance to entertain us. He also prepared an armado by sea to set upon us. It were long to tell you how we were preserved. If I live, I shall make it known. My brains are broken, I cannot write much. I live yet, and I told you why.

Whitney, for whom I sold all my plate at Plymouth, and to whom I gave more credit and countenance than all the captains of my fleet, ran from me at the Granadoes, and Wollaston with him. So as I am now but five ships, and one of those I have sent home, my flyboat, and in her a rabble of idle rascals, which I know will not spare to wound me, but I

---

7 But because ... other] *Sloane; not in Harley*        25 If I ... known] *Harley; not in Sloane*

[4] Ralegh has merged what he learned of Keymis's motives after his death with the excuses Keymis actually offered. See the postscript to the Winwood letter.

[5] Henry Percy, ninth earl of Northumberland; the 'wizard earl', another victim of James, who with Ralegh made the Tower a centre of learning and scientific enquiry. He was not released until 1621.

[6] Silvanus Scory, whose attempt in verse to keep Ralegh in England is printed in E. Edwards, vol. i, 598. Keymis wrote to him from Guiana (Harlow, pp. 160–1).

[7] Sir John Leigh or Lee was knighted for his part in the Cadiz expedition of 1596.

care not. I am sure there is never a base slave in all the fleet hath taken the care and pains that I have done, hath slept so little and travailed so much. My friends will not believe them, and for the rest I care not. God in heaven bless you and strengthen your heart.

Your

W. Ralegh

## 4. *The Apology*
### (Written at Salisbury, 28–31 July 1618)

If the ill success of this enterprise of mine had been without example, I should have needed a large discourse, and many arguments for my justification. But if the vain attempts of the greatest princes of Europe, both among themselves and against the great Turk, are in all modern histories left to every eye to peruse, it is not so strange that myself, being but a private man and drawing after me the chains and fetters whereunto I have been thirteen years tied in the Tower, being unpardoned and in disgrace with my sovereign lord, have by other men's errors failed in the attempt I undertook.

For if that Charles the Fifth returned with unexampled loss (I will not say dishonour) from Algier in Africa;[1] or if King Sebastian lost himself and his army in Barbary;[2] if the invincible fleet and forces of Spain in eighty-eight were beaten home by the Lord Charles Howard, admiral of England; if Mr Strozzi,[3] the Count Brizack,[4] the Count of Vimioso, and others, with a fleet of fifty-eight sail and six thousand soldiers, encountered with far less numbers, could not defend the Terceres; leaving to speak of a world of other attempts furnished by kings and princes; if Sir Francis Drake, Sir John Hawkins, and Sir Thomas Baskervile,[5] men for their experience and valour as eminent as England had any, strengthened with divers of her majesty's ships and filled with soldiers at will, could not possess themselves of the treasure they sought for, which in their view was embarked in certain frigates at Puerto Rico; if afterward they were repulsed with fifty negroes upon the mountains

---

[1] The Emperor was forced to abandon his expedition against Barbarossa in 1541.
[2] The battle of Alcázar-el-Kebir in Morocco, 1578.
[3] Filippo Strozzi, general in the service of the French, brought the Portuguese pretender, Dom António, to the Azores but was heavily defeated by the Spanish fleet under Santa Cruz in 1582.
[4] Charles de Cossé, Duke of Brissac.
[5] He took over command of the ill-fated expedition after the death of Drake.

of Vasques Numius[6] or Sierra de Capira in their passage towards Panama;[7] if Sir John Norris (though not by any fault of his) failed in the attempt of Lisbon, and returned with the loss, by sickness and otherwise, of eight thousand men;[8] what wonder is it, but that mine (which is the least), being followed with a company of volunteers who for the most part had neither seen the sea nor the wars, who, some forty gentlemen excepted, were the very scum of the world; drunkards, blasphemers, and such others, as their fathers, brothers, and friends thought it an exceeding good gain to be discharged of them with the hazard of some thirty, forty or fifty pounds, knowing they could not have lived a whole year so cheap at home—I say what wonder is it if I have failed, where I could neither be present myself nor had any of the commanders whom I most trusted living or in state to supply my place?

Now whereas it was bruited, both before and since my departure out of England, and by the most men believed, that I meant nothing less than to go to Guiana, but that being once at liberty and in mine own power, having made my way with some foreign prince, I would turn pirate and utterly forsake my country; my being at Guiana, my returning into England unpardoned, and my not taking the spoil of the subjects of any Christian prince, hath (I doubt not) destroyed that opinion.

But this is not all; for it hath been given out by an hypocritical thief, who was the first master of my ship,[9] and by an ungrateful youth which waited upon me in my cabin (though of honourable and worthy parents), and by others, that I carried with me out of England twenty-two thousand pieces of twenty-two shillings the piece, and therefore needed not, or cared not, to discover any mine in Guiana, nor make any other attempt elsewhere. Which report, being carried secretly from one to another in my ship, and so spread through all the ships in the fleet which stayed with me at Trinidado while our land-forces were in Guiana, had like to have been my utter overthrow in a most miserable fashion. For it was consulted,[10] when I had taken my barge and gone ashore (either to discover or otherwise as I often did) that my ship should have set sail and left me there, where either I must have suffered famine, been eaten with

5 least] *1650*; last *1751*+

[6] Named after Vásquez or Vasco Núñez de Balboa, discoverer of the Pacific.

[7] Baskerville's force was routed by the Spaniards at the pass of Capirilla in Jan. 1596. See notes to p. 234/1.

[8] This is the fiasco of 1589.

[9] The name of the master of the Destiny, as given in *News of Sir Walter Ralegh* (1618), was Robert Burwick. There is no mention elsewhere of Ralegh replacing the master.

[10] Planned (*OED*, v. 4).

wild beasts, or have fallen into the hands of the Spaniards and been flayed alive, as others of the English which came thither but to trade only had formerly been.

To this report of riches I make this protestation: that if it can be proved, either now or hereafter, that I had in the world, either in my keeping or in my power, either directly or indirectly, in trust or otherwise, above one hundred pieces when I departed London, of which I had left forty-five pieces with my wife and fifty-five I carried with me, I acknowledge myself for a reprobate, a villain, a traitor to the king, and the most unworthy man that doth live or ever hath lived upon the earth.  10

It is true that such as thought to find some great deceit in me in the detaining a great part of the monies adventured, in perusing the bills of adventure written by scriveners, found above fifteen thousand pounds more than all my charge demanded came unto. But of the money I never received any penny, for the monies and provisions adventured with all the other captains amounted to very nearly twenty thousand pounds, for the greatest part whereof I gave the bills.[11]

Now whereas the captains that left me in the Indies, and Captain Bailey that ran away from me at Lancerota, have, to excuse themselves, objected (for the first) that I lingered at Plymouth when I might have  20 gone thence, and lost a fair wind and time of year,[12] or to that effect; it is strange that men of fashion and gentlemen should so grossly belie their own knowledge; that had not I lived nor returned to have made answer to this fiction, yet all that knew us in Plymouth and all that we had to deal withal knew the contrary; for after I had stayed at the Isle of Wight divers days, the Thunder, commanded by Sir Warham St Leger, by the negligence of her master was at lee in the Thames;[13] and after I arrived at Plymouth, Captain Pennington was not come then to the Isle of Wight, and being arrived there, and not able to redeem his bread from the bakers, he rode back post to London to entreat help from my wife to  30 pay for it; who having not so much money to serve his turn, she wrote to Mr Wood of Portsmouth, and gave him her word for thirty pounds (which she soon after paid him); without which, as Pennington himself protested to my wife, he had not been able to have gone the journey.

11  It is true ... bills] *1829; not in 1650, 1751*

[11] The preceding paragraph has puzzled editors (see text note). Cayley and Harlow give a quite different version which seems to be an attempt at a rewriting.

[12] i.e. the proper season.

[13] The master had failed to take advantage of the winds and the ship had become windbound.

Sir John Ferne I found there without all hope of being able to proceed, having neither men nor money and in great want of other provision; insomuch as I furnished him by my cousin Herbert with a hundred pounds, having supplied him also in Wales with a hundred pounds before his coming to Plymouth and procured him a third hundred pounds from the worthy and honest Dean of Exeter, Doctor Sutcliffe.[14] Captain Whitney, whom I also stayed for, had a third part of his victuals to provide; insomuch as, having no money to help him withal, I sold my plate in Plymouth to supply him.

10    Bailey I left at the Isle of Wight, whose arrival I also attended here some ten or twelve days as I remember. And what should move Bailey only to leave me as he did at the Canaries, from whence he might have departed with my love and leave, and at his return to do me all the wrong he could devise, I cannot conceive. He seemed to me from the beginning not to want anything; he only desired of me some ordnance and some iron-bound cask, and I gave it him. I never gave him ill language nor offered him the least unkindness to my knowledge. It is true that I refused him a French shallop which he took in the Bay of Portugal outward bound; and yet after I had bought her of the French and paid

20    fifty crowns ready money for her, if Bailey had then desired her he might have had her. But to take anything from the French or from any other nation, I meant it not.

True it is, that as many things succeed both against reason and our best endeavours, so it is most commonly true that men are the cause of their own misery, as I was of mine, when I undertook my late enterprise without a pardon; for all my company, having heard it avowed in England before they went, that the commission I had was granted to a man who was *non ens* in law; so hath the want thereof taken from me both arms and actions;[15] which gives boldness to every petty companion to

30    spread rumours to my defamation and the wounding of my reputation in all places where I cannot be present to make them knaves and liars.

It hath been secondly objected, that I put into Ireland and spent much time there, taking care to revictual myself and none of the rest.

Certainly I had no purpose to see Ireland when I left Plymouth, but being encountered with a strong storm some eight leagues to the westward of Scilly (in which Captain Chudleigh's pinnace was sunk, and Captain King thrust into Bristol), I held it the office of a commander of

[14] Matthew Sutcliffe, who supported the colonizing of Virginia and New England. He was imprisoned by James in 1621 for his opposition to the Spanish marriage.
[15] i.e. official punishment and legal redress.

many ships, and those of divers sailings and conditions, of which some could hull and try,[16] and some of them beat it up upon a tack,[17] and others neither able to do the one nor the other, rather to take a port and keep his fleet together than either to endanger the loss of masts and yards, or to have it severed far asunder and to be thrust into divers places. For the attendance of meeting them again at the next rendezvous would consume more time and victual (and perchance the weak ships might be set upon, taken, or disordered) than could be spent by recovering a harbour and attending the next change of wind.

That the dissevering of fleets hath been the overthrow of many 10 actions, I could give many examples, were it not in every man's knowledge. In the last enterprise of worth undertaken by our English nation,[18] with three squadrons of ships, commanded by the earl of Essex, the earl of Suffolk,[19] and myself, where was also present the earl of Southampton, if we, being storm-beaten in the Bay of Alcashar[20] or Biscay, had had a port under our lee, that we might have kept our transporting ships with our men of war, we had in all likelihood both taken the Indian fleet and the Azores.

That we stayed long in Ireland it is true, but they must accuse the clouds and not me for our stay there, for I lost not a day of a good wind. 20 And there was not any captain of the fleet but had credit, or might have had, for a great deal of more victuals than we spent there, and yet they had of me fifty beeves among them, and somewhat else.

For the third accusation, that I landed in hostile manner at Lancerota; certainly Captain Bailey had great want of matter when he gave that for an excuse of his turning back; for I refer myself to Mr Barney, who I know will ever justify a truth, to whom, when he came to me from Captain Bailey to know whether he should land his men with the rest, I made this answer: that he might land them if it pleased him or otherwise keep them aboard, for I had agreed with the governor for a proportion of 30 victual which I hourly expected. And it is true, that the governor being desirous to speak with me with one gentleman with him, with their rapiers only, which I accepting, and taking with me Lieutenant Brad-shaw, we agreed that I should send up an English factor (whose ship did

[16] Lie to, head to wind, under minimum sail.
[17] Sail to windward by tacking.
[18] The Islands voyage of 1597. The fleet ran into heavy storms at the outset and the ships eventually returned to Plymouth.
[19] Lord Thomas Howard.
[20] Arcachon.

then ride in the road) and that whatsoever the island could yield should be delivered at a reasonable rate. I sent the English factor according to our agreement, but the governor put it off from one morning to another, and in the end sent me word that except I would embark my men which lay on the sea-side, the islanders were so jealous[21] as they durst not sever themselves to make our provisions. I did so, but when the one half were gotten aboard, two of our sentinels were forced, one slain,[22] and the English factor sent to tell me that he had nothing for us, whom he still believed to be a fleet of the Turk's, who had lately taken and
10 destroyed Puerto Sancto. Hereupon all the companies would have marched towards the town and have sacked it, but I knew it would not only dislike[23] his majesty, but that our merchants having a continual trade with those islands, that their goods would have been stayed, and amongst the rest the poor Englishman riding in the road, having all that he brought thither ashore, would have been utterly undone.

Hereof I complained to the governor of the Grand Canaries, whom I also desired that we might take water without any disturbance. But instead of answer, when we landed some hundred men, far from any habitation and in a desert place of the island where we found some fresh
20 water, there ambush was laid, and one Fisher of Sir John Ferne's ship wounded to death; and more had been slain had not Captain Thornhurst and Master Robert Hammond, my son's lieutenant, two exceeding valiant gentlemen, who first made head against them, seconded by Sir Warham St Leger and my son, with half a dozen more, made forty of them run away.

From hence, because there was scarcity of water, we sailed to Gomera, one of the strongest and best defenced places of all the islands, and the best port, the town being seated upon the very wash of the sea. At the first entrance of our ships, they shot at us, and ours at them; but as
30 soon as I myself recovered the harbour, and had commanded that there should be no more shooting, I sent a Spaniard ashore (taken in a bark which came from Cape Blank) to tell the governor that I had no purpose to make war with any of the Spanish king's subjects, and if any harm were done by our great ordnance to the town, it was his fault, which by shooting first gave the occasion. He sent me for answer that he thought

23 Hammond] *Hayman 1650+*

[21] Suspicious (of Ralegh's intentions).
[22] In his journal (p. 202), Ralegh lays the responsibility for the violence on an English sergeant, and says that two were killed.
[23] Displease.

we had been the Turkish fleet which destroyed Puerto Sancto; but being resolved by the messenger that we were Christians and English, and sought nothing but water, he would willingly afford us as much as we pleased to take, if he might be assured that we would not attempt his town and spoil it, with the churches and other religious houses, nor destroy the gardens and fruits.

I returned him answer that I would give him my faith, and the word of the king of Great Britain my sovereign lord, that the people of the town and island should not lose so much as one orange or a grape without paying for it.[24] For if any man of mine should injure them, I would hang 10 him up in the market street. Now, that I kept my faith with him, and how much he held himself bound unto me, I have divers of his letters to show, for he wrote unto me every day. And the countess being of an English race (a Stafford by the mother, and of the house of Horn by the father) sent me divers presents of fruits, sugar and rusk; to whom I returned (because I would not depart in her debt) things of greater value. The old earl at my departure wrote a letter to the Spanish ambassador here in England, how I behaved myself in those islands. There I discharged a bark of the Grand Canaries, taken by one of my pinnaces, coming from Cape Blank in Africa; and demanding of him 20 what prejudice he had received by being taken, he told me that my men had eaten of his fish to the value of six ducats, for which I gave him eight.

From the Canaries, it is said that I sailed to Cape de Verte knowing it to be an infectious place, by reason whereof I lost so many of my men ere I recovered the Indies. The truth is that I came no nearer to Cape de Verte than Bravo, which is 160 leagues off. But had I taken it in my way, falling upon the coast, or any other part of Guiana, after the rains, there is as little danger of infection as in any other part of the world, as our English that trade in those parts every year do well know. There are few places in England or in the world near great rivers, which run through 30 low grounds, or near moorish or marsh grounds, but the people inhabiting near are at some time of the year subject to fevers; witness Woolwich in Kent and all down the river on both sides. Other infection there is not found either in the Indies or in Africa, except it be when the

---

5 and spoil ... religious] *1829*; *not in 1650, 1751, Cayley*
9 grape ... hang] *1751*; grape without paying for it, I would hang *1650*; grape, and if any man took from them, were it but an orange or a grape, without paying for it, I would hang *1829*          33 river] *Cayley*; rivers *1650, 1751, 1829*.

[24] I surmise that 1829 is following an early copyist who wished to save Ralegh from an unintentionally comic statement.

easterly wind or breezes are kept off by some mountains from the valleys, whereby the air wanting motion doth become exceeding unhealthful, as at Nombre de Dios[25] and elsewhere.

But as good success admits no examination,[26] so the contrary allows of no excuse, how reasonable or just soever. Sir Francis Drake, Mr John Winter, and John Thomas, when they passed the Straits of Magellan,[27] met with a storm which drove Winter back, which thrust John Thomas upon the islands to the south where he was cast away, and drove Sir Francis near a small island upon which the Spaniards landed their
10 thieves and murderers from Baldivia.[28] And he found there one Philip, an Indian,[29] who told him where he was and conducted him to Baldivia, where he took his first prize of treasure; and in that ship he found a pilot called John Grege[30] who guided him all that coast over, in which he possessed himself of the rest; which pilot, because he should not rob him of his reputation and knowledge in those parts, resisting the entreaties and tears of all his company, he set him ashore upon the island of Aegulus, that is, Alligator, to be by them devoured.[31] After which, passing by the East Indies, he returned into England, and notwithstanding the peace between us and Spain, he enjoyed the riches he brought,
20 and was never so much as called to accompt for cutting off Doughty's head at Port St Julian, having neither martial law nor other commission available.[32]

Mr Candish, having passed all the coasts of Chile and Peru and not gotten a farthing, when he was without hope and ready to shape his course by the east homewards, met a ship which came from the Philippines at California, a thousand pounds to a nutshell. These two in these two voyages were the children of fortune and much honoured. But when Sir Francis Drake in his last attempt might have landed at

---

4 examination] *1650, 1751, Cayley*; examination of errors *1829*　　　　7 met] *1751, Cayley*; meeting *1650, 1829*　　　10 thieves] *Cayley, 1829*; chains *1650, 1751* 20 accompt] *1650*; an account *1750+*

[25] Spanish port on the north-eastern side of the Panama isthmus.
[26] Investigation. If you succeed, Ralegh argues, no one enquires how you got there.
[27] This is the circumnavigation of 1577–80.
[28] Valdivia, Chile.
[29] See Nuna de Silva's account, in Hakluyt, vol. xi. 138.
[30] 'John Griego a Greeke borne' (ibid. 114).
[31] This looks like hearsay. According to Nuna de Silva, John the Greek was put into a ship from Panama which Drake took at Lima (ibid. 143).
[32] After Drake's circumnavigation John Doughty tried in vain to bring an action against Drake for the murder of his brother Thomas. See Andrews 1967, pp. 67–8.

Cruces[33] by the river of Chiagra, within eight miles of Panama, he notwithstanding set the troops on land at Nombre de Dios, forty miles off, and received the repulse aforesaid, and died for sorrow. The same success had Candish in his last passage towards the Straits. I say that one and the same end they both had, to wit Drake and Candish, when chance had left them to the trial of their own virtues.

For the rest, I leave it to all worthy and indifferent[34] men to judge by what neglect or error of mine the gold mine in Guiana which I had formerly discovered was not found and enjoyed. For after we had refreshed ourselves in Caliana (otherwise in the first discovery called Port Howard), where we buried Captain Hastings, Captain Pigott, and Captain Snedall, and there recovered the most part of our sick men, I did embark six companies, of fifty to each company, in five ships; to wit, the Encounter, commanded by Captain Whitney, in the Confidence, by Captain Wollaston, in two flyboats of my own, commanded by Captain Samuel King,[35] and Captain Robert Smith in a carvel. Which companies had for their leaders Captain Charles Parker; Captain North; my son; Captain Thomas Thornhurst; Captain Pennington's lieutenant, Bradshaw; and Captain Chudleigh's lieutenant, Pridieux.

At the Triangle islands I embarked the companies for Orenoque, between which and Caliana I lay aground twenty-four hours, and if it had not been fair weather we had never come off the coast, having not above two fathom and a half of water; eight leagues off from whence I directed them for the river of Surinam, the best port of all that tract of land between the river Amazones and Orenoque; there I gave them order to trim their boats and barges, and by the Indians of that place to understand the state of the Spaniards in Orenoque, and whether they had replanted or strengthened themselves upon the entrances or elsewhere; and if they found no Indians there, to send in the little flyboat or the carvel into the river of Dissekebe, where they should not fail to find pilots for Orenoque.

11 buried] *1829*; tarried *1650*; tarried for *1751*    24 tract] *1650*; track *1751*+
30 Dissekebe] Dissebecke *1650*+

[33] In the centre of the Panamanian isthmus, on the River Chagre, about 20 miles NW of Panama. The reason why Drake did not try to reach Panama via the Chagre is that he knew the Spaniards were aware of his plans; incredible though it may seem, the information had come to them from Ralegh, who casually told Antonio de Berrio (then his prisoner) about the projected attack while at Trinidad in 1595. See Andrews 1972, pp. 14–15.    [34] Impartial.
[35] The second flyboat was commanded by Captain Hall (see the journal, p. 213/25).

For with our great ships we durst not approach the coast, we having been all of us aground, and in danger of leaving our bones upon the shoals, before we recovered the Triangle islands as aforesaid. The biggest ship that could enter the river was the Encounter, who might be brought to eleven foot. The depth of the water upon the bar we could never understand, neither by Keymis, who was the first of any nation that had entered the main mouth of Orenoque,[36] nor by any of the masters or mariners of our fleet which had traded there ten or twelve years for tobacco; for the Chudley, when she came near the entrance, drawing but twelve foot, found herself in danger, and bore up for Trinidado.

Now whereas some of my friends have been unsatisfied why I myself had not gone up with the companies I sent, I desire hereby to give them satisfaction, that besides my want of health and strength (having not recovered my long and dangerous sickness, but was again fallen into a relapse) my ship shoaled and laid aground at seventeen foot water, seven leagues off the shore, so as the master nor any of my company durst adventure to come near it, much less to fall between the shoals on the south side of the river's side and sands on the north side called Puncto Anegado, one of the most dangerous places in all the Indies.[37] It was therefore resolved by us all that the five greater ships should ride at Puncto Gallo in Trinidado, and the five lesser should enter the river. For if Whitney and Wollaston at eleven foot lay aground three days in passing up, in what case had I been, which drew seventeen foot, a heavier ship and charged with forty pieces of ordnance? Besides this impossibility, neither would my son nor the rest of the captains and gentlemen have adventured themselves up the river (having but one month's victuals, and being thrust together a hundred of them in a small flyboat) had not I assured them that I would stay for them at Trinidado, and that no force should drive me thence except I were sunk in the sea, or set on fire by the Spanish galleons; for that they would have adventured themselves upon any other man's word or resolution, it were ridiculous to believe.

Having in this sort resolved upon our enterprise, and having given instructions how they should proceed both before and after their entrance into Orenoque, Keymis having undertaken to discover the

---

2 bones] *Cayley*; Bands *1650, 1751*; bows *1829*; beaues *Harlow*

[36] In 1596 Keymis gave the bar as 'not full two fathom' at low tide, rising 5 ft. at normal high tide (Hakluyt, vol. x. 463).

[37] See the journal, p. 214/8.

mine with six or eight persons in Sir John Ferne's shallop, I better bethinking myself, and misliking his determination, gave him this order, *viz.*:

Keymis, whereas you were resolved after your arrival into Orenoque to pass to the mine with my cousin Herbert and six musketeers, and to that end you desired to have Sir John Ferne's shallop, I do not allow of that course, because you cannot land so secretly but that some Indians on the river side may discover you, who giving knowledge of your passage to the Spaniards, you may be cut off before you can recover your boat. I do therefore advise you to suffer the captains and the companies of the English to pass up to the westwards of the mountain 10 Aio, from whence you have no less than three miles[38] to the mine, and to lodge and encamp between the Spanish town and you, if there be any town near it; that being so secured you may make trial what depth and breadth the mine holds, and whether or no it answer our hopes. And if you find it royal,[39] and the Spaniards begin to war upon you, then let the sergeant-major repel them, if it be in his power, and drive them as far as he can. But if you find that the mine be not so rich as it may persuade the holding of it, and draw on a second supply,[40] then shall you bring but a basket or two to satisfy his majesty that my design was not imaginatory[41] but true, though not answerable to his majesty's expectation, for the quantity of which I never gave assurance, nor could.

On the other side, if you shall find that any great number of soldiers be newly 20 sent into Orenoque, as the cacique of Caliana told us that they were, and that the passages be already forced,[42] so that without manifest peril of my son, yourself and other captains, you cannot pass toward the mine, then be well advised how you land; for I know (a few gentlemen excepted) what a scum of men you have; and I would not for all the world receive a blow from the Spaniards to the dishonour of our nation. I myself for my weakness cannot be present, neither will the company land except I stay with the ships, the galleons of Spain being daily expected. Pigott the sergeant-major is dead, Sir Warham my lieutenant without hope of life, and my nephew your sergeant-major now but a young man. It is therefore on your judgement that I rely, whom I trust God will direct for the best.                                                                                    30

Let me hear from you as soon as you can. You shall find me at Puncto Gallo, dead or alive; and if you find not my ships there, yet you shall find their ashes, for I will fire with the galleons if it come to extremity, but run away I will never.[43]

---

19  imaginatory] *1650, 1751, Cayley*; imaginary *1829*        23  passages ... forced] *1650, 1751*; passage be reinforced *1829*

[38]  Harlow reads 'you have less than three miles'. I have no doubt that 'no less than' is correct—but that Ralegh meant 'no more than'.

[39]  Of the highest quality and potential.        [40]  i.e. and that you need reinforcements.

[41]  *OED* has only one other, later, example of the word.        [42]  Strengthened.

[43]  It looks as though Ralegh has reworked these instructions; he had no need to tell Keymis that Pigott was dead.

That these my instructions were not followed was not my fault. But it seems that the sergeant-major, Keymis and the rest were by accident forced to change their first resolution, and that finding a Spanish town, or rather a village, set up twenty miles distant from the place where Antonio Berreo, the first governor by me taken in my first discovery, had attempted to plant, to wit, some two leagues to the westward of the mine, they agreed to land and encamp between the mine and the town, which they did not suspect to be so near them as it was.[44] And meaning to rest themselves on the river's side till the next day, they were in the night set 10 upon and charged by the Spaniards, which being unlooked for, the common sort of them were so amazed, as had not the captains and some other valiant gentlemen among them made a head and encouraged the rest, they had all been broken and cut in pieces.

To repel this force, putting themselves in order, they charged the Spaniards, and following them upon their retreat, they were ready to enter the town ere they knew where they were. And being then charged again by the governor and four or five captains which led their companies, my son, not tarrying for any musketeers, ran up in the head of a company of pikes, where he was first shot, and, pressing upon a 20 Spanish captain called Erinetta[45] with his sword, Erinetta, taking the small end of his musket in his hand, struck him on the head with the stock and felled him; whom again John Plessington, my son's sergeant, thrust through with his halbert. At which time also, the governor Diego Palomeque and the rest of the Spanish captains being slain, and their companies divided, they betook themselves into a house or hold[46] adjoining to the market-place, where with their murderers and muskets (the houses having loopholes cut towards the market-place) they slew and wounded the English at their pleasure, so as we had no way to save ourselves but by firing those houses adjoining; which done, all the 30 Spaniards ran into the bordering woods and hills, keeping the English still waking with perpetual alarms.

25 divided ... hold] *1650*, *1751*, *Cayley*; divided themselves into the houses *1829*
26 where] *1650*; whereby *1751*; whence *Cayley*, *1829*        26 with ... market-place]
*Cayley*, *1829*; *not in 1650*, *1751*

[44] In his second letter (Latham, pp. 109–10) Keymis said San Thomé had been moved. But he did not say 20 miles, and it is impossible to make sense of what Ralegh has written here. If San Thomé had been so moved it would be 14 miles *east* of the mine, and the only way Keymis could in that case have camped between mine and town would have been to sail past the town and land to the *west* of it.

[45] Arias Nieto.

[46] Fort or stronghold (*OED* 10).

The town (such as it was) being in this sort possessed, Keymis prepared to discover the mine, which at this time he was resolved to do, as appeareth by his letter to me of his own handwriting, hereafter inserted. He took with him Captain Thornhurst, Master William Herbert, Sir John Hampden and others; but, at his first approach near the bank where he meant to land, he received from the wood a volley of shot which slew two of his company, hurt six others and wounded Captain Thornhurst in the head, of the which he languished three months after.[47]

Keymis his Letter                     10
dated the eighth of January,
from Orenoque.[48]

All things that appertain to human condition, in that proper nature and sense that of fate and necessity belongeth unto them, being now over with your son, maketh me choose rather with grief to let you know from me this certain truth than uncertainties from others; which is, *viz.*, that had not his extraordinary valour and forwardness, which, with constant vigour of mind, being in the hands of death, his last breath expressed in these words, *Lord have mercy upon me, and prosper your enterprise*, led them all on when some began to pause and recoil shamefully, this action had neither been attempted as it was, nor performed as it   20
is, with his surviving honour.

This Indian pilot whom I have sent, if there be occasion to use his service in anything, will prove sufficient and trusty. Peter Andrews, whom I have sent with him, can better certify your lordship of the state of the town, the plenty, the condition of our men, &c., than I can write the same.

We have the governor's servant prisoner, that waited on him in his bed-chamber and knows all things that concerned his master.[49] We find three or four refiners' houses in the town, the best houses of the town. I have not seen one piece of coin or bullion, neither gold or silver, a small deal of plate only excepted.

Captain Whitney and Wollaston are but now come to us, and now I purpose,   30
God willing, without delay to visit the mine, which is not eight miles from the

14  fate and necessity] *1650, 1751, Cayley*; fatal necessity *1829*

[47]  According to the account of Father Pedro Simon (Harlow, p. 178), this ambush was off the island of Seiba, west of the Caroní River.

[48]  Possibly the first page of this letter has been suppressed. It would have given details of the San Thomé battle and more direct news of young Walter Ralegh's death.

[49]  This is Christoval Guayacunda, who at Trinidad gave Ralegh information about the Spanish mines near San Thomé (see the letter to Winwood, and below, p. 242/10). He went with Ralegh to England and there witnessed his execution. He returned to New Granada in 1622 and became the major source of information for Pedro Simón's detailed account of the doings of the English in San Thomé (see Harlow, p. 197).

town. Sooner I could not go by reason of the murmurings, the discords, and vexations, wherewith the sergeant-major is perpetually tormented and tired, having no man to assist him but myself only. Things are now in some reasonable order, and so soon as I have made trial of the mine I will seek to come to your lordship by the way of the river of Macareo, by which river I have appointed Peter Andrews to go and to search the channels, that if it be possible, our ships may shorten the course for Trinidado, when time serves, by those passages. I have sent your lordship a parcel of scattered papers (I reserve a cart-load), one roll of tobacco, one tortoise, and some oranges and lemons, praying God to give
10 you strength and health of body, and a mind armed against all extremities. I rest ever to be commanded, this 8th of January, 1617.

Your lordship's,

Keymis

Now it seems that the death of my son, fearing also (as he told me when he came to Trinidado) that I was either dead of my first sickness, or that the news of my son's death would have hastened my end, made him resolve not to open the mine, to the which he added for excuse (and I think it was true) that the Spaniards, being gone off in a whole body, lay in the woods between the mine and their passage. It was impossible,
20 except they had been beaten out of the country, to pass up the woody and craggy hills without the loss of those commanders which should have led them; who had they been slain, the rest would easily enough have been cut in pieces in their retreat. For, being in the possession of the town, which they guarded with the greatest part of three companies, they had yet their hands full to defend themselves from firing, and the daily and nightly alarms wherewith they were vexed.

He also gave forth the excuse that it was impossible to lodge any companies at the mine for want of victual, which from the town they were not able to carry up the mountain, their companies being divided.
30 He therefore, as he told me, thinking it a greater error to discover it to the Spaniards, themselves neither being able to work it nor possess it, than to excuse himself to the company, said that he could not find it.[50]

All which his fancies when I rejected, and before divers of the

1 discords] *1650, 1751, Cayley*; disorders *1829*      9 lemons] *1650, 1751, Cayley*; limes *1829*    24 three] *1650, 1751, Cayley*; their *1829*    27 forth the] *1650, 1751*; for an *Cayley*; for the *1829*    30 thinking] *1751, Cayley*; thought *1650, 1829*

[50] Is it conceivable that Keymis's position was that he thought it impracticable and inadvisable to go to the mine and try to work it, so he told his men that he could not find it? See Introduction, p. 187.

gentlemen disavowed his ignorance[51]—for I told him that a blind man might find it by the marks which himself had set down under his hand; then I told him that his care of losing so many men in passing through the woods was but feigned; for after my son was slain, I knew that he had no care at all of any man surviving; and therefore, had he brought to the king but one hundredweight of the ore, though with the loss of one hundred men, he had given his majesty satisfaction, preserved my reputation, and given our nation encouragement to have returned this next year with greater force and to have held the country for his majesty, to whom it belonged—and of which himself had given the testimony that    10 besides the excellent air, pleasantness, healthfulness, and riches, it hath plenty of corn, fruits, fish, fowl (wild and tame), beeves, horses, sheep, hogs, deers, conies, hares, tortoises, armadiles, wanas,[52] oils, honey, wax, potatoes, sugar canes, medicaments, balsamum, simples, gums, and what not. But seeing he had followed his own advice and not mine, I should be forced to leave him to his arguments, with the which if he could satisfy his majesty and the state, I should be glad of it, though for my part he must excuse me to justify it, that he, if it had pleased him, though with some loss of men, might have gone directly to the place.

With that he seemed greatly discontent, and so he continued divers    20 days. Afterward he came to me in my cabin and showed me a letter which he had written to the earl of Arundel,[53] to whom he excused himself for not discovering of the mine, using the same arguments and many others which he had done before, and prayed me to allow of his apology. But I told him that he had undone me by his obstinacy, and that I would not favour or colour in any sort his former folly. He then asked me whether that were my resolution. I answered that it was. He then replied in these words, "I know not then, sir, what course to take,"[54] and

28 I know not then] *1650, 1751, Cayley*; I know then *1829*

[51] This does not make sense if Ralegh was right in saying that Keymis was only pretending ignorance to his colleagues, but it is more likely that this is the way it really went: namely that Keymis's twofold argument was that it had become too difficult to work the mine, and that in any case he had become uncertain where exactly it was located.

[52] Iguanas.

[53] Thomas Howard, second earl, 1585–1646. We should dearly like to see Keymis's letter; presumably Ralegh destroyed it.

[54] See text notes. The omission of the negative in what has become the standard version of the Apology is indefensible. If Keymis had announced in this melodramatic way that he knew what course to take, Ralegh could not have been in any uncertainty when he heard the pistol-shot. In the letter to Winwood, Ralegh said that Keymis 'then told me that he would wait on me presently and give me better satisfaction'. There is no hint of the determination conveyed in the 1829 version.

went out of my cabin into his own, in which he was no sooner entered but I heard a pistol go off. I sent up (not suspecting any such thing as the killing of himself) to know who shot a pistol. Keymis himself made answer, lying on his bed, that he had shot it off because it had been long charged, with which I was satisfied. Some half hour after this, his boy going into his cabin, found him dead, having a long knife thrust under his left pap through his heart, and his pistol lying by him, with which it appeared that he had shot himself, but the bullet lighting upon a rib had but broken the rib, and went no further.

Now he that knew Keymis did also know that he was of that obstinate resolution, and a man so far from caring to please or satisfy any man but himself, as no man's opinion from the greatest to the least could have persuaded him to have laid violent hands on himself.[55] Neither would he have done it when he did it, could he have said unto me that he was ignorant of the place, and knew no such mine; for what cause had I then to have rejected his excuses, or to have laid his obstinacy to his charge?[56] Thus much I have added because there are some puppies which have given it out that Keymis slew himself because he had seduced so many gentlemen and others with an imaginary mine. But as his letter to me the 8th of January proves that he was then resolved to open it—and to take off all these kinds of objections, let Captain Charles Parker, Captain George Ralegh, and Captain King, all living and in England, be put to their oaths whether or no Keymis did not confess to them coming down the river, at a place where they cast anchor, that he could from that place have gone to the mine in two hours.

I say then, that if the opening of the mine had been at that time to any purpose, or had they had any victuals left then to bring them away, or had they not been hastened by seeing the king of Spain's letters before they came to my hands—which I am assured Keymis had seen, who delivered them to me, whereof one of them was dated at Madrid the 17th of March, before I left the river Thames, and with it three other dispatches, with a commission for the strengthening of Orenoque with

---

[55] 'Opinion' means judgement, or valuation. Ralegh's argument is that Keymis would not have been influenced in his actions by what anyone thought of him.

[56] I take the meaning of this very difficult sentence to be as follows: 'If Keymis had been honest and sincere in saying he did not know where the mine was, he would never have killed himself. For I could not then have challenged him as I did. He *did* know, but he had made up his mind that it wouldn't do to seek it out. It was because I rejected his reasons and excuses as untenable that he killed himself.' This tortuous paragraph is to discredit the idea that there was no mine, that Keymis knew there was no mine, and that in the end he slew himself in shame and guilt for having misled so many people.

one hundred and fifty soldiers, which should have come down the river from the new kingdom of Granada, and one other one hundred and fifty from Puerto Rico, with ten pieces of ordnance, which should have come up the river from the entrance by which with two troops they might have been enclosed—I say, had not the rest seen those despatches, and that having stayed in the river above two months they feared the hourly arrival of those forces, why had they not constrained Keymis to have brought them to the mine, being as himself confesses within two hours march?[57]

Again, had the companies' commanders but pinched the governor's  10 man, whom they had in their possession, he could have told them of two or three gold mines and a silver mine not above four miles from the town, and given them the names of their possessors, with the reason why they forbore to work them at that time, and when they left off from working them, which they did as well because they wanted negroes as because they feared lest the English, French, or Dutch would have forced them from those, being once thoroughly opened, having not sufficient strength to defend themselves. But to this I have heard it said since my return, that the governor's man was by me persuaded, being in my power, to say that such mines there were when indeed there was no  20 such thing. Certainly they were but silly fools that discovered this subtlety of mine, who having not yet by the long calenture[58] that weakened me lost all my wits, which I must have done if I had left my reputation in trust with a mulatto who for a pot or two of wine, for a dozen of hatchets, or a gay suit of apparel, would have confessed that I had taught him to speak of mines that were not *in rerum natura*—No, I protest before the majesty of God that without any other agreements or promise of mine than well usage, he hath discovered to me the way to five or six of the richest mines which the Spaniards have, and from whence all the mass of gold that comes into Spain in effect is  30 drawn.

Lastly, when the ships were come down the river as far as Carapana's country (who was one of the natural lords, and one that resigned that

27  agreements] *1650, 1751*; arguments *Cayley, 1829*              32  resigned] *1829*; reserved *1650, 1751, Cayley*

[57]  The impenetrable density of this paragraph comes about from the conflict of two opposing arguments: (*a*) there was a mine and they were too pusillanimous to attempt it; (*b*) there were very strong reasons for their not getting to the mine.

[58]  Tropical fever, with delirium.

part of Guiana to her majesty)[59] hearing that the English had abandoned St Thomé and left no force in the country, which he hoped they would have done, he sent a great canoe with store of fruits and provisions to the captains, and by one of his men which spake Spanish (having as it seemed been long in their hands) he offered them a rich gold mine in his own country, knowing it to be the best argument to persuade their stay; and if it pleased them to send up any one of the English to view it, he would leave sufficient pledges for his safe return; Master Leak, Master Molineux, and others offering themselves. Which
10 when the greater part refused (I know not by what reason led), he sent again, leaving one of his men still aboard, to entreat them to tarry but two days and he himself would come to them and bring them a sample of the ore (for he was an exceeding old man when I was first in the country some twenty four years since). Which being also neglected, and the ships under sail, he notwithstanding sent a boat after them to the very mouth of the river, in hope to persuade them. That this is true, witness Captain Parker, Captain Leak, Master Tresham, Master Maudict, Master Molineux, Master Robert Hammond, Master Nicholas, Captain King, Peter Andrews, and I know not how many others.
20     But to set aside[60] his offer also there hath not been wanting an argument, though a foolish one, which was that the Spaniards had employed the Indians with a purpose to betray our men. But this treason had been easily prevented if they had stayed the old man's coming, who would have brought them the gold ore aboard their ships; and what purpose could there be of treason, when the Guianians offered to leave pledges six for one? Yea, one of the Indians which the English had aboard them, whom they found in fetters when they took the town of St Thomé, could have told them that the cacique which sent unto them to show them the gold mine in his country was unconquered, and an
30 enemy to the Spaniard, and could also have assured them that this cacique had gold mines in his country.
    I say then, that if they would neither force Keymis to go to the mine when he was by his own confession within two hours march of it, if they neglected to examine from whence these two ingots of gold which they

20 But ... aside] *1751*, *Cayley*; But besides *1650*; But against *1829*

[59] In *The Discovery*, Ralegh had called Carapana 'a man very wise, subtle, and of great experience', and also an 'old fox'. He looked on his co-operation with the Spaniards as a matter of expedience, and thought that if 'we return strong, he will be ours'. But it does not appear that he 'resigned' his country to England! (Schomburgk, pp. 35, 103–4.)

[60] i.e. discredit.

brought me were taken, which they found laid by for king's quinto, or fifth part, or those small pieces of silver which had the same marks and stamps; if they refused to send any one of the fleet into the country to see the mines which the cacique Carapana offered them; if they would not vouchsafe to stay two days for the coming of Carapana himself, who would have brought them a sample of the gold ore; I say, that there is no reason to lay it to my charge that I carried them with a pretence of gold, when neither Keymis nor myself knew of any in those parts. If it had been to have gotten my liberty, why did I not keep my liberty when I had it? Nay, why did I put my life in manifest peril to forgo it? If I had had a purpose to have turned pirate, why did I oppose myself against the greatest number of my company, and was thereby in danger to be slain or cast into the sea because I refused it?

A strange fancy had it been in me to have persuaded my son, whom I have lost, and to have persuaded my wife to have adventured the eight thousand pound which his majesty gave them for Sherborne, and when that was spent to persuade my wife to sell her house at Mitcham, in hope of enriching them by the mines of Guiana, if I myself had not seen them with my own eyes. For being old and weakly, thirteen years in prison and not used to the air, to travail, and to watching, it being ten to one that I should ever have returned, and of which by reason of my violent sickness and the long continuance thereof no man had any hope, what madness could have made me undertake this journey but the assurance of the mine, thereby to have done his majesty service, to have bettered my country by the trade, and to have restored my wife and children their states they had lost, for which I have refused all other ways and means; for that I had no purpose to have changed my master and my country, my return in the state I did return may satisfy every honest and indifferent man.

An unfortunate man I am, and it is to me a greater loss than all I have lost that it pleaseth his majesty to be offended for the burning of a Spanish town in Guiana, of which these parts bordering the river of Orenoque and to the south as far as the Amazones doth by the law of nations belong to the crown of England, as his majesty was well resolved when it pleased him to grant a great part thereof to Mr Harcourt;[61] and as his majesty was also resolved when I prepared to go thither; otherwise his majesty would not have given me leave to have landed there; for I set

19 weakly] *1650, 1751, Cayley*; sickly *1829*        37 me leave] *Cayley*; once leave *1650, 1751*; leave to me *1829*

[61] See the Introduction, p. 179.

it down under my hand that I intended that enterprise and nothing else, and that I meant to enter the country by the river Orenoque; and it was not held to be a breach of peace neither by the state here nor the Spanish ambassador, who knew it as well as I that I pretended[62] the journey of Guiana, which he always held to be a pretence. For he said it to Master Secretary Winwood and to others of my lords that if I meant to sail to Guiana and had no intent to invade any part of his majesty's West Indies, nor his fleets, I should not need to strengthen my self as I did, for I should work any mine there without any disturbance, and in peace.

10    To which I made answer that I had set it under my hand to his majesty that I had no other purpose, nor meant to undertake anything else. But for the rest, if Sir John Hawkins in his journey to St John de Loa,[63] notwithstanding that he had leave of the Spanish king to trade in all parts of the West Indies, and having the plate fleet in his power did not take out of it one ounce of silver, but kept his faith and promises in all places, was set upon by Don Henrico de Martines, whom he suffered (to save him from perishing) to enter the port upon Martines' faith and inter-changed pledges delivered; had Jesus of Lubeck, a ship of her majesty's of a thousand ton, burnt; had his men slain which he left on the land; lost

20    his ordnance, and all the treasure which he had got by trade—what reason had I to go unarmed upon the ambassador's promises, whose words and thoughts, that they were one, it hath well appeared since then, as well by the forces which he persuaded his master to send to Guiana to encounter me and cut me off there, as by his persecuting me since my return, who have neither invaded his master's Indies nor his fleet, whereof he stood in doubt.

True it is, that the Spaniards cannot endure that the English nation should look upon any part of America, being above a fourth part of the whole known world; and the hundredth part neither possessed by the

30    Spaniards nor to them known,[64] as Acosta the Jesuit in his description of the West Indies doth confess and well knows to be true.[65] No, though the king of Spain can pretend no other title to all that he hath not conquered than the Pope's donation, for from the straits of Magellan to the river of Plate, being a greater territory than all that the Spaniards

---

[62] Intended, meant, purposed. It is unfortunate that Ralegh then uses 'pretence' with its modern meaning of deceit.

[63] San Juan de Ulúa, Mexico. This is 1568.

[64] i.e. 'and not the hundredth part possessed or known'. The Spaniards occupy or know only one per cent.

[65] José de Acosta's history (1590) was translated into English in 1604 as *The Natural and Moral History of the East and West Indies.*

possess in Peru or Chile, and from Cape St Augustine[66] to Trinidado, being a greater extent of land than all which he possesses in Nova Spain or elsewhere, they have not one foot of ground in their possession, neither for the greatest part of it so much as in their knowledge.

In Orenoque they have lately set up a wooden town and made a kind of fort, but they have never been able either to conquer the Guianians nor to reconcile them. But the Guianians before their planting there did willingly resign all that territory to her majesty, who by me promised to relieve them and defend them against the Spaniards. And though I were a prisoner for this last fourteen years, yet I was at the charge every year, 10 or every second year, to send unto them to keep them in hope of being relieved. And as I have said before, the greatest of the natural lords did offer us a rich mine of gold in his own country in hope to hold us there. And if this usurped possession of the Spaniards be a sufficient bar to his majesty's right, and that thereby the king of Spain calls himself king of Guiana, why might he not as well call himself duke of Brittain,[67] because he took possession of Blavet[68] and built a fort there, and call himself king of Ireland because he took possession at Smerwick[69] and built a fort there?

If the ambassador had protested to his majesty that my going to 20 Guiana before I went would be a breach to the peace, I am persuaded that his majesty, if he had not been resolved that Guiana had been his, would have stayed me. But if it be now thought to be a breach of peace, not for the going thither (for that cannot be, because I had no other intent, and went with leave), but for taking and burning of a Spanish town in the country, certainly, if the country be the king of Spain's, it had been no less a breach of peace to have wrought any mine of his, and to have robbed him of his gold, than it is now called a breach of peace to take a town of his in Guiana and burn it. And with as good reason might I have been called a thief and punished for a thief and a robber of the king 30 of Spain if the country be not his majesty's as I am now pursued for the invasion. For either the country is the king of Spain's or the king's. If it be the king's, I have not then offended; if it be not the king's, I must have

---

17 Blavet] *Cayley*; Blewet *1650, 1751, 1829*     18 Smerwick] Smereck *1650, 1751*; Limerick *1829*     32 the king . . . king's] *1650, 1751, Cayley*; the king or not the king's *1829*

[66] On the Brazilian coast near Recife (Pernambuco).
[67] Brittany.
[68] Port Louis, at the mouth of the Blavet.
[69] Ralegh took part in the massacre of the Spanish garrison in 1580.

perished if I had but taken gold out of the mines there though I had found no Spaniards in the country.

For conclusion, if we had had any peace with the Spaniards in those parts of the world, why did even those Spaniards which were now encountered in Guiana tie six and thirty Englishmen out of Master Hall's ship of London and mine back to back, and cut their throats, after they had traded with them a whole month, and came to them ashore having not so much as a sword or any other weapon among them all? And if the Spaniards to our complaints made answer that there was nothing
10 in the treaty against our trading in the Indies, but that we might trade at our peril, I trust in God that the word peril shall ever be construed to be indifferent to both nations.[70] Otherwise we must for ever abandon the Indies, and lose all our knowledge and our pilotage of that part of the world. If we have no other peace than this, how can there be a breach of peace, since the Spaniards with all nations, and all nations with them, may trade upon their guard?[71] For to break peace where there is no peace is impossible.

The readiest way that the Spaniard's ambassador could have taken to have stayed me from going to Guiana had been to have discovered the
20 great practices[72] which I had with his master against the king my sovereign lord in the first year of his majesty's reign of Great Britain, for which I lost my estate and lay thirteen years in the Tower of London, and not to urge my offences in Guiana, to which his master hath no title other than his sword, with which to this day he hath not conquered the least of these nations, and against whom, contrary to the Catholic profession, his captains have entertained and do entertain whole nations of Cannibals.[73] For in a letter of the late governor's to the king of Spain, of the eighth of July, he not only complaineth that the Guianians are in arms against him, but that even those Indians which under their noses
30 live do in despite of all the king's edicts trade with *los flamencos e ingleses enemigos*, with the Flemish and English enemies, never once naming the English nations but with the epithet of an enemy.

But in truth, the Spanish ambassador hath complained against me to no other end than to prevent my complaints against the Spaniards, who, landing my men in a territory appertaining to the crown of England, they

---

[70] i.e. either side has the right to get rough in self-protection.
[71] i.e. at their own risk. It is up to everyone to look to his own defence in the violent situation brought about by Spain's illegal insistence on sole rights.
[72] Evil schemes.
[73] Supposedly fierce tribes, as against the peaceful Arawaks.

were invaded and slain before any violence offered to the Spaniards. And I hope that the ambassador doth not esteem us for so wretched and miserable a people as to offer our throats to their swords without any manner of resistance. Howsoever, I have said it already and I will say it again, that if Guiana be not his majesty's, the working of a mine there and the taking of a town there had been equally perilous; for by doing the one I had robbed the king of Spain and been a thief, and by the other, a disturber or breaker of the peace.

## 5. *Letter to George, Lord Carew*[1]
(Summer 1618)

Because I know not whether I shall live to come before the Lords, I have for his majesty's satisfaction here set down as much as I can say, either for mine own defence or against myself, as things are construed.

It is true that though I acquainted his majesty with my intent to land in Guiana, yet I never made it known to his majesty that the Spaniards had any footing there,[2] neither had I any authority by patent to remove the Spaniards from thence, and therefore his majesty had no interest in the attempt of Saint Thomé by any foreknowledge thereof in his majesty.

But knowing his majesty's title to the country to be the best and most Christian, because the natural lords did most willingly acknowledge 10 Queen Elizabeth to be their sovereign, who by me promised to defend them from the Spanish cruelty, I made no doubt but that I might enter the land by force, seeing the Spaniard had no other title but force (the Pope's donation excepted), considering also that they got a possession there divers years since my possession, taken for the crown of England. For, were not Guiana his majesty's, then might I as well have been questioned for a thief for taking of gold out of the king of Spain's mines, as the Spaniards do now call me a peacebreaker; for from any territory confessed to be the king of Spain's it is no more lawful to take gold than lawful for the Spaniards to take tin out of Cornwall. 20

Now, were this possession of theirs a sufficient bar to his majesty's

---

[1] George, Lord Carew of Clopton (later earl of Totnes), 1555–1629. Ralegh's cousin and lifelong friend. He was a member of the Privy Council.

[2] Harlow (p. 250) thought footing meant foothold, and therefore found this denial of Ralegh's inexplicable and inexcusable. The word means an agreed status, or contractual position. Ralegh's argument is that he had never conceded the legal right of the Spaniards to the possession of Guiana. So far as Ralegh was concerned, the King had not been apprised that the Spaniards had a rightful tenure in the country. Therefore he could not be accused of being a party to the expulsion of the rightful owners of San Thomé!

right, the kings of Spain might as well call themselves dukes of Britain because they held Bluette and fortified there, and kings of Ireland because they possessed Smericke and fortified there; and so in other places.

That his majesty was well resolved of his right there, I make no kind of doubt, because the English both under Mr Charles Leigh and Mr Harcourt had leave to plant and inhabit the country.

That Oronoque itself had long ere this 5,000 English in it, I assure myself, had not my employment at Cales the next year after my return
10 from Guiana, and after that our journey to the Islands, hindered me for those two years. After which Tyrone's rebellion made her majesty unwilling that any great number of ships and men should be taken out of England till that rebellion were ended. And lastly, her majesty's death and my long imprisonment gave time to the Spaniards to set up a town of stakes, covered with leaves of trees, upon the banks of Oronoque, which they called 'St Thomé', but they have reconciled nor conquered any of the caciques or natural lords of the country, which caciques are still in arms against them, as by the governor's letter to the king of Spain may appear.
20 That by landing in Guiana there can be any breach of peace, I think it under favour impossible. To break peace where there is no peace, it cannot be.

That the Spaniards give us no peace there, it doth appear by the king's letter to his governor that they shall put to death all those Spaniards and Indians that trade *con los Engleses enimigos*—with English enemies. Yea, those very Spaniards which we encountered at St Thomé did of late years murder thirty-six of Mr Hall's men of London, and mine, who landed without weapon, upon the Spanish faith to trade with them. Mr Thorne also, of Tower Street in London, besides many other English,
30 was in like sort murdered, the year before my delivery out of the Tower.

Now if this kind of trade be peaceable, there is then a peaceable trade in the Indies between us and the Spaniards. But if this be cruel war and hatred and no peace, then there is no peace broken by our attempt. Again, how doth it stand with the greatness of the king of Spain first to call us enemies, when he did hope to cut us in pieces, and then, having failed, to call us peacebreakers? For to be an enemy and a peacebreaker in one and the same action is impossible. But the king of Spain, in his letter to the governor of Guiana dated at Madril the 19th of March, before we left the Thames, calls us *Engleses inimigos*.
40 Had it pleased the king of Spain to have written to his majesty in six

months time (for we were so long in preparing) and have made his
majesty know that our landing in Guiana would draw after it a breach of
peace, I presume to think his majesty would have stayed our enterprise
for the present. This he might have done with less charge than to levy
300 soldiers and transport ten pieces of ordnance from Puerto Rico;
which soldiers, added to the garrison of St Thomé (had they arrived
before our coming) had overthrown all our raw companies. And there
would have followed no complaint.

For the vain point of landing near St Thomé, it is true that we were of
opinion that we must have driven the Spaniards out of their town before    10
we could pass the thick woods upon the mountain of the mine; which I
confess I did first resolve upon. But better bethinking myself, I referred
the taking of the town to the goodness of the mine, which if they found to
be so rich as it might persuade the leaving of a garrison there, then to
drive the Spaniards thence. But to have it burnt was never my intent;
neither could they give me any reason why they did it.

Upon the return, I examined the sergeant-major and Keymis why
they followed not my last directions for the trial of the mine before the
taking of the town. And they answered me that although they durst
hardly go to the mine leaving a garrison of Spaniards behind them and    20
their boats, yet they said they followed those latter directions and did
land between the town and the mine; and that the Spaniards without any
manner of parley set upon them unawares and charged them, calling
them *peros engleses*; and by skirmishing with them drew them on to the
very entrance of the town, before they knew where they were. So as, if
any peace had been in those parts, the Spaniards first brake the peace
and made the first slaughter. For as the English could not but land to
seek the mine, being come thither to that end; so, being first reviled and
charged by the Spaniards, they could do no less than repel force by
force.                                                                      30

Lastly, it is a matter of no small consequence to acknowledge we have
offended the king of Spain by landing in Guiana. For, first, it weakens
his majesty's title to the country, or quits it. Secondly, there is no king
that hath ever given the least way to any other king or state in the traffic
of the lives and goods of his subjects—to wit, as in our case, that it shall
be lawful for the Spaniards to murder us either by force or treason, and
not lawful for us to defend ourselves and pay them with their own coin.
For this superiority and inferiority is a thing which no absolute monarch
ever yielded to or ever will.

Thirdly, it shows that the English bears greater respect to the    40

Spaniard, and is more doubtful of his forces, than either the French or the Dutch is, who daily invade all parts of the Indies without being questioned at their return. Yea, and at my being at Plymouth, a French gentleman called Florie went thence with four sail and 300 landsmen with commission to land, to burn and to sack all places in the Indies that he could master; and yet hath the French king married a daughter of Spain.

This is all that I can say, other than I have spent my poor estate, lost my son and my health, and endured as many sorts of miseries as ever
10 man did, in hope to do his majesty service; and have not, to my understanding, committed any hostile act other than the entrance upon a territory belonging to the crown of England, where the English were first set upon and slain by the usurping Spaniards.

I invaded no other part of the Indies pretended by the Spaniards. I returned into England with the manifest peril of my life, with a purpose not to hold my life by any other act than his majesty's grace, and from which no man nor any peril could dissuade me. To that grace, and goodness, and kingliness, I refer myself; which if it shall find that I have not suffered enough, it may if it please add more affliction to the
20 remainder of a wretched life.

## 6. *Letter to King James I*
(24 September 1618)

May it please your most excellent majesty:

If in my journey outward bound I had of my men murdered at the islands, and spared to take revenge; if I did discharge some Spanish barks taken, without spoil; if I forbare all parts of the Spanish Indies, wherein I might have taken twenty of their towns on the sea coast, and did only follow the enterprise which I undertook for Guiana, where without any direction from me a Spanish village was burnt, which was newly set up within three miles of the mine—by your majesty's favour, I find no reason why the Spanish ambassador should complain of me.
10 It it were lawful for the Spanish to murder twenty-six Englishmen, tying them back to back, and then to cut their throats, when they had traded with them a whole month, and came to them on the land without so much as one sword amongst them all; and that it may not be lawful for your majesty's subjects, being forced by them, to repel force by force, we may justly say, *O miserable English*!

5 to land] *MS; omitted E. Edwards, Harlow*

If Parker[1] and Metham took Campeach and other places in the Honduraes seated in the heart of the Spanish Indies, burnt towns, killed the Spaniards, and had nothing said to them at their return; and that myself forbore to look into the Indies because I would not offend; I may justly say, *O miserable Sir Walter Ralegh*!

If I had spent my poor estate, lost my son, suffered by sickness and otherwise a world of miseries; if I had resisted with the manifest hazard of my life the robberies and spoils which my companies would have made; if when I was poor I could have made myself rich; if when I had gotten my liberty, which all men and nature itself doth so much prize, I   10 voluntarily lost it; if when I was master of my life I rendered it again; if I might elsewhere have sold my ship and goods and put five or six thousand pounds in my purse, I have brought her into England; I beseech your majesty [not] to believe[2] that all this I have done because it should be said to your majesty that your majesty had given liberty and trust to a man whose end was but the recovery of his liberty, and who had betrayed your majesty's trust.

My mutiners told me that if I returned for England I should be undone, but I believed more in your majesty's goodness than in their arguments. Sure I am that I am the first that being free and able to enrich   20 myself, yet hath embraced poverty and peril. And as sure I am that my example shall make me the last. But your majesty's wisdom and goodness I have made my judges, who have ever been and shall ever remain,

Your majesty's most humble vassal,

W. Rauleigh.

1 Metham] *PRO (2)*, *Jones B60*; Mutton *PRO (1)*          8 robberies] *PRO (2)*;
rebells *PRO (1)*          21 and peril] *PRO (2)*; *not in PRO (1)*

[1] William Parker. This expedition was in 1596. See Hakluyt, x. pp. 277–80.
[2] The insertion of a negative before 'believe' is the simplest way of saving Ralegh's impossible syntax which (if it has been correctly copied) has sunk under its own weight.

# References

| | |
|---|---|
| Abbe and Gillis | Ernst C. Abbe and Frank J. Gillis, 'Henry Hudson and the Early Exploration and Mapping of Hudson Bay, 1610–1631', in J. Palmer (ed.), *Merchants and Scholars: Essays in the History of Exploration and Trade*. Minneapolis: University of Minnesota Press, 1965, pp. 87–116. |
| Andrews 1966 | K. R. Andrews, *Elizabethan Privateering: English Privateering during the Spanish War 1585–1603*. Cambridge: Cambridge University Press, 1966. |
| Andrews 1967 | K. R. Andrews, *Drake's Voyages*. London: Weidenfeld & Nicolson, 1967. |
| Andrews 1972 | K. R. Andrews, *The Last Voyage of Drake and Hawkins*. Cambridge: Hakluyt Society, 1972. |
| Andrews 1984 | K. R. Andrews, *Trade, Plunder and Settlement: Maritime Enterprise and the Genesis of the British Empire, 1480–1630*. Cambridge: Cambridge University Press, 1984. |
| APC 1592–3 | *Acts of the Privy Council, 1592–3*. London: HMSO, 1901. |
| Asher | G. M. Asher, *Henry Hudson the Navigator*. London: Hakluyt Society, 1860. |
| Brushfield | T. N. Brushfield, *A Bibliography of Sir Walter Ralegh Knt.* 2nd edn., Exeter: J. G. Commin, 1908. |
| Cayley | Arthur Cayley, *The Life of Sir Walter Ralegh, Knt.* 2 vols., London: Cadell & Davies, 1806. |
| Christy | Miller Christy, *The Voyages of Captain Luke Fox ... and Captain Thomas James ... in search of a North-West Passage, in 1631–2*. 2 vols., London: Hakluyt Society, 1894. |
| CSP Dom., 1601–3 | *Calendar of State Papers, Domestic, 1601–3*. London: Longman & Co. [&c], 1870. |
| CSP Spanish | *Calendar of State Papers, Spanish, 1587–1603*. London: HMSO, 1899. |
| Cuvelier | Eliane Cuvelier, *Thomas Lodge: Témoin de son temps*. Paris: Didier Érudition, 1984. |
| Dodge | Ernest S. Dodge, *Northwest by Sea*. New York: Oxford University Press, 1961. |
| Donno | Elizabeth Story Donno, *An Elizabethan in 1592: The Diary of Richard Madox*. London: Hakluyt Society, 1976. |
| Dyke | Gwenyth Dyke, 'The Finance of a Sixteenth-century Navigator, Thomas Cavendish of Trimley in Suffolk'. *The Mariners' Mirror*, 44 (1958), 108–15. |

Eccles          Mark Eccles, 'Brief Lives, Tudor and Stuart Authors'. *Studies in Philology*, 79 (1982), 1–133.

E. Edwards      Edward Edwards, *The Life of Sir Walter Ralegh ... together with his Letters*. 2 vols., London: Macmillan, 1868.

P. Edwards      Philip Edwards, 'Unfortunate Travellers: Fiction and Reality'. *Huntington Library Quarterly*, 50 (1987), 295–307.

Ewen            C. L'Estrange Ewen, *The North-West Passage: Light on the Murder of Henry Hudson from Unpublished Documents*. [London:] Printed for the Author, June 1938.

Franco          Guiomar de Carvalho Franco and Francisco de Assis Carvalho Franco, *Vária Fortuna e Estranhos Fados de Anthony Knivet*. São Paulo, Brazil: Editora Brasiliense, 1947.

Gardiner        Samuel R. Gardiner, *History of England from the Accession of James I to the Outbreak of the Civil War, 1603–1642*. 10 vols., London: Longmans, Green, 1883–4.

George          James George, 'Additional Materials on the Life of Thomas Lodge between 1604 and 1613', in *Papers Mainly Shakespearian*, collected by G. I. Duthie. Edinburgh: Oliver & Boyd, 1964, pp. 90–105.

Gilman          W. H. Gilman, *Melville's Early Life and 'Redburn'*. New York: New York University Press; London: Oxford University Press, 1951.

Greenblatt 1980 Stephen Greenblatt, *Renaissance Self-fashioning: From More to Shakespeare*. Chicago and London: University of Chicago Press, 1980.

Greenblatt 1985 Stephen Greenblatt, 'Invisible Bullets: Renaissance Authority and its Subversion, *Henry IV* and *Henry V*', in J. Dollimore and A. Sinfield (eds.), *Political Shakespeare: New Essays in Cultural Materialism*. Manchester: Manchester University Press, 1985, pp. 18–47.

Grosart         A. B. Grosart, *The Lismore Papers*. 2nd series, 1887, vol. ii. [Private circulation.]

Hadow           G. E. Hadow, *Sir Walter Ralegh: Selections from his 'Historie of the World', his Letters etc.* Oxford: Clarendon Press, 1917, reprinted 1926.

Hakluyt         Richard Hakluyt, *The Principal Navigations, Voyages, Traffiques & Discoveries of the English Nation*. 12 vols., Glasgow: MacLehose, 1903–5.

Hakluyt 1589    Richard Hakluyt, *The Principall Navigations, Voyages and Discoveries of the English Nation*. London, 1589.

Hakluyt 1598–   Richard Hakluyt, *The Principal Navigationes, Voiages, Traf-*
1600            *fiques & Discoveries of the English Nation*. 3 vols., London, 1598–1600.

| | |
|---|---|
| Harlow | V. T. Harlow, *Ralegh's Last Voyage*. London: Argonaut Press, 1932. |
| Hemming | John Hemming, *Red Gold: The Conquest of the Brazilian Indians*. Cambridge, Mass.: Harvard University Press; London: Macmillan, 1978. |
| Hulme | Peter Hulme, *Colonial Encounters: Europe and the Native Caribbean, 1492–1797*. London and New York: Methuen, 1986. |
| Hunter and Rawson | G. K. Hunter and C. J. Rawson (eds.), *The Yearbook of English Studies*, 13, Colonial and Imperial Themes Special Number. London, Modern Humanities Research Association, 1983. |
| Kastner | L. E. Kastner, 'Thomas Lodge as an Imitator of the Italian Poets'. *Modern Language Review*, 2 (1907), 155–61. |
| Kemp | Peter Kemp, *The Oxford Companion to Ships and the Sea*. Oxford: Oxford University Press, 1976. |
| Kermode | Frank Kermode, *The Genesis of Secrecy: On the Interpretation of Narrative*. Cambridge, Mass.: Harvard University Press, 1979. |
| Latham | Agnes M. C. Latham, 'Sir Walter Ralegh's Gold Mine: New Light on the Last Guiana Voyage', in G. Tillotson (ed), *Essays and Studies*. London: Murray, For the English Association, 1951, pp. 94–111. |
| Lefranc | Pierre Lefranc, *Sir Walter Ralegh écrivain: L'œuvre et les idées*. Paris: Armand Colin, 1968. |
| Lewis | C. S. Lewis, *English Literature in the Sixteenth Century*. Oxford: Clarendon Press, 1954. |
| Lorimer 1978 | Joyce Lorimer, 'The English Contraband Tobacco Trade in Trinidad and Guiana, 1590–1617', in K. P. Andrews, N. P. Canny, and P. E. H. Hair (eds.), *The Westward Enterprise*. Liverpool: Liverpool University Press, 1978, pp. 124–50. |
| Lorimer 1982 | Joyce Lorimer, 'The Location of Ralegh's Guinea Gold Mine'. *Terrae Incognitae*, 14 (1982), 77–95. |
| Marienstras | Richard Marienstras, *New Perspectives on the Shakespearean World*, tr. Janet Lloyd. Cambridge: Cambridge University Press; Paris, Éditions de la Maison des Sciences de l'Homme, 1985. (Previously published as *Le Proche et le lointain*, 1981.) |
| Markham | A. H. Markham, *The Voyages and Works of John Davis the Navigator*. London: Hakluyt Society, 1880. |
| Martin | Wallace Martin, *Recent Theories of Narrative*. Ithaca and London: Cornell University Press, 1986. |

| | |
|---|---|
| Nagel | Thomas Nagel, *The View from Nowhere*. New York and Oxford, Oxford University Press, 1986. |
| OED | *The Oxford English Dictionary*, 1884–1928; 13 vols., 1933; with Supplement, 4 vols., 1972–86. |
| Paradise | N. Burton Paradise, *Thomas Lodge: The History of an Elizabethan*. New Haven: Yale University Press; London: Oxford University Press, 1931. |
| Pollack | Claudette Pollack, 'Lodge's *A Margarite of America*: an Elizabethan Medley'. *Renaissance and Reformation*, 12 (1976), 1–11. |
| Powys | Llewellyn Powys, *Henry Hudson*. London: John Lane, The Bodley Head, 1927. |
| Purchas | Samuel Purchas, *Hakluytus Posthumus or Purchas his Pilgrimes*. 20 vols., Glasgow: MacLehose, 1905–7. |
| Purchas 1625 | Samuel Purchas, *Hakluytus Posthumus or Purchas his Pilgrimes*. 4 pts., London, 1625. |
| Quinn 1947 | D. B. Quinn, *Ralegh and the British Empire*. London: English Universities Press, 1947; Harmondsworth: Pelican Books, 1973. |
| Quinn 1955 | D. B. Quinn, *The Roanoke Voyages 1584–1590*. 2 vols., Cambridge: Hakluyt Society, 1955. |
| Quinn 1975 | D. B. Quinn, *The Last Voyage of Thomas Cavendish 1591–1592*. Chicago and London: University of Chicago Press, 1975. |
| Quinn 1979 | D. B. Quinn, *New American World: A Documentary History of North America*. 4 vols., London: Macmillan, 1979. |
| Sandison | Helen E. Sandison, 'Ralegh's Orders Once More'. *The Mariners' Mirror*, 20 (1934), 323–30. |
| Schomburgk | R. H. Schomburgk, *'The Discovery ... of Guiana...' by Sir W. Ralegh, Knt*. London: Hakluyt Society, 1848. |
| Sisson | Charles J. Sisson, *Thomas Lodge and Other Elizabethans*. Cambridge, Mass.: Harvard University Press, 1933. |
| Strathmann | E. A. Strathmann, 'Ralegh Plans his Last Voyage'. *The Mariners' Mirror*, 50 (1964), 261–70. |
| Tenney | E. A. Tenney, *Thomas Lodge*. Ithaca, New York: Cornell University Press, 1935. |
| Walker | Alice Walker, 'The Reading of an Elizabethan: Some Sources of the Prose Pamphlets of Thomas Lodge'. *Review of English Studies*, 8 (1932), 264–81. |
| Wallis 1951 | Helen M. Wallis, 'The First English Globe: A Recent Discovery'. *The Geographical Journal*, 117 (1951), 275–90. |
| Wallis 1955 | Helen M. Wallis, 'Further Light on the Molyneux Globes'. *The Geographical Journal*, 121 (1955), 304–11. |

White       Hayden White, *Tropics of Discourse: Essays in Cultural Criticism*. Baltimore and London: Johns Hopkins University Press, 1978.

Williamson       James A. Williamson, *English Colonies in Guiana and on the Amazon, 1604–1668*. Oxford: Clarendon Press, 1923.

# Index

(References to the inhabitants of the lands touched on during the three voyages are collected under the heading 'Indigenous peoples')